ENTERTAINING
the TRIUNE MYSTERY

GOD, SCIENCE, AND THE SPACE BETWEEN

D1570943

ENTERTAINING the TRIUNE MYSTERY

GOD, SCIENCE, AND THE SPACE BETWEEN

JEFFREY C. PUGH

TRINITY PRESS INTERNATIONAL
A Continuum imprint
HARRISBURG • LONDON • NEW YORK

Trinity Press International, P.O. Box 1321, Harrisburg, PA 17105
Trinity Press International is a member of the Continuum International Publishing Group.

Cover design: Tom Castanzo

Library of Congress Cataloging-in-Publication Data
Pugh, Jeffrey C., 1952–
     Entertaining the triune mystery : God, science, and the space between / Jeffrey C. Pugh.
          p. cm.
     Includes bibliographical references and index.
     ISBN 1-56338-401-9 (pbk.)
     1. Religion and science.   I. Title.
BL240.3.P84   2003
261.5'5—dc21
                                        2003008787
Printed in the United States of America
03 04 05 06 07 08   10 9 8 7 6 5 4 3 2 1

To Miriam and Joy,

mysteries of grace for which I am profoundly grateful

CONTENTS

PREFACE

In the Lenten season of 2002 I was invited to lead a study on the topic of theology and science at a local congregation in Chapel Hill, North Carolina, where I live. I have done many different series before, but I was especially challenged by this experience because of the robust debate that arose around the ideas I was presenting. It was out of those experiences that this book began to take shape. I was already at work on the initial stages of a book about how we define God, but the questions raised by the congregation helped to shape the distinct form of this work. The members of the Episcopal Church of the Holy Family are serious about their faith in a way that is rare in the American church, and I benefited from their desire to understand how faith and science might relate to one another.

When I was thinking about my audience for this book, I found myself going back to their questions, their frustrations with what they were hearing, and my desire for Christian faith to escape its present captivity to elements in culture and tradition that keep it tethered to what I feel is an idolatrous frame of mind. I have tried in this book to offer fresh perspectives that we can draw upon not only to understand, but also to manifest the presence of God in the world. One possible path for those perspectives is recovering a sense of mystery about the world that Christians claim is a creation.

I am sure many of those in the Lenten series will find it a curious and puzzling step for me to argue that the world that is being revealed to us by the currents of scientific inquiry moving through the world gives us an opportunity to deepen our spirituality. Yet, this is in some measure *one* of the arguments of the work in front of you.

My initial research began at the library of the University of North Carolina, Chapel Hill. After typing in religion and science in the book search, I found to my dismay that 1,764 entries popped up. At first this was a tad daunting; surely I had nothing new to add to the conversation that is taking place in the field of science and religion. I am not a scientist, though I appre-

ciate very much what I learn from them. I even think theologian is too
grand a title for what I do, but I had a contract to write this book and it was
hubris on my part to think I had anything original to say in the first place.
So, on I plunged into what was to be an exciting time of discovery for me
and I hope the readers of this book.

My first interest in this field came from a class I taught at Elon University
with Pranab Das, a colleague of mine from the physics department, under
the auspices of the course grant program of the Templeton Foundation.
Since that course I have sought further understanding about the intersections of religion and science, particularly within my own faith community
of Christianity. The more I read and study, the more indebted I am to those
who pioneered what has become a burgeoning field.

These names are familiar to those who work this area: Ian Barbour,
Nancey Murphy, Arthur Peacocke, John Polkinghorne, Robert J. Russell,
John Haught, Philip Clayton, and countless others have been my teachers
over the last several years and I am grateful for their work. But I come from
a world of theologians and my debt to them is as great. In fact, the percep-
tive reader of this book will discern Dietrich Bonhoeffer's influence in the
pages of this work even though there will be no mention of his name.

With great interest I plunged on to explore the borders of theology and
science. What emerged surprised me. The first chapter of this book sets up
the questions and struggles that inform the rest of the work. How do we
understand the life of God in the world? When so much seems to run
counter to belief in any sense of meaning or purpose, wouldn't it make
more sense to take the way of the skeptics and argue that at bottom the
processes of life are inherently meaningless? Given the vast amount of waste
and suffering we find in the world of exploding galaxies and deadly viruses,
of predator and prey, how can faith speak a word of hope?

Perhaps part of our problem comes from the ways we have defined God.
The second chapter is a historical excursus concerning the ways in which various faith and philosophical traditions have conceived and articulated the
being of God. This chapter will probably constitute the greatest challenge for
the reader; however, I believe it will be worth the effort. There have been a
diversity of images of God in these traditions, but subsequent development
of doctrine and history has narrowed these options somewhat. It has been
only recently, for example, that the suffering of God has reappeared as a central subject of theological reflection. Indeed, this subject was a crucial aspect
of Bonhoeffer's later struggles. It is in this chapter that I raise one of the
major concepts that I will use to think about God in relation to science.

This concept is the one that revolves around our partial interpretation of God on the basis of the energies of God found in the fields, forces, and processes of life within which we are embedded. This distinction is not a novel one; the Cappadocian theologians of the fourth century used this notion in their understanding of God as Trinity. The distinction between God's essence and energies allows us to grasp the life of God in ways that are compelling in a scientific age.

The rest of the book explores the intersections of science and faith in conversation with the past and present to maintain that the life of God revealed in the world through the Scriptures and tradition can also be seen in the world we are presently exploring under the auspices of science. This strikes some as a curious claim, for the two inquiries do not really share common ground in the minds of many. As the reader will soon discover, I believe that there is a space between interpretations that will have to remain a space of tension and discussion. This should not necessarily put people of faith on the defensive, for I believe our interpretations of the world are as warranted as others placed before us.

The tough part about this is that Christian faith is rooted in the commitment to realities that are, in the words of our creeds, "things seen and unseen." Surely those things that are seen comprise not only the world we grasp, but also those aspects of the world that we barely comprehend. We simply don't know the total workings of the processes that bring life to being and the sustaining power that allows it to continue. Christianity has the tradition of understanding God as Creator, Redeemer, and Sustainer of life and it is in this context that I explore a few simple and distinct questions.

I do this with the realization that science, like theology, should be an open discipline, standing ready for revision and fresh concepts, even while it remains true to its traditions. There is still much that is mysterious to us, though we know far more than we used to. The latest cutting edge scientific work in such matters as consciousness and evolution reveals a far different perspective than the science of the past. We will have to become comfortable with the ambiguity even of our science.

In both science and theology, interpretations of the world are offered that will differ depending on how the data gets treated. But we do have this inescapable world within which we all are embedded. The anguish of the father who sits beside his daughter's bed as she is wracked by disease calls for more pastoral response than simply saying that this is just the way the world works. The sublime feeling that occasionally wraps itself around us as we observe a morning sunrise or observe a starry night can be accounted for in more ways than just biological processes. This is territory Christian faith should not vacate and there are many in the burgeoning field of science and religion who are bringing their interests and expertise to show the possibilities of grasping toward the reality behind all things seen and unseen.

The work you are holding in front of you does not profess to be breaking any new ground; much of what is in here will be familiar territory for the specialists. But this is a book written for those like the parishioners at Holy Family who question whether faith and science should even be on the same playing field. I believe they should be because we miss much about the world without them both.

In that respect I hope interested readers might start a journey from what they read in these pages. Reflection upon the deep mysteries of the universe might work to restore to Christian faith a sense of the passion of God for the world. Part of the mystery that will unfold throughout this book suggests that the Trinity does not have to be an obscure theme spoken of in ancient times; it is a revealing of God that speaks to God's deep involvement in the world. It rests at the heart of Christian identity and I hope to offer reasons why this is the case.

Although I hope scholars in the field might find food for thought in these pages, this is not a book for them. This is a book for people like my students and those who worship at Holy Family who wonder about the connection between their faith and vocations. This is a book meant for those who entertain the mystery of the cosmos and our place in it. In that sense I believe that this book assumes dimensions of a spiritual rather than a systematic theology. My desire as it took shape was that it might illumine for some a new way of understanding the life of God in the world, for others a renewed passion for manifesting the ultimate energy of God, which is love.

I also became more aware of the unfinished nature of books as I came to the end of this work. There is much I did not say about the ways in which God's presence is made manifest on Earth. The whole issue of the way in which the mind/body analogy might offer us clues for how God acts in the world will have to wait for another time. I believe that God does act in the world today, but I also believe that we must be careful about how we define that belief.

It is a fiction that books belong solely to their authors. There is a community of persons behind this work. First and foremost is Henry Carrigan, who I am sure is taking a chance by publishing yet another book in the area of science and religion. My thanks also to Amy Wagner for all her hard work on the book. Elon University has been my vocational home for many years and I am deeply grateful for all the colleagues and friends that I have made there. Special thanks go to all those at Elon—faculty, staff, and students—who have taught me over the years more than I could ever have imagined

Deep appreciation is also due to my colleague J. Christian Wilson, whose close reading and critique of the original manuscript prevented me from errors I would have regretted. His support and friendship over the years have probably saved me countless dollars in therapy. James Pickens of the psychology department has been invaluable both in his reading of this work and subsequent discussions. Others at Elon have also contributed in their own way to this text. My department chair, James Pace, ensured I would be unfettered with work during my sabbatical semester, and made valuable suggestions. Rebecca Todd Peters, G. Chad Snyder, L. D. Russell, Pranab Das, Dan Wright, Anthony Weston, and many others have been faithful conversation partners and have taught me much. The ongoing support of Thomas Tiemann, Steve DeLoach, and Paul Miller has been priceless. I am also grateful to James C. Logan and Shenandoah University colleagues John Copenhaver and Barry Penn Hollar for their contributions to my journey.

Students have also been a part of this project as well. Special appreciation goes to Brooke Droy, who spent time on the first draft of the first three chapters arguing with me about why I wanted to focus on Christian faith. Michael Polanis, Cynthia Briggs, and Michael Holly read the manuscript carefully and asked good questions that helped me better explain myself. If it were not for the time and investment of these persons, the project would have been much poorer. Deep gratitude is also due to Timothy Kimbrough, rector at Holy Family, who has inspired me with his music, his preaching, and his spirit.

My life has been made richer for what I have been taught by Ryan and Kristen Godwin. My children Miriam and Joy have given me far more to celebrate about my life than they know. This book is dedicated to them for all they have given me over the years. Finally, as I entertain the great mystery of the universe, I am deeply grateful for the gift of my wife, Jan Rivero. Conversations with her about this material enhanced the work immeasurably. Her presence in the world is a manifestation of God's healing mercy not only to me, but to all whom she touches.

Lent 2003

1

ENTERTAINING MYSTERY

Scientific research is simply a form
of religious contemplation.
—Simone Weil

Man's last good and highest parting
is when for God's sake, he takes leave of God.
—Meister Eckhart

The mother of a child born with congenital heart defects suffers greatly as she watches her son go through his fourth operation in a year. Through all her struggles she hears from well-intentioned persons that God must have a reason, one even being so insensitive as to suggest that there must be some hidden sin in her life for God to give her such a baby. She silently sits, staring at the wall, and wonders about God's way in the world. Surely God could have prevented this, but if not, then there must be some healing for this all-encompassing pain and suffering. But as she tosses out this silent cry to the universe, there is no response. God, seemingly, is silent.

Another parent, a father, sits two chairs over from the woman and he, too, is lost in thoughts about his daughter, who had been struck down by a virus that came upon her suddenly and took her life within a week. He wonders about the way of the universe and why God creates disease only to strike down those we love. His mind takes him to places that are uncomfortable. "Is disease God's way of thinning the herd?" he asks ruefully, and no reply comes forth. He concludes that the universe really has no meaning and that the stories he heard as a child about the God who watches and protects the world were really fairy tales, meant to allay the fears of young children.

A scientist sits late at night and peers into her telescope, looking out into space and searching interstellar galaxies for signs, hints, clues, to the origin of the world. She wants to understand how the universe works because she is so fascinated by the energies present in what she sees. She ponders the vast collisions of particles seen and unseen and marvels at the amazing destruction and chaos before her. And yet, out of that chaos emerges life and wonder. Even given her scientific training she cannot help but ponder the night sky in ways that can only be described as aesthetic, the beholding of great beauty or art. She reflects on how a universe of such strange beauty and complexity came into being.

Every day on this terrestrial ball of dirt and gas millions of persons peer into the deepest spaces of the human heart, or the most intricate behavior of cellular life, or the vast regions and expanses of space and find themselves confronting the age-old question of human existence: Why? Why do things work the way they do? Why does space and time behave the way it does? Why do the innocent suffer through no fault of their own? Why can't God eradicate unnecessary suffering? Why do we even believe in the existence of that which we have called by various names, whether it is the Tao, Yahweh, Allah, or God?

These questions emerge from the recesses of our hearts and minds, seeking answers to puzzles that have been a part of the human journey for millennia. We do not seem to be any closer to solving them now than we have been in the past. One thing, however, remains a constant. For millions of people all over the planet, spanning ages and cultures, their thoughts will turn to that which functions in humankind's life as the ultimate symbol and answer to these types of questions. God is, to put it somewhat indelicately, the final answer. And yet this symbol seems more elusive to us than ever. We live as orphans in the cosmos, hoping for a sign from beyond this life and finding silence instead.

Many believe in God because for them such belief answers the question of why there is something rather than nothing. Why is there a universe at all? It is God, the one who stands outside of time, who creates the heavens and the earth, who is without beginning or end, who creates and brings into being all that is. This answer has the benefit of being a rock-solid place to stand, and so this image must be protected against those who would reduce the majesty and wonder of the Almighty.

Many go even further to claim that God is the divine designer who, through omnipotence and omniscience, governs and directs the processes of life, animate and inanimate. In diverse cultures and civilizations this belief in God has given rise to religious life that even in its polytheistic forms still points back to the One. Call it Brahman, Jehovah, or Allah, humankind has conceptualized an entity that is the source of something rather than nothing.

In the culture of Western civilization, where the monotheistic traditions have arisen, this symbol has taken on certain characteristics and attributes that many take for granted as an accurate way of describing ultimate reality. While we are barely aware of it in our conscious thought, our images of the Divine have been shaped for centuries by traditions and habits of thought informed by philosophy, theology, and sacred Scripture. What is perhaps more surprising to us is that our images of God have also been shaped by our reflections upon nature.

In this history we have fashioned images of God and God's way with the world that rarely, if ever, get questioned or critiqued. At worst these are the images that are quickly jettisoned when the circumstances of life confront us with levels of tragedy deeper than we have previously faced. When we are confronted with something that conflicts with the images of God we have developed, we respond sometimes as though we were waiting for the first excuse to take leave of faith.

Consider the well-publicized case of television mogul Ted Turner, who, responding to queries about his life, talked about how his faith in God was lost after watching his sister go through a difficult and painful illness when he was young. He said he could no longer believe in a God who would allow so much suffering for one so young. His experience is probably all too typical of many today.

Part of the problem comes from our tradition, which has defined God in such a way that God can sometimes become little more than a metaphysical construct, abstract and lifeless, which, when portrayed in such concepts as power and knowledge, leaves little room for compassion and love. God becomes a philosophical abstraction and only allows for what reason requires. In this way our definitions of God remove God from the ordinary life of the world, and do not allow for the imagination to discover the shape of God's presence in the world. This is the type of presence that is not only found in the explosions of galaxies, but in the deepest places of our souls, cultivated and welcomed in the midst of great suffering and receiving all that life brings us with gratitude.

There is a danger when God becomes captive to our metaphysical systems. God becomes defined in terms of natural or moral laws and we find the power of symbol, mystery, or even narrative being peeled away from human existence. Everything must be explained literally, and a sense of the mystery of life is lost. In the history we are going to touch on later, God becomes captive to metaphysical systems and human thought. Newton, when he looked at the mechanics of things, wanted to work out a notion of God consistent with his understanding of the natural order. In this way he mirrors Aristotle's approach by seeing nature as entirely passive and God as the sole agent of things in motion. God becomes the Divine Mechanic. The Creator is reduced to a mechanistic function and mystery gets treated to the back door. As a result, God can become so impersonal as to have no meaning in the struggles of our lives.

There is also the other problem with personal elements of understanding God. It does not take a particularly observant person to look at the history of the world to see the dangers inherent in the personification of God. How many places can we look and see where God has become employed by us to justify our wars, our prejudices, our violence and willful dehumanizing of others? God has ended up serving our desires and even the very narratives of religion reflect this tendency. Never mind the political or social narratives that have allowed the oppression of millions in the name of "manifest destiny" or "ethnic cleansing"; there are also the biblical accounts that self-consciously portray God in such ways that cast doubt on the full humanity of others. None of us who are Christians like to admit such a thing, but our images of God have led to murder and violence against those who are of different faiths. The tragedy is that this is a continuing moment in the life of the planet.

The other difficulty is that personification of God makes such an easy target for those who are rightly suspicious of belief in God. Who would sign up for such a belief, knowing that you would have to hate someone else? Even more, when so much about our beliefs shows up in our prejudices, fears, and bigotries, who could not agree with Freud that our images of God are little more than projections of inner emotional and psychological states? We create the God we want so we will feel safe and secure in the world. God will be the principle of order that will keep the terror of death away from our doors. God will reward the righteous (of which we believe ourselves to be a part), and punish the wicked (all those we really don't like). God has chosen our country for special favor because we are a "city set on a hill," or our tribe, or even our race, because God loves us more than the others.

This use of the ultimate symbol of all that is for our own purposes has caused many to abandon belief in any such reality, and, in truth, who could blame them? Those like Nietzsche who call our attention to the ways in which we construct an idol from our own interests and demand obedience to it and all it entails should be carefully considered. Their voices contain needed truth if God is to have a life in the world reflective of something other than our own agendas.

Other words have been used to try to get at this tension between the impersonal and the personal dimensions of the deity, but the abstraction of transcendence and immanence has its own particular set of problems as well. These tensions emerge because human ideas about God do not of necessity correspond to the reality of whatever ineffable life/thought exists for which we use the word symbol, God.

An interesting illustration comes from the life of St. Thomas Aquinas. Late in his career he traveled extensively through France, Italy, and Germany. During this time, after mass on the feast of St. Nicholas in December 1273, he put away his writing instruments and stopped dictating. According to the material we have, Thomas answered queries about his health by saying, "I cannot go on. . . . All that I have written seems like so much straw compared to what I have seen and what has been revealed to me." Interpretations of this event vary among scholars of St. Thomas; however, if we take him at his word, he experienced a moment of profound discovery about God. Try as we might, we cannot exhaust the reality of God through our minds and language.

All through the history of our struggle with the mystery of God those who most clearly see understand that God does not exist in any way we can adequately capture or conceive. So, if nothing else, this tells us that the images of God we speak of ought to be held lightly, with creativity and imagination. But in practice we have held tightly to our images of the Divine, so tightly that we are unable to let go when new images present themselves as ways of enlarging our vision of God in the world. This is nothing new; we have been doing it since the ancient texts were first being written. There are today new images that are emerging in a curious place. As humankind reflects on its images of God, we find that scientific inquiry into the world has offered rich resources for entertaining the mystery of God.

What Does Science Have to Do with Religion?

In what follows I am asking you to take the most improbable of journeys with me. I want us to think again about the Christian understanding of God in the context of the world of science, or perhaps more precisely, the world

science is revealing to us through its investigations. It is admittedly a difficult concept for many to grasp, that these two disciplines have something in
common. There are those who have both of their feet so planted in one field
of study they cannot imagine stepping into the other to learn from it. For
others the whole image of Galileo being silenced by the church, and the subsequent repression that went with it, remains a lingering obstacle to dialogue. Neither point of view allows them much room for their imaginations
to overcome the images of conflict and move to a new story.

The world that has been described by some as postmodern has revealed
that the boundaries we so firmly held onto were also the result of our wish
fulfillment. We are finding that while we may have desired absolute truth,
absolute truth is very difficult to come by. There are new possibilities and
spaces open now for a reconsideration of the heritage bequeathed to us by
the past.

These new fields of possibility are being seeded by those who realize that
the images of God we have been struggling with for millennia can be
images that can never capture the totality of the One who stands at the
boundaries of thought. Both theologians and scientists who are willing to
be patient and enter the mystery of the universe are finding that a God
imprisoned by the constructs of metaphysics or Freudian projection can
paradoxically be freed by looking at the universe through the lenses that
scientific inquiry is revealing to us.

Care must be taken here, for I don't wish to make this connection firmer
than it need be. Part of the dilemma with the relationship between science
and religion has come when too much has been claimed on either side. Religion has sometimes constructed an image of God that was so closely identified with science that when the scientific perspective changed, the images
collapsed along with it. Perhaps, though, if models of God are held with a
balance between attachment and detachment, then we will find a path that
enlarges our theology and faith. A theology of nature can allow for changing perspectives in the scientific community if it bases its theology on the
biblical witness and subsequent tradition.

What I am suggesting is that there is much in the exploration of the
world and its strange and peculiar wonders that opens us to a sense of mystery, and sometimes anguish. Some would like to know, for example, why
suffering and death seem to be such a part of life. Others, contemplating the
sheer energy of life in the cosmos, find themselves amazed that consciousness exists at all. Those who consider our world in its deepest forms find
there an entertaining mystery.

We have discovered that creative scientific breakthroughs occur in those almost mystical moments of insight when things emerge in new ways to speak of themselves.[1] Those scientists and theologians who are willing to allow a place for an imaginative listening and attending to the world are finding more that intrigues them every day. It will be the argument of this book that in this dialogue Christians and others have a way of responding to the overpersonification and impersonal abstraction of God that has been a part of the legacy of the monotheistic tradition. This way is offered partially by the world that scientists and others are interpreting to us. In this exploration of life and space, blood and bone, cell and star, we find ourselves in the realm of mystery.

This word makes some uncomfortable, for it is difficult to exist with mystery. Dictionaries may define the word as something secret and impossible to understand, or something that arouses curiosity through its obscure nature. Certainly mystery indicates the puzzling, hidden, unknown, though possibly intuited dimensions of existence. However we define it, mystery puts us into the realm of searching for a reality we presently apprehend but dimly.

Theologians and scientists alike work this territory, each in their own way, though their understandings may be quite different. Entertaining mystery is not very comfortable to us, though we get a hint of it when we look at the night sky, or we pause long enough in our particularly busy lives to reflect upon some distinct moment that makes us question the trajectories of our lives and the shape they have taken.

Living in the mystery means we have to make use of our imagination, and cultivate the heart of a poet. It means becoming willing to think metaphorically about things that can escape logical thought. It can mean that we struggle with new ideas, thoughts, and concepts so that fresh perspectives may arise to enhance our faith. It may mean that dogma and the dogmatic spirit need to be revisited, for both disciplines of science and theology are understanding now that our sight is sometimes limited by what we are willing to see. If we stay locked in the prisons of what we are, we can never become what God calls us to be. The type of vision that is emerging in the world now, the vision seen in the life of subatomic particles or cosmic strings, the life of cells and information systems, could even be called revelatory.

Perhaps we can look at the inquiries of both religion and science to make a modest claim. Both are involved in an enterprise that seeks to understand the boundaries of existence by using the best available understandings and sources of human knowledge. In some measure, intersections are likely to result even though there are scholars on both sides of the divide who say there should be no intersection between the two disciplines.[2]

But is increasing understanding of the universe helpful in filling out our metaphorical images of God? Can science in its understanding of chaos and complexity theory, or the principle of self-organization, point out possible fruitful avenues for thinking about God's relations with the world? Can we affirm through a rigorous and reflective examination of the immense complexity of the world something new, not thought of before about the ultimate symbol of humankind?

Such questions may not seem worth asking, or for Christians may constitute an alien agenda for theology. Does the universe itself contain data that calls for theological interpretation? Someone like Wolfhart Pannenberg argues that the natural world and its properties are best understood in their relation to God. The corollary is that our understanding of God increases the more we know about the world.[3] For others such an approach constitutes a potential danger for Christianity. Outside of revelation, they would argue, nothing about God can be properly known from the natural world.[4]

Still the natural world does exist as data for interpretation and Christian faith must respond to it in some way. But the skeptic will surely ask, haven't we been down this road before? Every age says this and theologians are always seeking to take advantage of that which does not properly belong to them. Surely those images of God that we have built on the edifices of science pass away into the mists of history when the advances of science write a new and revised script. After all, we don't really believe in Newton's god anymore, do we? Why bring science into it at all? We are only setting ourselves up for a fall when the world revealed to us will cause us to revise our notion of God's action in the world.

And as in all things there is some truth to this point of view. New concepts will replace old ones and any construction of God built upon interpretations of the newest understandings of science runs the risk of being overturned just like the deist god of the Enlightenment. When construals of God make no sense, they should stand for critique and reevaluation. But science moves ahead because in its reevaluations it builds on what has gone before. Newtonian mechanics was not tossed out the window because of quantum mechanics, but the deeper relationships present in the universe emerged to give us a more complete picture. Revision does not of necessity lead to dissolution.

And this is perhaps the place to make a further assertion about the project in front of you. My approach is going to assume that theology can be the disciplined imagination working within the tradition of Christian faith to allow for a deeper spiritual sense of being in the world and in God. Theology is reflection upon the way reality is to be construed, understood, and interpreted. This is territory that science believes it has a proprietary claim over and does not wish to vacate. As the argument of this book continues, we will look more closely at these competing claims. But at the outset it must be stated that Christian theology does its interpreting on the basis of a narrative given it in the Scriptures and focused specifically on the reality of God revealed in the life, teaching, death, and resurrection of Jesus Christ.

Furthermore, this narrativity extends through the tradition of Christian faith, establishing the contours for our interpretations of God and the world in their relation to one another. This does not mean that the tradition is sacrosanct and cannot be questioned, for it can and it will be. But it does mean that the affirmations or negations we make about God have to take into account those formulations of God that have shaped and informed us.

One of the central beliefs that has guided the Christian tradition is that the nature of God is expressed in the belief of God-as-Trinity. It is this that many believe to be a central and guiding metaphor, reality, or revelation for Christian reflection. Careful consideration of this doctrine can lead us to spaces that will allow for deeper understandings about God's life in the world, and even the cultivation of a deeper spirituality. Our doctrine of God does affect our inner lives, for our theologies establish the ways we will be in the world and to what we will give our allegiances. The attention being paid to this doctrine in the last several years has allowed for a recovery of new ways of understanding Trinity that do not necessarily lead us into a morass of ancient terminology that obscures a deeper understanding of God's being in the world.[5]

The Space Between

For many there are simply no grounds for contending that science has the potential to enhance the mystical element that Christianity seems to have lost. But my argument is going to proceed on the basis that scientific exploration of our world has opened the space for thinking about the triune God in terms of God's actions in the world. Many scientists would be particularly horrified by that statement, for that is not the goal of scientific inquiry, and yet the sense of wonder that any scientist encounters when the universe speaks to her, either through star or cell, can truly be a mystical moment. Many theologians might be equally horrified because this statement would seem to move the issue into some vague spiritualism unhinged from the church's witness to God the Father, Son, and Holy Spirit.

And yet the church's witness has always been oriented to the saving actions of God, or what has been termed the "economy" of God. Seen in this respect there has always been a creative tension in the tradition between the immanent and economic forms of the Trinity. Karl Rahner in his ground-breaking exploration of this subject made the statement that "the economic Trinity is the immanent Trinity and vice-versa."[6] Another way of under-standing this is to realize that the history of the world has been the mani-festation of the redemptive acts of the triune God.

The questions we will be exploring in the next few chapters go to the heart of the stories that opened this chapter. In what way is God's presence manifested in the world? Or better still, how can we see with the eyes of faith that something is at work amid all the destruction and chaos that surrounds us in the world of nature and in our own personal lives? Perhaps we cannot, but we should not be prevented by our imaginations or our doctrines from revisiting the ultimate symbol of religious reflection. If we do, we may find there a path for thinking anew about the reality of God. While we are care-ful not to invest too deeply in claiming to know the essence of God, is there room in this exploration for reflecting on the energies of God?

This distinction, the one between God's essence and God's energies, is not a new or novel one. Philo of Alexandria used the distinction and in Christianity the entire tradition of the Eastern Orthodox Church drew upon this distinction in its theological formation. While the Western tradi-tion was concentrating on defining God in terms of attributes or essence, another stream of the Christian tradition saw God making Godself known to us in the continual presence of earthly life.[7]

The question can be raised of whether the life of the cosmos with its fif-teen billion-year history of evolving development can be seen as a clue to the divine life. We do not seem to have access to God's essence, but the ener-gies of God are present to us in a rather inescapable way. While the tradition of natural theology in Christianity has shared the same limitations of loca-tion and history as do all forms of human inquiry, it does not seem intel-lectually naïve to study the natural world and ask questions of it, or better, to become such a part of it that it speaks to us.

This is where care must be taken in some ways not to claim too much. I am not advocating a theology that looks to nature to vindicate belief in God's existence; rather, I am starting from the position of accepting that there is a dimension of existence that still calls us to reflect on that which we have called God. Given this acceptance, is it possible for us to see the cosmos as we presently understand it and make any connections between what we are finding and faith? Deeper still, is there a reality about the natural order that calls for us to respond?[8]

The difficulty of the contemporary world is that we are beginning to understand how much our interpretations of things affect exactly what it is we will be able to see. Some talk of this as the observer/participant dynamic. Essentially, our observation of something changes the thing itself. Thus we are interpreting the world, but the world is also in some measure interpreting us.

Surely when this is done the results are mixed, for not only does reflection upon the universe produce awe and wonder, it can also produce anger and despair. If the energies of God are going to be teased out of the world, surely we will have to reflect on what John Polkinghorne calls "the cruciform pattern of life."[9] Any cursory view of the universe reveals to us that from cells to stars, life comes through death.

No better observer of this view is found in culture today than Annie Dillard, who first explored these themes in her Pulitzer Prize-winning book, *Pilgrim at Tinker Creek,* and later extended them in her book *For the Time Being.* She writes about this paradoxical intuition, "Life's cruelty joins the world's beauty and our sense of God's presence to demonstrate who we're dealing with, if dealing we are. God immanent and transcendent, God discernible but unknowable, God beside us and wholly alien. How this proves his mercy I don't understand."[10] She joins many who just don't understand.

How do we reconcile a universe that seemingly appears to be one vast realm of destruction with the notion of self-conscious, purposeful being? How this One is understood as the primary force behind all that is is one of the largest tensions facing Christian theology. If we were to take just the testimony of nature, we might conclude that God is a sadistic monster, intent on finding ever new and creative ways of making the creation suffer.

Part of the problem may come from the ways we have conceptualized the world and God and the relationship between them. In the next couple of chapters we are going to take a closer look at the tradition that emerged out of the Judeo-Christian ethos to trace out the path the Western world took in defining its understanding of God. But for now, whether in theology or science, however we define God, certain ideas may emerge that have a way of limiting God or forcing God to be consistent with whatever the demands of a particular theology, science, or even interpretation of nature call for. The result has been that we have con-

fused our images and metaphors for the reality, thus missing the opportunity for expanding our vision. The truth is that God eludes all attempts
at comprehensive definition.

Knowing this means that we should be careful about how concrete we
make our images of God. Even when we make the argument that the traditional ways of conceiving God and the relationship between God and the
world are in need of revising, care must be taken not to allow our new
insights to become so solidified that they become for us God's new prison.
The Swiss theologian Karl Barth once said that God is like a bird in flight.
We are constantly aiming at a moving target and we can never pin it down.

The irony of the present age is that many have pinned down their image
of God with concepts that emerged in ancient cultures, yet the world is no
longer thus. Rather than a static universe, it now "appears the universe is
much more like a series of continuing thoughts, not all of them related or
even coherent in themselves, than a machine. And if this is so, the critical
question becomes, metaphorically but intriguingly: Is there someone thinking these thoughts?"[11]

It may be difficult for us to realize that, like science, religion has a history.
In the life of religious communities ideas emerge, some finding root, some
disappearing. The symbol "God" has had a history as well, for the stories
told about God have shaped the lives of individuals and cultures. These narratives have established laws, social structures, and relationships; literally
every part of human life has been affected in some fashion by the ways that
we have interpreted our ultimate symbol.

In accepting the stories on the authority of those who have gone before
us, we have often been unaware of the path that has been traveled to bring
us to where we are. When doubt is cast upon a story, we can be very resist-
ant because this story carries with it the imprimatur of absolute truth. Any
doubt about the ideas of God represented in the story, any revision of these
inherited images, results in the charge of blasphemy, or the fear that some-
how God is being diminished.

Theology, in its search for understanding, does examine its sacred texts
and traditions, claiming that the Holy Spirit has inspired the community of
faith to articulate and interpret events in such a way that the reality of God
is known. In this way interpretation of mundane things becomes the
ground for new responses to the God who calls all life into existence.[12]

This idea constitutes one of the fundamental spaces between science and
theology today. It is the fundamental interpretation of what is being
observed that causes the space between to seem almost impossible to

breach. Indeed, one of the critiques of all human knowing is that the very way we look for things can be determined by what we believe is actually there in the first place. Part of the attraction of science as a means of knowing is that it offers through its methods of testing means by which interpretations can be proven to be accurate readings of the way things are.

Even though many in the contemporary world would point to a plurality of interpretations of the universe and argue that we cannot divest ourselves of background assumptions, cultural constructions, and language to escape our limitations, the fact remains that science has established its methods as a seemingly accurate means of interpreting reality.

Theology offers a differing interpretation that may have its own truth, but which lacks the benefit of testable hypothesis, repeatable experimentation, and other results of scientific method. In science theories are put out into the public arena for all comers to verify or falsify. Even given the awareness that in some measure science shares the limitations of all human knowing, its methods have issued in such success as to assume in the minds of many an almost omnipotent competence to explain the processes of life.

In our search for truth we are finding that all forms of human inquiry need to be careful about their claims and pretense at pure objectivity. We can do the best we can at trying to escape the boundaries of our past, or our humanity, but we should always be aware of the fact that many unconscious factors play a role in our understanding of the world. Truth is stranger than it used to be, but there is still truth to be had, even in the intersections of what we now assume to be the natural world. A variety of truth claims emerge in the contemporary world because there are a variety of perspectives and interpretations.

In reflecting upon whether a thing can be true, we are met with this diversity of interpretations. Truth can be construed from our language, our cultural perceptions, even our empirical senses, but there is a sense in which it can also be discovered, revealed, and uncloaked.[13] Even granted the notion of apprehension of reality, there are no means whereby theology or science can access reality uninfluenced by background assumptions and presuppositions of which we may in fact be unaware. The truths that emerge from our observations will make different claims on us, but there simply exist no transcendental points from which we stand able to comprehend accurately everything that is taking place in front of us.

There will always be that which is hidden from us because the universe itself is not absolute, but relative and ambiguous, and our knowledge of it will always be interpretive and contextual. According to Morton Tavel,

The laws and theories of physics are maps of a reality that we will probably never fully understand. These laws and theories are very useful for getting around in that reality, but we must never confuse them with reality itself. For one thing, the laws and theories are constantly changing, whereas the reality presumable is not.

In addition, there are theories for large-scale reality and theories for reality on a microscopic scale, whereas reality itself is presumable unified. For example, physicists have developed a complex and picturesque hierarchy of elementary particles, ranging down to a small group of what are called "quarks" and "leptons" which they consider more fundamental than all others. . . . It could very well turn out that elementary particles have no reality at all other than the fact that they were created by physicists to help explain reality at some deeper inner level.[14]

The scientific perspectives that have emerged over the last century have seen a move to this type of understanding. Matters have moved from seeing things as fixed systems to a more fluid understanding of reality. Things are not as hard and deterministic as previously believed and indeterminacy and interconnectedness presently serve as defining marks of the universe in which we live.

Theology should take this point of view into account when it is exploring the nature of reality and the connection between God's action and the world. Territory opens up when we rethink ideas about whether God is locked in some metaphysical box that tradition has constructed. I will contend, for example, that the Trinity offers a way of reflection upon God and the world that addresses some of our deepest concerns but calls for a new understanding that many in the Christian faith do not believe. This call does not necessarily have to mean the abandonment of Christian faith, but can be an enhancement of our continuing story. This story is ultimately rooted in the life of the triune God and it is this notion that seems so distant from the life of the church.[15]

There is a space between the interpretations that science and theology bring to their differing accounts of the way things are. Science and theology incorporate different metaphors of what they are trying to understand, yet if both are honest, they will acknowledge that at the heart of all things rests a dimension of mystery that is beyond our ability to control or even dominate, even though we believe in the illusion that we can.

It seems to be a part of it all that our very concepts and theology of God keep us at a distance from the thing itself. Should we take the step of letting go of our ideas, of entertaining the mystery, or perhaps of letting the mystery entertain us, of even allowing ourselves the painful process of letting go of God? If so, we may find that the God we believed in was nothing more than an idol, built from the storehouse of our fears and self-protective impulses.

This is a curious claim coming from someone who will argue that recovery of God-as-Trinity may enhance our deep sense of mystical awareness of the life of God in the world. What is even odder, I suppose, is that for all the seeming distance between the worlds of theology and science, it may be that science can be a guide to letting go of our idols and it is the burden of this book to show why. But in order to offer a new vision we must first see how it was that we came to accept certain images about God and whether those images should be candidates for reconstruction.

I will start by taking a look at the historical foundations of the development of the tradition of classical theism and the emergence of the doctrine of the Trinity. I will then move to consider the contemporary response to the issue of God. From there we will move to exploring such issues as creation and evolution, the sustaining energies of the universe discovered by scientific inquiry, and the relationships that we are discovering lie at the heart of the universe. Our conversation will move back and forth between past and present in an attempt to be faithful to the tradition. However, I will argue that we need to recover aspects of our tradition that would allow us to understand the life of God in the world in a new way. Let us then turn to a further examination of why the images of God many believe in today have become for some an idol, for others an irrelevancy, and for still others a promise.

NOTES

1. See, for example, the story of Barbara McClintock, whose reflections on how life functions at the cellular level led her to a new realization of how things work. She was interested in function and organization and how genes and cells related to the larger environment. Her work, in which she discovered that information went to DNA as well as from it, led to the realization that wider environmental factors could indirectly bring about genetic changes. She felt she had apprehended a truth in which things were speaking to her, and she was acquiring a "feeling for the organism." Ian Barbour, *Religion and Science: Historical and Contemporary Issues* (San Francisco: HarperSanFrancisco, 1997), 148.

2. So, for example, there are those such as Stephen Jay Gould who speak of the nonoverlapping magisteria of the disciplines of religion and science. See, for example, *Rock of Ages: Science and Religion in the Fullness of Life* (New York: Ballantine, 1999). Even more stringent about the incompatibility, even the absolute futility of any dialogue, would be those represented by Richard Dawkins, whose often cited work, *The Blind Watchmaker: Why the Evidence of Evolution Reveals a Universe Without Design* (New York: W. W. Norton, 1987) speaks to this issue. The larger conversation can be seen in such works as Ian Barbour, *Religion and Science,* and Ted Peters, ed., *Science and Theology: A New Consonance* (Boulder, Colo.: Westview Press, 1998). Finally, a recent publication by Richard J. Coleman portrays the relationship between science and theology as sibling rivalry: *Competing Truths: Theology and Science as Sibling Rivals* (Harrisburg, Pa.: Trinity Press International, 2001).

3. See, for example, Wolfhart Pannenberg, *Toward a Theology of Nature: Essays on Science and Faith* (Louisville, Ky.: Westminster John Knox, 1993), 16, 48. This is a path taken by many. Nature should be interpreted in relation to Christian faith's understanding of the revelation of God, but there is much to discover there about God.

4. See Stanley Hauerwas, *With the Grain of the Universe: The Church's Witness and Natural Theology* (Grand Rapids, Mich.: Brazos Press, 2001). The Gifford Lectures given by Hauerwas in 2000–2001 form the text of this book. David S. Cunningham also believes that the question of how much the created order can shape our knowledge of God is contingent upon a prior commitment to the Christian revelation. The created order is interpretive substance, however, the interpretation is done under the beliefs and practices of the Christian church. It is not necessarily a matter where the world is used to illumine God, or the absoluteness of God throws light on the world; rather, there is a relationship between God and the world that is more deeply grasped the deeper we move into both of them. "Toward a Rehabilitation of the *Vestigia* Tradition," in *Knowing the Triune God: The Work of the Spirit in the Practices of the Church* (eds. James J. Buckley and David S. Yeago; Grand Rapids, Mich.: Eerdmans, 2001).

5. I will treat this subject more extensively in a later chapter, but a good survey of this renewed interest is found in such books as David Cunningham, *These Three Are One: The Practice of Trinitarian Theology* (Oxford: Blackwell Publishers Inc., 1998); Leonardo Boff, *Trinity and Society* (trans. Paul Burns; Maryknoll, N.Y.: Orbis Books, 1988); Robert W. Jenson, *The Triune Identity: God According to the Gospel* (Philadelphia: Fortress Press, 1982); Colin Gunton, *The Promise of Trinitarian Theology* (Edinburgh: T&T Clark, 1990). There are others that will be noted in the next chapter.

6. Karl Rahner, *The Trinity* (trans. Joseph Donceel; New York: Herder & Herder, 1970).

7. There are a number of places where this idea can be seen. A more specifically theological source for this notion can be found in Vladimir Lossky, *The Mystical Theology of the Eastern Church* (Cambridge: James Clarke, 1991). After I came across the concept of the energies of God in my reading of the Cappadocians, I started noticing it turning up with increasing frequency. I found it in Arthur Peacocke's *Paths from Science towards God: The End of All Our Exploring* (Oxford: Oneworld, 2001), and he has a slight discussion of the phrase in relation to his project on pp. 160–62. I also ran across this phrase in Philip Sheldrake's work, *Spirituality and Theology: Christian Living and the*

Doctrine of God (Maryknoll, N.Y.: Orbis Press, 1998). Finally, when I returned to Jürgen Moltmann's *God in Creation: A New Theology of Creation and the Spirit of God* (San Francisco: Harper & Row, 1985), I found he also treats this notion.

8. There is a long and complex history in recent theology concerning approaches to natural theology. Karl Barth was adamant in his opposition to any theology that would allow God to be "read off" the structures of nature or human institutions. One aspect of his critique was the belief that knowledge represents a form of power. We do not possess the power over God to define the terms in which God will be known to us. Knowledge of God is not to be found in the sciences because such an approach diminishes the revelation of God found in the one true word about God, Jesus Christ.

9. John Polkinghorne, *Belief in God in an Age of Science* (New Haven, Conn.: Yale University Press, 1998), 14.

10. Annie Dillard, *For the Time Being* (New York: Alfred Knopf, 1999), 123.

11. Jeffrey Sobosan, *Romancing the Universe: Theology, Science, and Cosmology* (Grand Rapids, Mich.: Eerdmans, 1999), 34.

12. One thinks, for example, of Alasdair MacIntyre's statement: "In the Bible men go on journeys, suffer greatly, marry, have children, die and so on. So far no difficulty. But they go on journeys because God calls them, suffer in spite of God's care, receive their brides and their children at the hand of God, and at death pass in a special sense into God's realm." Alasdair MacIntyre, "The Logical Status of Religious Belief," in *Metaphysical Beliefs* (ed. Stephen Toulmin, et al.; New York: Schocken Books, 1957), 133.

13. It is this distinction between construction and disclosure that truly does constitute one of the great divides between so much of the discussion today around the idea of postmodernity.

14. Morton Tavel, *Contemporary Physics and the Limits of Knowledge* (Piscataway, N.J.: Rutgers University Press, 2002). Quoted from the *Chronicle of Higher Education* XLVIII (July 19, 2002), B4. One interesting aspect of this possibility is the ongoing discovery that quantum "weirdness" is not limited to the smallest particles, but has been shown to function within atomic clusters as well. In experiments that won the 2001 Nobel Prize in physics, scientists used rarified gases and cooled them so that the motion of atoms became slower and slower. Each atom's wavelength widened until the wavelengths began to overlap, forming a Bose-Einstein condensate. Imagine two thousand billiard balls merging into one and you have the effect.

15. I say this because in much of Christianity today the doctrine of the Trinity is passed over fairly quickly. Theologians, of course, are heavily involved in articulating the importance of this belief in recent years, and this has the potential to lead to much renewal for the church. However, the person in the congregation does not normally root his or her understanding of God in this direction.

2

CONSTRUCTING GOD

*I consider it an act of insane folly
to investigate the nature of God.*
—Procopius

*Anyone who tries to describe
the ineffable light in language is a liar.*
—Gregory of Nyssa

In almost any class I teach, whether at the university, in adult forums in the local church, or even in retreat settings, I sometimes write the word "God" on a board or newsprint and then ask for reactions, or the first words or thoughts that come into people's minds. Usually I get the same type of responses. The words are predictable—infinite, all-powerful, all-knowing, omnipresent, perfect, unchanging, eternal, transcendent, even impassible. I am usually not surprised because I very rarely get words like changing, finite, emotional, immanent, relationship, or even Father, Son, and Holy Spirit.

When I start to probe a little deeper, I find that our thoughts and images of God have been born in a setting that is strongly affected by the monotheistic traditions of Judaism, Christianity, and even Islam. What I don't find is much knowledge about how those traditions have been shaped in turn by historical circumstances and human reflection. In what follows I want to offer a background for considering how we got our understand-

ings of a supreme being and suggest that there might be other ways to conceive of deity. In doing so I hope to show that our images of God, while
informed by the images of the past, do not have to stay chained to them. I
realize that I run the risk of simplifying a complex and rich history; however, others have written richly on these stories and the reader can refer to
them for further study.[1]

Even though Christian faith articulates its sense of God by the category
of revelation, we cannot ignore the fact that historical contingency and cultural context have had a formative impact upon the way we understand the
reality of God. It is within the space of culture that our conceptualizations
of God have arisen, and so in any treatment of the life of God we will have
to come to grips with the fact that God has, in a sense, been constructed.
This does not mean that theology is necessarily wrong in its understandings
of God, but it does mean that careful attention must be paid to the ways our
reflections upon the divine life are shaped by the milieu in which they arise.

Surely a part of the legacy for the Western world begins in the ancient
Near East area when a tribal group was led to adopt the notion that there
was a supreme God among all the other gods. Israel's religious development
then moved through a complex and varied number of influences. The story
of Yahweh's emergence as a national God above all the other gods was
strengthened by the rise of the prophetic voices who called Israel to remember the covenant with Yahweh. The challenge to remember Yahweh as the
true God extended itself deep into the social, economic, and political
spheres of Israel's life. Humankind may worship other gods, but these were
mere idols and thus were no gods at all.

Perhaps the most sublime moment in this development came in the story
of Moses at the burning bush, which is found in the Exodus accounts. After
Moses asks exactly who is sending him to Egypt to prophesy to Pharaoh, he
gets the cryptic answer, "I AM WHO I AM," and upon reflection this might
be all we should ever say about this One who calls creation to relationship.
I heard someone once say that after Mount Sinai all language about God is
ideology, or worse, idolatry.

Hebrew Scriptures would express a diversity of views about this God
that were developed in interaction with the various ancient Near Eastern
images of deity, but in the diversity there does emerge a central narrative
thread of a God who, as creator and sustainer of the world, seeks relationship with the people Israel, and the rest of humanity as well. As we read
Hebrew Scripture we see images of God emerging that speak to God's creative and relational energies.

We will discuss issues of creation in later chapters, but for now it is inescapable that the language used to describe God in Hebrew Scripture employs a vast diversity of metaphors and images. One of the most compelling images is the notion of God's response to humankind's refusal to commit fully to a relationship with the Creator. This creates great grieving on the part of the God who creates and calls persons into covenant.

God's grieving is shown most poignantly in the many calls of the prophets to Yahweh's people to enter into relationship. These prophets use many images to speak of God, but among the most striking is the one of a betrayed husband in the book of Hosea. Though this account may seem overly sexist to us, the author was trying to convey the depth of what he felt was the intimacy of the relationship between Yahweh and Yahweh's people.

As the author of this book renders the story, Hosea marries a woman who, by all accounts, is destined to be unfaithful to her husband. She does in fact betray her husband, but his love for her is steadfast and he never deserts her. He pursues her with the express purpose of maintaining the marriage covenant. As the prophet renders the story, God experiences similar emotions to those of a betrayed husband, and these emotions run the gamut from revenge to reconciliation. The amazing thing is that the prophet says God never gives up hope that the relationship between humankind and God will be restored.

Not just in Hosea, but in other Scriptures, the writers use the type of imagery that compels the readers and hearers of their words to enter into God's own emotional life and consider that the relationship between God and humankind is one that involves vulnerability on God's part as well as our own. In the deepest sense possible we are given an image of God allowing a relationship of such depth and even mutuality that God is affected by the human response. This is the type of thing that many today cannot accept about God, because the definition of God has by far been weighted on the side of power, sovereignty, and control. A God who waits to see how humans will decide does not seem a likely candidate for our understandings of deity.

Indeed, many would feel this gives too important a place to human and other life. Those uncomfortable with these images will find places in Scripture that appeal to their sense that God must never be seen in such a way that allows for such vulnerability as emotions to be a constituent part of the divine life. Surely the one who creates out of nothing, who brings worlds into existence, cannot be subject to the changing currents of life that involve us. And yet the whole history of Israel's theology is one that portrays Yahweh in dynamic and not static ways. Drawing heavily on the use of metaphor to describe the life of God, the writers of the Hebrew Scriptures have some surprising images of the Divine for our consideration.[2]

It is undeniable that the stream that flows from Judaism forms one of Western culture's most important sources for thinking about God, and a reading of Hebrew Scripture reveals a host of images that seek to convey God and God's relationship with humankind. The question is have we considered the wide variety of ways that Israel sought to express its growing sense of exclusive monotheism when we formulate our ideas of God in the contemporary context? Some of these images we have used; others we may find troubling; and others, such as God's emotional suffering and response to rejection, do not seem to be part of our mental furniture.

Why have we not been able to draw upon this tradition to understand the willingness of God to suffer with God's creation? Part of the problem may rest with the early strands of Israel's tradition wherein God is portrayed in such a way as to require absolute cruelty to other tribes and peoples. Yahweh seems to exhibit and encourage an approach to other peoples that can only be called genocidal. And yet over the years the images that emerge in the biblical writers are those that seek to call forth the responses of compassion and pathos for not only human life, but for more-than-human life as well.[3]

The images found in Hebrew Scripture are not philosophical abstractions about utter transcendence. All theology concerning Yahweh and the human community is set within a specific context. The created order is the act of a free decision of Yahweh that structures the ongoing covenant relationship with humankind. In this sense the vital importance is that God is sovereign over all creation, and all actions of God arise not from a philosophical necessity of what it is "proper" for God to be, but of what type of God exists within the context of redemption and relationship.

This does not mean that God is utterly and remotely transcendent over creation, nor is God dependent on creation. God is not radically separate from the created order, but allows for a distance in order to let the creation have its own freedom. Still, even given this relationship, the majesty of God was such that embodiment in the world would have been too close to the religious life of Israel's enemies for comfort: "Nonetheless, the idea of God becoming focally incarnate in the world, even in the form of a particular person, or the idea of modeling God's relation with the world on an inner dialectical (trinitarian) structure, lies beyond the Hebrew texts."[4]

We shall have opportunity to pursue these ideas later in this book, but for right now I want to suggest that while this part of the Hebraic tradition was vital to the formation of Christian identity, it was not to be the only influence to shape the Christian idea of God.

Another Tradition, Another Image

At about the same time that these developments were marking the history of Israel, another tradition was developing concepts that would greatly influence the future of human thought about its ultimate symbol. While the cultures of Babylon, Egypt, Sumeria, Israel, and numerous others were creating narratives of ultimate concern, addressing the issue of origins and destinies, the culture of Greece was taking a turn to consider its own mythology and the picture of the world that these stories portrayed. Confronted by the changeableness of the world and the capriciousness of the gods, some thinkers started searching for something more stable, thus launching serious critical inquiry into the world.

Around the year 585 B.C.E., the philosopher Thales of Miletus offered an explanation of the world that changed perspectives for the ages. He assumed all things were made of a single substance and that the processes of change came from within the substance itself. He seemed to think that the principle of motion and change was inherent in the basic material of which the universe is made. This would mean that the gods were not responsible for the changes in the world; rather, the order of change was inherent in the thing itself.

The significance of this move is found in the notion that previously accepted perspectives of change were accounted for on the basis of supernatural causes. The gods, goddesses, demigods, and spirits affected the course of the sun, stars, moon, and all of natural life. By turning to natural explanations of the world's change, Thales and those who followed him would in some measure remove the arbitrariness of the gods from the natural order. These philosophers described a world that was orderly and predictable, and one in which things behaved according to their natures. The tyranny of divine intervention was being replaced by a world of order and regularity. Thus *chaos* was being replaced with *kosmos*.[5]

Future reflection on the fundamental problems such as the origins of things, or the underlying reality behind the continuing changing order of life, resulted in vacating nature of any personification or anthropomorphisms. There were no divinities directing the fates of humankind, but there were matter and mathematics and geometry, all of which had far better powers of prediction. There was also the need to test empirical observation and try to explain the need for change.

From this soil sprung the classical Greek tradition represented by Socrates, Plato, and Aristotle, among others. We begin with Plato.[6] Among his many ideas, which are difficult to compress, Plato conceptualized two worlds, the world of matter and the world of ideas where perfection rests.

The material world is the imperfect manifestation of the world of eternal ideas or forms. This world of our senses is the one in which change and transition are featuring marks. The other world, eternal, unchangeable, is barely perceived by us.

Plato used his famous allegory of the cave found in Book VII of *The Republic* to illustrate this concept. In this allegory he maintained that humankind is imprisoned within a deep cave, chained to a wall, and only able to glimpse the shadows of real things going on outside the cave. Not knowing any better since they have never experienced another reality, the inhabitants of the cave mistake the shadows they see for reality itself. They do not know that the shadows are incomplete representations of objects we, as humans, cannot see. To move beyond the illusion to a higher reality, to perceive finally the eternal realities, we must be freed from the cave.

The implications of this and other ideas had a profound impact on how Western civilization conceptualized God. In the material world there exists the order of change and imperfection, but in the other world, call it the realm of ideas, or the life of God as a symbol of perfection, there is unchangeableness and ultimate reality. How this idea ties in to the notion of God is difficult to assess in Plato, however, and there is no uniform agreement because Plato himself can sound at various times like a polytheist, a monotheist, or a mystic pantheist. He has been interpreted a number of different ways, and it would be difficult to offer a thumbnail sketch, but Plato's construal of the Divine aimed at a couple of things. In some ways he set up a system that would banish the capriciousness of the Homeric gods, but he also wanted to make sure that he maintained order and purpose in the cosmos.

Plato depicted the cosmos as the handiwork of a divine craftsman, the Demiurge, a rational God who struggles against the limitations of the material world. The Demiurge is a master mathematician who constructs the world on the basis of geometric principles. It would appear, however, that behind the Demiurge is another principle at work, the Good, which represents Plato's ultimate metaphysical principle.

As Plato described it, God is in every way perfect. Being perfect, God cannot change because perfection thus defined means change can only be for the worse, not the better. Given his philosophical perspective of the Ideal, Plato deduced implications from that perspective and then conceived of deity as measuring up to that ideal. Drawing upon values held in high esteem by his culture such as immutability, timelessness, and impassability, almost to the point of divine apathy, Plato fashioned a notion of the Divine that is not affected by human life, but undergirds it and accounts for the rationality of the cosmos.

Through an early method of reasoning and inquiry into the way the world works, Plato sought to banish the capriciousness of the deities and remove the absolute from anything so changeable as emotions, because this would disturb God's perfection. He spoke in different ways about the interaction of God in the affairs of human life. While wishing to remove anthropomorphic expression from deity, he conceptualized God as the best that we can imagine, perfectly good and thus impervious to change. God is all-knowing and all-powerful in the sense that God knows all that can be known, and these qualities exist timelessly in God because God exists outside of time.

Owing to the distinction between such terms as the Demiurge, the World Soul, and the Good, it is difficult to get an exact fix on a definition of the Divine. In fact in Plato the concept of God needs to be held lightly because it is hard to read him as talking about God the way that later thinkers who used his thoughts would. His attempts to work out satisfactory explanatory metaphysical principles led to speculations that probably put him outside the notion of theism in the way it is understood today. Nevertheless, the ideas that arose from Plato's mind have worked their way into the consciousness of Western culture. That these ideas arose in no small part from early reflection on nature should be no surprise. Furthermore, these early ideas about nature pointed the way for the future of scientific inquiry as exemplified by Plato's student and contemporary, Aristotle.

Aristotle was eighteen when he went to Athens to join Plato's Academy, where he became an astute pupil. He left the Academy at thirty-eight and ended up on the island of Lesbos, where he became a keen observer of marine life. He stressed scientific research and the teaching of scientific method. He took great delight in the particulars of things and would generalize from there, which was somewhat different than the path of his teacher Plato. In his mind, abstract concepts of change, actuality, potentiality, causality, being and becoming, deduction, and induction were formulated, and played a significant role in the foundation of the sciences.

Aristotle was dissatisfied by Plato's theory of forms, and was intrigued by the process of change. But he relied on his powers of observation with regard to the particular things he saw around him. He was still interested in the problem of change and continuity, but he thought more in terms of potentiality and actuality rather than in ideas, forms, and matter. A child becomes an adult, an acorn becomes an oak, but the basic material is still present. Nature seemed to have a purpose in motion, each individual thing developing its potential toward an actuality it could become.

In his theories God functions as symbolic of metaphysical principles that emerged as the final answer for all movement and change that Aristotle saw around him. Just as in Plato and Thales, the theistic understanding of God was not really present in Aristotle. God was the Unmoved Mover, the Prime Mover, pure being and thought. This Unmoved Mover causes all activity and motion in the world and serves as the ultimate attraction (final causality) for all that is. The notion of purpose is rooted in Aristotle's teleology.

In some ways this God had little religious relevance. This Unmoved Mover did not create the world, since that would have involved some sense of change and temporal activity. There was no certainty, no notion of providence or direction in the world. God's immateriality was pure actuality, for potentiality would have involved the notion of change. Thus God could receive nothing from the world and was certainly not in relationship to it in any way. For Aristotle, God is literally apathetic, impassible, to the world.

While Aristotle's achievements are breathtaking in the area of natural philosophy, physics, biology, geology, astronomy, and scientific reasoning, his notion of God entailed this particular symbol as a metaphysical necessity in his system to explain motion. The eternal and unmovable, impassible and unalterable certainly may create awe in us, but it does not necessarily move us to relationship.[7]

While these two philosophers were working out the boundaries that would help determine how much of the world thought, there were others in the Greek world who were also conceptualizing deity in a new way, casting about for more personal terms to understand God. One of the most important groups for later theology were the Stoics. Their perspective, difficult to distill over several centuries of formulation, understood God as being in the world, ordering it providentially, as the one principle behind it and constituent of it. God as the eternal and uncreated One creates the plentitude of all that is. Proceeding from God, this plentitude returns ultimately to its source of origin. Sometimes this world reason was identified with Zeus, who predetermined and ruled everything through his law.

This strong sense of determinism and predestination tended to conceptualize God in more personal terms, but the Stoic belief in the notion of causal determination led to the notion that everything that happens, happens for a reason, which is known only to the deity. This is a thought that still holds a controlling interest in many minds, especially when tragedy strikes. This is the way we comfort ourselves. When we use the word stoic in our context, it usually means someone who is able to reconcile himself or herself to his or her fate. Though suffering may happen, it does no good to protest it, since it is part of the divine plan. According to Chrysippus, even bed bugs support the divine Logos by keeping the slothful from wasting away life.

Another major element in Stoic thinking was the realization that feelings such as desire, pleasure, regret, and compassion are pathological states from which we must be free to reach the goal of imperturbability *(apatheia)*. Freedom from the entanglement of the negative results of emotion would enable us to rise above the transitory conflicts of the moment.[8]

Centuries of Greek thought concerning the world and nature left its imprint on the collective consciousness of the Western world in ways we are barely aware of, yet we do know that Greek thought has affected our views of God, life, and the meaning and purpose of our being in the world. Stoicism became the philosophical underpinning for Hellenistic theology and culture, and through them to the wider world from which Christianity would develop.

One way to get a handle on this is to read the narratives of Greek culture and mythology to gain an insight on how they viewed certain forces in the world. In the Greek stories the tale is told of Chronos (Time), who devoured his own children, thus indicating that time destroys what it creates. The desire to move the ultimate principle out of the realm where change and time conspired to corrupt meant that God would be defined by timelessness and immutability (nonchanging, since any change implies weakness).

This in turn meant that everything observable by our empirical senses in some way changes, therefore God must be beyond that which we have the power to observe. God was absolute Being, unchangeable and not subject to the vagaries of life. All other than God was becoming and changing. Deity could not have the principle of becoming as an attribute, since this would imply weakness. In this world of becoming, of potentialities becoming actualities, there rested that principle of rational order that was above and beyond, out of the reach of the changing and decaying corruptions of everyday life. Perhaps this order was accessible through mathematical inquiry, or geometry, which was one of the principles of creation.

This was the realm of the eternal, the immutable, the impassible, and the supremely rational order of the world. This One was an abstraction of the highest order and could never enter into the emotional life of humans. The ability to do so would have marked the path back to the capriciousness of the gods and what was sought was an escape from all that was superstitious. All ability to comprehend the world through natural science meant that God was the One, the principle of rationality, but also the remote, the impersonal, and the inaccessible.

So now we have the two principles mentioned earlier, the personal and the impersonal, and part of the story we are telling about science and reli-

gion carries this tension. On the one hand we have a portrayal of the ultimate symbol of human thought framed in such stories as the prophets and
visionaries tell. This God fights for the people, argues with them, bargains
with them, is even identified as their spurned husband.

Admittedly, this deity undergoes significant revision from the early
strands of the tradition and is seen in less provincial terms as the tradition
progresses, but the reality of Israel's God is that God is emotionally involved
and hopes for a relationship with that which God creates. The contours that
define this One are steeped with the shape of humanity. The primary mode
of self-disclosure is not an impassive reason, but an impassioned revelation
given to prophets, seers, and ordinary people doing ordinary things.

On the other hand we have the images of God that emerge from Greek
reflection on the deity, starting with Thales, continuing with Plato and Aristotle, and on through the Stoics and beyond. God is impassible, not touched
with the fickleness of human emotion. God is timeless and immutable, not
weakened by temporality. God is perfect and can neither be added unto or
subtracted from. God is omnipotent, perfect in power, such that everything
that happens does so because God wills it. God is barely more than a metaphysical principle meant to explain the continuity that rests behind the
world of change.

This does not necessarily mean that the Greeks were exclusive monothe-
ists; indeed, they maintained a more inclusive monotheism that had a place
for the intermediary forces. As important as his concern with the realm of
perfection was, Plato believed that intermediate beings existed who were
able to communicate with human beings on behalf of the gods. Aristotle, in
contrast, was not as important for his theological concepts as he was for
being a natural scientist. But in the midst of centuries of philosophical and
theological speculation, Hellenism developed a complex of ideas and concepts that Christians would employ for their concepts of God.

Crossing the Divide: Bridging Traditions

One of the great mysteries of the story we are telling is how the formula-
tors of Jewish, Christian, or philosophical perspectives would pave the way
for what would become the controlling notion of millennia of cultures.
Certainly part of this story can be found in the history of Greek and Jewish interaction, extending even back to the time of Alexander the Great's
defeat of Darius III of Persia. The Hellenist influence would find purchase

in those Jews who loved Greek philosophy and sought to fashion a synthesis between the two.

One of the most prominent individuals in this regard is Philo of Alexandria (30 B.C.E.–45 C.E.) an older contemporary of Jesus who bridged the gap between Judaism, Hellenism, and, indirectly, Christianity. A Platonist with a strong Stoic influence in his philosophical orientation, Philo sought to synthesize Hebraic and Greek ideas. One of the most prominent ways he met this tension was to distinguish God's unknowable essence, that which will always remain inaccessible to us, from God's energies, that which we can observe, reflect upon, and intuit. Philo was able to maintain Greek ideas in his thought by appealing to the ineffableness of God, God as absolutely transcendent and beyond our conceptual understanding. But God does not leave us without witness. Through energies and intermediaries, God reveals God's activities to us.

Philo thus defined God by the classical Greek categories of timelessness, perfection, omnipotence, omniscience, immutability, impassiveness, and others, while still maintaining the sense of relationality he believed in as a Jew. He wrote an entire treatise on the subject of God's immutability and impassability in which he dealt with the interaction of God in the world. He wanted to articulate the notion of God's love, truthfulness, and faithfulness, but he also wanted to maintain a rational sense of order that avoids the lesser human emotions of fickleness and uncertain behavior.[9]

In doing so he used the concept of the *logos,* the master plan of creation. While at times Philo can be contradictory about this notion, the concept worked its way into later Christian theology in a number of ways. While the details of Philo's perspective cannot be fully explored here, it is important to recognize that the attempt he made to synthesize Greek and Jewish ideas would figure prominently in the formation of the tradition of classical theism carried forth by the Christian tradition.

This trajectory, whereby Greek philosophical constructs emerge into the religion of Christianity, is a topic of much debate, and not everyone agrees with the assessment that theism's origins are the Bible and Greek philosophy. The differences of opinion among the church fathers meant there was not an unqualified reception of Greek philosophy by the earliest Christians. But the diversity of perspectives does point to the fact that the nascent Christian community was trying to respond to the cultural milieu within which it found itself. The various strands of thinking about God in the theological development of Christianity reflect various symbolic universes and cultural influences.

In the earliest streams of Christianity, the Greek tradition, while present—for example, in the writings of Paul—was not really an integral part of things. However, as the religion of Christianity developed, especially after the fall of Jerusalem in 70 C.E., it ended up moving its emphasis from Judaism to the communities of which it was a part. From this point on, the church would find its center shifting away from Jerusalem and its Jewish roots to the culture of the Roman world.

Regarding the culture of paganism, the church fathers wanted to show that belief in the God of Scripture was more compatible with the monotheistic perspective of Hellenist culture than with its polytheistic dimensions. In the earliest strata of the tradition found in the Christian Scriptures we find Paul the apostle referring to an unknown god worshiped on Mars Hill and making the claim that this God could be known through Jesus Christ (Acts 17).

Of course, some have read this story as a not particularly successful appeal, but nevertheless the story serves to show that Christianity was engaged in making its narrative attractive to the world in which it found itself. Certainly it was Christian belief that the fulfillment and ultimate revelation of Greek philosophy was to be found in the Christian God. But this belief was complicated by the fact that the syncretism of much of the culture had not left persons with any such thing as a clear and accepted image of the word God.

Nonetheless, because they had to deal in the coin of the realm, the early church fathers saw as one part of their explanation and defense of Christian belief the need to respond to the models of God permeating the culture. This defense, or apologetic, meant among other things that the God of history and revelation had to be explained in such a way that those who saw God as metaphysical principle would see the connection. In taking this path, the earliest Christian thinkers, known as apologists, adopted and adapted the philosophical vocabulary at hand.[10]

In the earliest expressions of theologians such as Ignatius and Justin Martyr, God is described as impassible, unchangeable, eternal, timeless, incomprehensible, unchanging, and even anonymous. While these early theologians sought to maintain the biblical rendering of God, allowing for such capacities as love and compassion, they still tried to steer a way between the thought forms of their own context and the context of their faith.

As the story of Christian engagement with pagan culture continues, even such writers as Tertullian, no great friend of classical philosophy and famous for the line "What has Athens to do with Jerusalem?" found themselves understanding God at times in ways that are reminiscent of classical thought.

At points Tertullian, for example, railed against Plato and idealism and sought to break free of the notions of impassability and immutability, arguing for a sense of divine responsiveness to the world.[11] He also wrote that God the Father, God the Son, and God the Holy Spirit are incapable of suffering and that while Jesus' humanity suffers, his divinity does not.[12] The notion that God suffers was not acceptable for many of the early church writers and would figure prominently in the Arian controversy in the fourth century.

In struggling with this tension of the impassability of God, Tertullian found himself in the company of many of the earliest Christians who tried to reconcile the biblical images of God with the constraints of Hellenistic thought. Specifically, the rejection of Greek mythology meant that images in Scripture that refer to such things as God repenting and suffering were to be seen as anthropomorphisms and figures of speech, not to be taken literally.[13]

This struggle to relate Christian belief to the thought forms of the culture in which the Christians found themselves would continue throughout the history of the church and would lead to some of the greatest conflicts found in Christian tradition. From the Arian controversy in the fourth century, to the rise of the Cappadocian fathers, and right up to Augustine, the tension between Hellenist-informed metaphysical systems and biblical renderings of God emerges from the church's desire to explain that the God of philosophical reflection is found in biblical revelation. While the church wanted to tell the story of a God who enters into relationships with human beings, it also wished to protect the majesty of God from being confused with what it thought were the vulgarities of Greek mystery religions.[14]

In addressing specifically the notions of change (immutability) and emotion (impassability), the church weighted these ideas far more on the human side of the scale. Since God was absolutely transcendent and unchangeable, change must occur on the human pole of the relationship. God cannot change and is not subject to the corruptions of time or the weakness of emotion. Especially after the Arian controversy and the Nicene Council, language about God became more abstract and even Christian understanding of Jesus tended to be slanted more to the eternal, divine, Son of the immanent Trinity, rather than to the historical Jesus of Nazareth.

Constructing Trinity

Even while theological reflection upon God led to the contours influenced by Greek philosophy, there was the knowledge that the word God itself pointed to a reality that was at best ambiguous, at worst, indefinable. The definition of God in this way proceeded as much by negation *(apophasis)* as by affirmation *(cataphasis)*. Sometimes the church found itself using these as interchangeable (and contradictory) modes of speaking about the ineffable.[15]

Thus it was God's ineffability that stood as the preeminent apophatic condition. Try as we might, the divine essence is unknowable. Gregory of Nazianzus asserted that it was "difficult to conceive God, but impossible to define God in words." When Christian faith came to the task of defining that which was beyond all human thinking and yet related to the world, it finally centered itself upon the notion of God-as-Trinity.

While an extended historical treatment of this doctrine is beyond the scope of this work, it is necessary to sketch out some of the main themes that I will use to speak of the Christian mystery. The doctrine of the Trinity arose within the first three centuries of the Christian faith not so much from rigorous biblical interpretation, though it rests there in embryo, as through a reflection on how, exactly, Jesus was related to God.[16] It is the explication of that relationship that led to so many different perspectives emerging from the early church.

This primary relationship was crucial for Christian self-definition because the struggle to maintain the unity and oneness of God while trying to conceptualize the revelation of God as existing within a community of relationship was extraordinarily difficult. Christianity over the centuries saw its doctrine of God having to allow for the diversity of relations that grounds the Trinity. This was not an abstract, impersonal, and rational belief. God, though given attributes and definitions from the cultural context, was not totally defined by it. How were the early Christians to express the One in the many?

Because the relationship of God to Jesus was of utmost importance, God was defined christologically, not as a philosophical principle of motion, nor as the principle of perfection, but as the One who incarnates and embodies self within the world. Here is the appearance of something that for all its parallels in the Near Eastern world does move beyond the cultural context. The need to explain this definition of God led to many different attempts to express how God's presence and character is manifest in the teachings of Jesus.

One of these attempts, modalism, posited that God is timeless and unitary so that Father, Son, and Spirit refer to three successive modes of divine expression in the temporal world. One proponent of this idea, Sabellius, contended that these modes of action in the world did not indicate inherent distinctions within the being of God, but were to be understood as the ways in which God manifested Godself to the world in time.

Other writers such as Origen also had schemes for incorporating the language of Father, Son, and Spirit and sought vigorously to try and maintain the unity of God. In so doing, the tradition wrestled with such ideas as the preeminence of the Father and the subordination of the Son, and the eternalness of the Son with the Father.

Matters would come to a head at the Council of Nicaea in 325 C.E. The debate, which was identified as a dispute between Arius and Athanasius, but was really about three centuries of disagreements, oscillated around some major concepts. Athanasius in his understanding argued that God is complex and trinitarian. There is both distinction and dynamism within the divine life and this allows for the understanding that God does not just exist in a static transcendence to all life. God is relational within Godself, not only internally, but also externally to the creation as well. Athanasius accepted the fact that the eternal reality of God is fundamentally Father, Son, and Spirit.

The role that Jesus plays as the Son was the great issue before the council. In the debate between Arius and Athanasius, the view brought forward was that there is an inner mutuality within God that exists before the creation emerges. Jesus is embodied in the flesh, but the Son is coeternal with the Father and the Spirit. God not only shares in the sociality of mutual relations, but also relates to the world as its Creator, Redeemer, and Sustainer.

God in God's own being is present in the incarnation. In this way the Logos is a manifestation of eternity, but it is an eternity with an immanent reality, a corporeal reality that was indeed flesh. This doctrine represents a huge distinction from all forms of Gnosticism that speak to flesh being an inherently corrupt source for God's life to be expressed.[17]

Matters were left unfinished at Nicaea and significant development of the doctrine emerged in the various regions of the church, but some of the most important work was done by the Cappadocians, Basil, Gregory of Nazianzus, and Gregory of Nyssa. While they constructed a rather elaborate theology based primarily on such terms as *ousia* and *hypostases*, Trinity for them was not important as a single divine "essence"; rather, the active and dynamic inner life of the Trinity was of utmost interest. In terms of Cappadocian thought on the Trinity, the manner of God's inner life being expressed in the world was important.[18]

This pushed the Greeks not in the direction of increasing rationalism, but to the boundary of a mystical perspective. They used the Trinity as a means of maintaining the mind in mystery and a realization that the human intellect could never understand the nature of God: "The mystery of divine being transcended not only the rational and philosophical constructs of Classical natural theology but the revealed and orthodox truth of the church's dogmatic theology itself."[19] It is for this reason that Gregory of Nyssa argued against Eunomius that the mystery of the Christian faith was not exactness of doctrines, even the doctrine of the Trinity.[20]

But even as the doctrine of the Trinity was being worked out by the Cappadocians, there was a positive connection that speaks to what I want to address in this book. For the Cappadocians, Trinity and cosmology were correlative doctrines. Basil in his reflections on the creation stories of Genesis asserted that God had welded all the diverse parts of the universe into a harmony and kinship among all created things. Even though creation was contingent, it was still, in its entirety, the manifestation of the triune God, which conferred upon it a single grace extending equally through all creation "that thus the earthy might be raised up to the Divine and so one certain grace of equal value might pervade the whole creation."[21]

One of the results of this move is that it allowed for an understanding of God that was more than negation. If the human mind was to understand the incomprehensible reality, it was "absolutely necessary for us to be guided to the investigation of the divine nature by its actions *(energeiai).*"[22] These actions are not confined to the incarnation and subsequent events; rather, the creation itself is included in the divine economy of salvation. Thus the inner life of the Trinity is manifested in the entirety of history, time, space, energy, and matter.

This connection between what God is and what God does provides interesting reflection for the relationship of science and theology. If the Trinity constitutes a genuine opening into the being of God, no matter how ineffable Godself may be, then doors open to deepen our understandings of God and world that have been neglected through centuries of captivity to a static metaphysics, bequeathed not by Christian Scripture or revelation but by certain metaphysical constraints. This is not a unique claim; in fact, it is a rather standard one. The curious thing seems to be that it doesn't emerge in the life of the church in any significant way.

If God is Creator, Redeemer, Sustainer, eternally in God's own identity, such that the triune God is present at every moment, then reflection upon the mysteries and energies present in the world is in the deepest sense reflection upon God and God's action of salvation for all things:

> Everything that is, exists and lives in the unceasing inflow of the energies and potentialities of the cosmic Spirit. This means that

we have to understand every created reality in terms of energy, grasping it as the realized potentiality of the divine Spirit. Through the energies and potentialities of the Spirit the Creator himself is present in his creation. He does not merely confront it in his transcendence; entering into it, he is also immanent in it.[23]

The significance of this will become fleshed out as we proceed, but for now the argument before you is that trinitarian theology in recent decades has moved away from abstract discussion regarding the terminology of *hypostases, ousia, substantia,* or *essentia* and seeks rather to relate trinitarian language to the contemporary world and its context. This does not constitute surrender to the culture. It means rather that within the traditions engendered by Christianity there are resources for fresh understanding. The theology of the Trinity is important not so much for the sake of doctrinal precisions found in Augustine or the Cappadocians, though these function as our touchstones for furthering the tradition, but for the life of the church and the spiritual life of Christians.

We can appreciate the Greek belief that the Trinity functions as boundary on all human attempts to define God in words or concepts. We can even see how this works itself out in the Greek attempt to link cosmology and theology. The Trinity functions to prevent theological idolatry because we are always poised on the porch of mystery, contemplating the darkness in front of us and delighting in the small sparks of light whether they are fireflies or stars.

Because God-as-Trinity is seen in ways that reflect a sociality and relationality both internal and external to God's own being, God's life is expressed in the world to the extent that the spiritual life is to be found in total immersion within the world, not gnostic withdrawal from it. If the triune God dwells within all things, a way opens to show that all processes of what we understand energy and matter to be are themselves manifestations of the energies of God and God is accomplishing God's will through them. The material world cannot be interpreted apart from God's redemptive intent for it. Of course, one of the great ironies of Christian history is that about the time that the tradition was struggling with these problems, the monastic movement, a journey away from the world, strengthened.

For some this immediately raises the suspicion that behind this approach there is essentially a type of pantheism masquerading as Christianity. Does this approach not bring the Creator and the creation in too close identification with one another? Is there not the danger of collapsing God and creation into an indefinable mess? Even worse, does not this understanding of

God raise the whole issue of evil and suffering, with God being directly responsible for the waste and suffering experienced by the universe?

More will be said about this later; however, for right now I ask you to think about a theological notion that has been crucial in Christianity. The tensions between God's transcendence and immanence have been with us from the beginning. It was one of the reasons for the emergence of the doctrine of the Trinity. But the triune God is able to hold these tensions. Pantheism, in contrast, sees simple eternal divine presence without differentiation. There is no distance between God and creation.

The trinitarian understanding moves us to consider that while the infinite One is manifested in all the created order, this One is also constituted by relationships that speak to the destiny and intention for that order. Transcendence and immanence are held together in such ways that not only are the particles of the material world created by the Creator, but the relationships among them are created as well.

It is this notion of relationality within God that has been so explored in recent years. It is an important concept but simplistic notions of it should be avoided.[24] Community and relationship are intrinsic to the being of God and offer us ways for thinking about the God who is not removed from the world, but related intimately to it, and, in contrast to some of the classical theistic notions of God, is even affected by it. The mutuality of God and the world offers us perspectives that allow for a new understanding.

One can see this in the works of Jürgen Moltmann, who contends that the Trinity functions not as a principle of subordination but as a means by which all trinitarian relations are equal, complete, and present at all moments, not manifested successively in time in a modalistic fashion. This position allows for a view that sees God's being in the world being expressed in terms of God's relations with the creation in the most intimate of ways.[25]

A recovery of trinitarian thought would allow the church to critique the simplistic theism that really functions as the concrete dimension from which most persons make statements about God's action and presence in the world. It also would allow us to make different types of assessments about the world that science is revealing in its explorations. We shall explore the implications of this presently, but for now perhaps these words from Catherine LaCugna express another dimension to this understanding of God:

> The Life of God—precisely because God is triune—does not belong to God alone. God who dwells in inaccessible light and eternal glory comes to us in the face of Christ and the activity of

the Holy Spirit. Because of God's outreach to the creature, God is said to be essentially relational, ecstatic, fecund, alive as passionate love. Divine life is also our life. The heart of the Christian life is to be united with the God of Jesus Christ by means of communion with one another. The doctrine of the Trinity is ultimately therefore a teaching not about the abstract nature of God, nor about God in isolation from everything other than God, but a teaching about God's life with us and our life with one another.[26]

According to LaCugna, as the subsequent theological tradition developed between the first two councils of Nicaea and afterward, the doctrine of the Trinity became separated from its first order of concern, the redemptive action of God in the world. The theologies spun off increasingly speculative ideas about the Trinity. The interest in God's essence became exceedingly important, but this was an essence defined in ways that were abstracted from God's redemptive intent. While it may be that we have no need to figure out what "went wrong," we should nonetheless ask if there are ways the ongoing process of tradition can enhance our understanding of God's life in the world. Before we finish our all too brief historical excursus, let us consider one final figure.

Augustine's Construction

The culmination of centuries of theological formation would find its destination in the man who set the table for the ensuing banquet of Christian tradition and theology, St. Augustine. All the tensions we have discussed will coalesce in the figure of Augustine of Hippo, who plays no small role in our story. It would be Augustine who would solidify the Western conceptualizations of God for subsequent generations, right to the present day. It would not be too great a stretch to argue that what most Christians today believe about God comes from the matrix offered them by Augustinian thought.

It would be in Augustine's disagreements with his opponents, like the Donatists and Pelagius, that he would fashion his images of God, but behind these arguments would be the storehouse of images he received from almost four centuries of Christian tradition. The importance of Augustine's impact on Christianity cannot be minimized, for the reality is that all of us are the children of Augustine. Even those who have long since left his theology find themselves affected by the imprint he has left on the heart and soul of civi-lization. Much of theology has been done in response to his legacy, either to affirm or overcome it.

There is no doubt that Augustine was much influenced by classical thought, especially the neoplatonism he learned from Plotinus. Like many who came before him, Augustine maintained the traditional list of attrib-utes, seeing God as impassible, omniscient, omnipotent, ineffable, self-suf-ficient, and timeless.[27] In Augustine's construction of God the attribute of immutability was of critical importance because it implied that God's will and knowledge never change and thus we can depend on them. The vision of divine life that emerges from his work would resonate strongly through-out his world and in the ongoing tradition. In Augustine's theology God knows all things in one eternal moment because God exists outside time. Past, present, and future are all known because God is eternal and not locked into time like we are. Augustine believed that divine foreknowledge and human freedom are not incompatible with one another.[28] Like many today, Augustine believed that God's knowledge of future events is not the cause of those events.

And yet the situation is a little more complex, because for Augustine, God is not that passive. Because he was being pushed in the Pelagian controversy to deal with this issue, Augustine finally took the position that humankind is so fallen away from God it cannot even do the right thing in accepting God's merciful invitation to grace. God must therefore do all the choosing because God, not humanity, is the sovereign power of the universe. God wills who is and who is not saved.

When he was faced with the problem of the suffering of the innocent, more specifically with the death of infants, Augustine fell back on the posi-tion that God, being God, has good reasons: "Perhaps God is doing some good in correcting parents when their beloved children suffer pain and even death."[29] When I was a pastor and went to my parishioners' homes after death or tragedy, I would often hear this type of idea expressed. God after all, controls everything, so everything must have a reason. Such is the legacy of Augustine down to the present day.

But the fact is that part of Augustine's construal of God as ultimate sym-bol was built on his understanding of what is and is not proper for God to be. This underlying assumption colors Augustine's interpretation of Scrip-ture, always weighing it on the side of God's impassability and immutabil-ity. How could God "repent" of an action that God foreknew throughout all eternity that God was going to take? The will of God is not dependent on anything human, or anything else in the created order for that matter, because God is radically independent from God's creation.

This emphasis on the sovereignty of God over the created order would have profound consequences for Christian belief in God, for with this understanding of omnipotence and predestination, "every event was charged with a precise meaning as a deliberate act of God, of mercy for the elect, of judgment for the damned."[30] Echoing the Stoics, everything that happens in the world does so by the will of an omnipotent God. And with this argument Augustine planted the Achilles heel into the heart of Christianity. Evil and suffering become the infection from which Augustine's image of God has yet to recover, yet it is that image that has formed so many of us.

In his structuring of the church's doctrine of God, Augustine built the dwelling for subsequent generations of Christians, yet he laid a difficult burden upon faith as well. Seeking to protect what he perceived to be the majesty of God, the sovereign will of the Divine, he portrayed an image of God that could not respond to human decision for all decisions were already predestined through foreknowledge by God. It is hard to believe in the notion that human and more-than-human decisions are freely made if they have already been determined through foreknowledge.

While Augustine wished to emphasize the certainty of God's grace and the corresponding impotence of human will with his understanding of God, he left many thoughtful and caring persons with only one option in the face of such a God, atheism. How could one believe in a God directly responsible for evil?

When Augustine dealt with the doctrine of the Trinity, he did so by a different emphasis than the Cappadocians. While they were more interested in the aspect of relationship among persons and the subsequent definition of God's being, Augustine was interested in the unity of the divine substance prior to the plurality of persons. In this he gave extensive attention to the vestiges of Trinity (vestigia trinitatis) found in the world, specifically the human being. This approach meant for some that Augustine moved the centrality of Christian salvation from the world to the individual: "In Augustine's theology, the true economy is that of the individual soul, whose interior structure discloses the reality of the Trinity."[31]

Has this emphasis on the personal dimension of redemption and the work of the trinitarian God led to an unbalanced understanding of God's action in creation? Is not Christianity in the West seen primarily as centrally concerned about the individual soul, but not about the entirety of the creation itself? Perhaps we need to rethink what the redemption of God looks like from God's perspective for all creation. As the subsequent generations of Christian development show, Augustine's understanding of God would continue to exercise its influence within the life of the Western world. Even to question the images of God emerging from the streams of Jewish, Greek, Christian, and later, Islamic tradition is for some to question the very reality of God. While this history is a complex and diverse one, I would argue that with only slight qualification or revision the idea of God that we have received from the classical theist tradition is the major idea that persons in the West believe to this day.

It is really to this image that most refer when they ask, "Where is God?" The ruling image of God in most minds influenced by Christian traditions is constituted by the metaphysics of perfection and its attendant shaping of God as the omnipotent, omniscient, infinite, utterly transcendent, impassible, and all-determining power of everything that happens in the world.

Whether they are conscious of it or not, most Christians today who sit in the church pew believe in a God who was constructed out of the Greek metaphysics of perfection. This metaphysics was present from the beginning of Christian thinking as the manifestation of the perfection of God, which in turn became a God who conformed to the strictures of human thinking about what constituted that perfection. Augustine helped to solidify this tradition and Thomas Aquinas baptized it.[32]

One of the great surprises of this history is that there were other images of God that were written about or manifested in the church. Much of trinitarian thought is lost to us because we have usually framed it in terms that are too abstract for most persons. Other than academically trained theologians, contemporary Christian existence mostly ignores the need for extending the tradition by further discussion concerning the Trinity. We simply cannot abstract God from the world, because this flies in the face of the reasons the Trinity was first formulated.

Sometimes ideas emerged from those who were a part of another stream altogether. Found in thinkers such as Meister Eckhart, Teresa of Avila, St. Francis of Assisi, Nicholas of Cusa, the Brethren of the Common Life, and many others, the ideas of the minority spoke of a God that was far different than the one of dominant tradition. That this alternative never became seriously considered was perhaps one of the most regrettable parts of the tradition, for had the church been able to exhibit a little flexibility in its official understanding, it might have been better able to engage in a fuller doctrine of the Trinity.

It is from this space that we will proceed. The mystery of God revealed in the universe is ultimately paradoxical. Diversity in unity, the One in the many, the personal in the impersonal forces of interstellar galaxies; in all these images we find ourselves entertaining the thoughts that cause us to become inarticulate. Everyone at some point has experienced those moments when deep intuition has led to speechlessness and amazement. It is in these moments, when we are barely able to grasp at what is there, that we find ourselves caught up in the triune mystery. And in that moment, for many of us, we find ourselves profoundly grateful for being a part of it all.

NOTES

1. See, for example, Karen Armstrong, *A History of God: The 4,000-Year Quest for Judaism, Christianity, and Islam* (New York: Knopf, 1993); George Newlands, *God in Christian Perspective* (Edinburgh: T&T Clark, 1994). These are fairly readable and accessible treatments that function as good introductions to the overall idea of God and God in Christianity. For a more philosophical treatment, see Sebastian Matczak, ed., *God in Contemporary Thought: A Philosophical Perspective* (New York: Learned Publications, Inc. 1977). See also, Jack Miles, *God: A Biography* (New York: Vintage Books, 1996).

2. One of the most well-known scholars working this territory over the last several years has been Walter Brueggemann. See, for example, his *Theology of the Old Testament: Testimony, Dispute, Advocacy* (Minneapolis: Fortress Press), 1997.

3. There are a number of places where the entirety of creation is described as sharing in the goodness of creation. Psalm 104 is a hymn to the creation. In Isaiah, the hope is raised that in God's Sabbath rest, peace will exist between all living things, 65:25; 66:3.

4. Philip Clayton, *God and Contemporary Science* (Grand Rapids, Mich.: Eerdmans, 1997), 30.

5. David C. Lindberg, *The Beginnings of Western Science* (Chicago: University of Chicago Press, 1992), 27.

6. There are numerous sources on this history. See, for example, the treatment of Plato's incorporation into the Christian ethos in John P. Rowan, "Platonic and Christian Theism," in Sebastian Matczak, ed., *God in Contemporary Thought*. See also, Dewey J. Hoitenga Jr., *Faith and Reason from Plato to Plantinga: An Introduction to Reformed Epistemology* (Albany, N.Y.: SUNY Press, 1991).

7. See Aristotle's *Metaphysics* 12.6–9; *Physics* 267b. Keith Ward has an interesting and very accessible treatment of Plato, Aristotle, and Augustine in his recent book, *God: A Guide for the Perplexed* (Oxford: Oneworld, 2002), 103–24. See also, Joseph Owen, "Aristotle on God," in Matczak, *God in Contemporary Thought*. Though Aristotle's influence was somewhat minimal in his own day, it became wider within Christianity

owing to the work of St. Thomas Aquinas and his recovery of Aristotle, aided by Islamic scholars such as Averroes and Avicenna.

8. See, for example, Helmut Koester, *History, Culture, and Religion of the Hellenistic Age* (Hermeneia 1; Philadelphia: Fortress Press, 1982), 144–51.

9. For a deeper study of Philo, see such works as Samuel Sandmel, *Philo of Alexandria* (New York: Oxford University Press, 1979); and Henry Wolfson, *Philo: Foundations of Religious Philosophy in Judaism, Christianity, and Islam* (2 vols.; Cambridge, Mass.: Harvard University Press, 1947).

10. Almost any church history book will contain an account of how these traditions were formed. Some of particular interest are Henry Chadwick, *Early Christian Thought and the Classical Tradition: Studies in Justin, Clement, and Origen* (New York: Oxford University Press, 1966); Frederick Copelston, *A History of Philosophy* (7 vols.; Garden City, N.Y.: Image, 1961). Perhaps the best of these is Jaroslav Pelikan, *The Christian Tradition: A History of the Development of Doctrine* (5 vols.; Chicago: University of Chicago Press, 1971). For an interesting account of the ways in which natural theology was informed by its encounter with the culture of the Cappadocian fathers, see Pelikan's *Christianity and Classical Culture: The Metamorphosis of Natural Theology in the Christian Encounter with Hellenism* (New Haven, Conn.: Yale University Press, 1993). This title constitutes the printed version of Pelikan's Gifford Lectures given in 1992–1993. Also, see John Sanders, "Historical Considerations," in *The Openness of God: A Biblical Challenge to the Traditional Understanding of God* (ed. Clark Pinnock; Downers Grove, Ill.: InterVarsity Press, 1994).

11. His most famous arguments are found in the work *Against Marcion.*

12. *Against Praxeas,* 29.

13. See, for instance, Origen, *De principiis* 2.4.4 or *Contra Celsum* 43.37, 72; 6.53

14. Pelikan, for instance, makes the point that while Christian theologians explicitly rejected the myths and religious cults of the Greeks, they did draw from and engage on many different levels the classical philosophical and scientific theories in the formation of their natural theologies. *Christianity and Classical Culture,* 24–25.

15. Justin Martyr, *First Apology* 1.61, "No One can utter the name of the ineffable God and if any one dare to say that there is a name he raves with hopeless madness." See, for example, Pelikan, *Christianity and Classical Culture,* 41.

16. While I certainly do believe that feminine images of God are found in Scripture and tradition, for instance in the use of the word *ruach* for the spirit, in my discussion of the historical development of the doctrine of the Trinity I employ the usage that emerged from the early church.

17. The sources on this are numerous. However, a few good introductory remarks can be found in Ted Peters, *God—The World's Future* (Minneapolis: Fortress Press, 1992); and Alister McGrath, *Historical Theology: An Introduction to the History of Christian Thought* (London: Blackwell, 1998). For more extended treatments see Ted Peters, *God as Trinity* (Louisville, Ky.: Westminster/John Knox, 1993); Jürgen Moltmann, *The Trinity and the Kingdom: The Doctrine of God* (trans. Margaret Kohl; San Francisco: Harper & Row, 1981); or Robert Jensen, *Systematic Theology* (2 vols.; Oxford: Oxford University Press, 1998–1999).

18. One of the best works concerning this history comes from Catherine M. LaCugna, *God for Us: The Trinity and Christian Life* (repr.; San Francisco: Harper SanFrancisco, 1993), to whom almost everyone is indebted. See also, Constantine N. Tsirpaulis, "God in Greek Orthodox Thought," found in Matczak, *God in Contemporary Discussion.* For a recent treatment of Orthodox theology and sophiology from a Russian perspective, see Sergius Bulgarov, *Bride of the Lamb* (trans. Boris Jakim; Grand Rapids, Mich.: Eerdmans, 2002).

19. Pelikan, *Christianity and Classical Culture,* 234. This is what allows Gregory of Nyssa to argue that every name we use for God, "whether invented by human custom or handed down by Scriptures, is indication of our conceptions of the divine nature." These names do not, however, capture the totality of the thing.

20. Gregory of Nyssa, *Contra Eunomium* 3.9.56; 59. Gregory argues for mystery in some sense because his opponent believed that accuracy of doctrine and clarity of logical expression were the way to salvation. Mystery was not really a viable category of theological expression for the Eunomians.

21. Gregory of Nyssa, *The Great Catechism* 6.4.

22. Gregory of Nyssa, "Ad Eustathium de Trinitatae," in *Gregorii Nysseni Opera* (ed. Werner Jaeger; 10 vols; Berlin and Leiden: E. J. Brill, 1921), 3:1.10–11. These energies are the uncreated energies such as grace, but they are energies in which God goes forth from Godself, manifesting, communicating, and giving Godself to the creation. In Book II of *Against Eunomius* Gregory addresses Eunomius's use of the term energy, arguing that energy cannot be used in abstraction from Person. The energies manifest in "all things visible and invisible are the work of the Son." Gregory took great delight in the beauty of nature, finding there that which educates the mind to a greater reality. See also his *On Infants Early Deaths,* or *Letters to Adelphus.* In St. Gregory Palama's doctrine of these energies, they have a world-creating, world-sustaining power that is the property of Sophia, the Wisdom of God. How can this be anything other than an involvement with the created order under the most intimate of connections?

23. Moltmann, *God in Creation,* 9. .

24. See LaCugna, *God for Us.* See also Elizabeth A. Johnson, *She Who Is: The Mystery of God in Feminist Theological Discourse* (New York: Crossroad, 1994); Karl Rahner, *The Trinity;* and Leonardo Boff, *Trinity and Society.*

25. Moltmann, *God in Creation,* 16. See also his *History and the Triune God: Contributions to Trinitarian Theology* (trans. John Bowden; New York: Crossroad, 1992).

26. LaCugna, *God for Us,* 1.

27. See, for example, *Confessions* 7.11; 11.18; 12.15; 13.16; *De Trinitate* 1.1.3; 5.2.3; 4.5–6; 7.5, 10. For secondary literature on Augustine there are several places where the reader might go. First among these would be Peter Brown, *Augustine of Hippo* (Berkeley: University of California Press, 1967); or Etienne Gilson, *The Christian Philosophy of Saint Augustine* (trans. L. E. M. Lynch; New York: Random House, 1960). A highly readable and accessible volume is Garry Wills, *St. Augustine* (New York: Lipper/Viking, 1999).

28. *City of God* 5.9–10.

29. *On Free Will* 3.68. Quoted from Sanders, "Historical Considerations," 82.

30. Peter Brown, *Augustine of Hippo*, 404.

31. LaCugna, *God for Us, 101*. Augustine does not begin with a treatment of the *vestigial* until after seven full books of his treatment of the Trinity. David Cunningham argues that this tradition actually can function as a positive interpretive tool for how we see the created order. "The *Vestigia Tradition*," 200.

32. See, for example, Thomas Franklin O'Meara, O.P., *Thomas Aquinas, Theologian* (Notre Dame: University of Notre Dame Press, 1997). This book should be the starting place for anyone interested in the theological shape of Aquinas's work. There are other sources too numerous to mention, but fine treatments of Aquinas are also found in Brian Davies, *The Thought of Thomas Aquinas* (Oxford: Clarendon Press, 1992); and Jean-Pierre Torrell, O.P., *Saint Thomas Aquinas: The Person and His Work* (vol. 1; trans. Robert Royal; Washington, D.C.: Catholic University of America Press, 1996). Aquinas will be looked at briefly in the next chapter.

3

ATTENDING GOD'S FUNERAL

O man-projected Figure, of late
Imaged as we, thy knell who shall survive?
Whence came it we were tempted to create
One whom we can no longer keep alive?
—Thomas Hardy,

I started out this book by telling the story of a friend who had given birth to a little boy who had severe medical difficulties from birth. He had about four heart operations in the first two years of his life and would be impaired in both hearing and speech for the rest of his life. His life was to be an endless round of doctors and special schools. While his mother was in the hospital recuperating from his birth, she was trying to struggle with the immediate sense of pain and anguish she felt. As she related the story to me, her pastor came to visit her and in the course of their conversation asked her what great sin she had committed that caused God to give her this baby.

As you read these words you probably respond the way most people do when I tell this story. There are usually audible gasps from listeners who are astounded by such insensitivity. And it seems on the face of it that horror and revulsion are the only appropriate response. Upon closer examination, however, something surprising happens. After I tell this story and get the type of response that signifies incredulity at such insensitivity, I ask a question. When was the last time something bad or tragic happened to you and your first response was, "What did I do to deserve this?" or "Why is this happening to me?" Usually a majority of people in the room respond that they have thought this way. The very fact that these questions often do form the first line of response shows how deep our unconscious images of God are.

The pastor was only echoing the friends of Job in Hebrew Scripture who come to comfort their suffering friend only to fall back onto tired religious clichés that offer justification for the one speaking. It is a story as old as time and one we strongly accept. If God rewards the righteous and punishes the wicked, then when I am doing well I must be accounted among the righteous, but when I am suffering I must have done something to bring this into my life. Much like Job and his "comforters," we struggle with our traditions when the experiences of life confront us with a reality that erases all our most cherished assumptions.

Many of us have experienced those moments when we took leave of the tradition because it made no sense for either our hearts or our minds. At such times, the boxes that we have put God in lay shattered on the floor of our lives and we find nothing there but emptiness. Of course, we never realize that our images of God can be built on the most ephemeral of things, and most of us never think to question whether other images of God are present for us to consider. We just accept the wisdom that we have received, much like Job and his friends had accepted the wisdom that they had received. But the most wonderful thing about that particular text in the Hebrew Scripture is that it functions as a demolition job on notions of God that have imprisoned God in a religious box.

Sometimes our images of God are more appropriately seen as the results of our own wishes and fears. We construct the image of God that provides us comfort and security and in the process we fashion an idol that keeps us from the reality of the truth itself. The German theologian Dorothee Soelle shares a story of the connection I am hoping to make for you when she relates the story of attending a conference where the question was raised: "Where was God at Auschwitz?" One of the attendees answered that Auschwitz was willed by God. Pressed further, she responded that if God had not willed it, it would not have happened. Nothing happens without God, she argued. Soelle calls this God the idol.[1]

With such ideas it is not hard to understand that for so many people today God is really not a viable option. We have been attending the funeral of God continually since Auschwitz, and as Richard Rubenstein eloquently stated in his book *After Auschwitz,* belief in God has been made impossible for future generations who think seriously about the issues raised by the sheer suffering of the innocent. Contemplation of the magnitude of the Holocaust brings one to the door of perplexity and tears.

I was going through the Holocaust Museum in Washington, D.C., a number of years ago when I came upon the display of children's shoes. I had maintained an odd sense of detachment up to this point; however, as I stood there, tears came to my eyes and I found myself responding in a visceral way, shaking my fist at the heavens and screaming inwardly, "If you had the power to prevent this and did not . . . " Old habits die hard and later I reflected that sometimes tears are the most symbolic manifestation of God. As such they are the only appropriate response of theology. But who or what exactly is it that we are grieving?

This is the question found in Dostoyevsky's *The Brothers Karamozov* when Ivan pushes his brother Alyosha to consider God's governance of the world. He gives his brother numerous instances of humanity's inhumanity, a child being hunted by a general's dogs, another being tortured by her parents. After this litany he asks his brother a tough question about God's governance:

> Look: if everyone must suffer in order for their suffering to purchase eternal harmony, what do young children have to do with it, tell me please? It is quite impossible to understand why they should have to suffer, and why should they have to purchase harmony with their sufferings? Why have they ended up as raw material, to be the manure for someone else's future harmony? Solidarity in sin among human beings I understand; I even understand solidarity in retribution, but I mean to say, there can be no question of solidarity in sin among young children, and if it is indeed true that they are in solidarity with their fathers in all the villainous actions of their fathers, then it goes without saying that therein is a truth that is not of this world and is impossible for me to understand.[2]

Much like Annie Dillard does in her comments, Dostoyevsky raises the issue we will never be through with in this life. These types of responses to the presence of undeserved suffering reveal our difficulty with all those attempts to understand and justify the life of God in the world. In the face of untold suffering by the innocent, we wonder where we will find a place to hold onto belief in God.

Because our images of God have been constructed from a multiple number of places, we can rightly ask the question if there are ways of conceiving God that may not be tied to our desires and self-regarding impulses, but could even demand of us more faith. Maybe there are ways of understanding our faith that seem consonant with our experience of suffering and randomness in the world. Part of the problem has been the legacy we have been bequeathed in the heritage of the metaphysics of perfection. If we have truly internalized those images as the truth about God, then it makes some of the ideas discussed in the last couple of chapters not just concepts, but truths.

Especially when we come to the problem of evil and suffering, we find how strong the pull of certain traditional perspectives are on us still. Most persons today have these traditional perspectives ingrained into them as their working model of God, not realizing that they offer just one image of what surely transcends all attempts at definition. In humankind's defining of God we embraced ideas that resulted in God being seen as the highest possible object of human thought. By defining God in a literal way we lost a sense of mystery and wonder. This wonder should have as its focus the world in which we live, but it can also have the corollary of enlarging our vision of God.

Consider the statements at the beginning of this chapter about God's action in the world. If we believe that God is the omnipotent and omniscient principle inherent in the world, then we will have this problem solved. God causes everything to happen and we must simply accept the will of the Supreme Being. We may talk about God willing something, or God allowing something, but the result is the same; God controls everything that happens. No wonder so many people have a difficult time with this idea.

For the person not inclined to blind belief, there are questions about the God who is "outside" the world, locked away in utter transcendence. One wonders about the places where God does not seem to be involved in the world. If God is "in" the world in some type of omnipotence, directing events as God wishes, then what are we to do about those times when the tornado hits my house and not my neighbor's? Why was this one healed and the other one not? The question of "Where was God when . . . ?" becomes particularly relevant. The suffering of the world must be the primary data for the theologian today, for a theology that does not respond to suffering is really unimportant to most people.[3]

In the model that many presently believe, including the woman who believed that God willed Auschwitz for nothing happens without God willing it, God has been defined in terms of infinity (for nothing finite can pertain to God), impassability (for suffering or the experiences of life cannot make God other than what God is), determinism (for God controls all things through absolute power, even though we have the illusion of freedom), and transcendence (for God is not involved in the world, save as God chooses to manifest power through action). But this model has increasingly come under examination by many from within the Christian community. Perhaps the hardest step to take is the one that addresses the notion that our ideas of God are in fact models or metaphorical images of our connection to the One in whom we live and move and have our being. These images, models, and metaphors are not in reality God, but our way of perceiving the Divine. One of the most difficult things for faith to embrace is the realization that there will always be that aspect of the divine life that is hidden from us, and so our definitions of God are based on images and models we develop, sometimes in concert with the narratives of Christian faith, sometimes out of the cultural storehouses of other sources.

In his book, *Religion and Science: Historical and Contemporary Issues,* Ian Barbour addresses this issue of models in both science and religion. According to Barbour, such models can be analogous in the sense that both operate in the realm of the imaginative, the intuitive, the metaphorical. They serve to extend theories in science and enlarge the perspective of religious communities. Models and theories can function as abstract symbol systems, not to be taken literally. This does not mean that models are total fictions, however, for they make tentative claims about the way things really are.

These models can emerge in stories and narratives that structure human life in ways that we are barely conscious of at first. The reason for this is that our models and images become so concrete that they are no longer seen as metaphor; they are actually the thing we have conceptualized. The result is a model or image that can give birth to a controlling paradigm that influences how we experience the world. In terms of what I have been reflecting about so far, consider the fact that the classical theist model we have examined is the controlling paradigm that so many assume represents God.

Historians of science have shown that once a model or image assumes the role of a controlling paradigm it becomes extraordinarily difficult to replace it. This is so in part because the paradigm, be it scientific or religious, that exercises so much influence can actually determine what we are willing to see or believe.[4]

In science one way to describe this phenomenon is to say that data is theory laden. In other words, our interpretation of what is going on in the physical world can be colored by what we believe we will find when we look at the data. This does not mean that new paradigms do not emerge, or that new theories do not occur in response to observation and investigation. It does mean that, when we are interpreting the world, we stand in the midst of a web of beliefs that affect us to the extent that the assumptions we make about the world can be difficult to revise.

Consider one of the most intriguing models to have emerged in the world of science in the last century. It involved the phenomenon of light. Isaac Newton and his followers thought that light might be composed of a stream of little particles. Christian Huygens and his followers believed that light might be a form of waves. Through subsequent experimentation it appeared that light was a form of wave energy.

However, the model was to undergo some revision in the twentieth century with the work of Max Planck and an obscure patent clerk in Berne, Switzerland, by the name of Albert Einstein. Building on the work of Planck, Einstein showed clearly that the ability of a beam of light to eject electrons from metals could be understood only if the beam were behaving as particles of light.

A period of great confusion ensued in which classical physics as exemplified by Newton gave way to quantum models and images, including a quantum mechanical account of light, and the first quantum field theory. This theory resolved the wave/particle paradox by showing that discrete and spread out field properties could both be applied to light. Thus a new paradigm began to take shape that would have profound implications for the discipline of science. We will take up some of the other implications and ideas of the quantum world later. However, for right now I want you to think with me about how we might use the revising of paradigms for extending our perspective about God.

Seen or Unseen?

I have been asking you to consider how we came to believe the way we do about that which by definition escapes all human constructs. Earlier I mentioned that the way humankind had defined its images of God in no small measure oscillates around two poles, the personal and the impersonal. The monotheistic traditions have sought to weight these definitions primarily on the personal side of the scale. However, there have been those in this tradition who have maintained the impersonal dimension because they have experienced the divine presence in ways that seem to transcend any personal description.

This sense of mystical union has been communicated to us by those who have had the experience of having been absorbed in all that is. In this space, all dualities are overcome as absolute union with God results in a holistic view of life. This experience of mystical union with God is spoken of in ways that are pantheistic and impersonal. God is not a being, God is Being itself. Escaping all attempts at positive definition, God can only be spoken of in terms of what God is not. As we saw earlier, this way of thinking is *apophatic*.

There is also the strong element of hiddenness in this experience. The impersonal God is not accessible to us in any way. All concepts, all ideas, all beliefs, all rituals will fall short because the totality of the thing cannot be known. There is that dimension of God that remains hidden and can never be known because all attempts at description will be partial and fragmentary. The realization that God is in simply everything and everything is in God results in a perplexing state of mind similar to that incurred when considering the quantum universe of which we are such a small part.

We have before us the realization that religion develops images and models that embody the tensions we have found elsewhere. Barbour makes connections between the wave/particle duality and the impersonal/personal duality in religion. In this way we might consider for a moment the fact that the symbol of God can be understood and experienced in ways that overcome our dualisms and definitions. God may incorporate all antinomies.

Consider some of the ideas we have spoken of so far. God is infinite, transcendent, perfect in power and knowledge, perfect in being, impassible, and a host of other images that speak to our desire to locate the object of religious knowledge and experience outside the world. But what would happen if we were to think in terms of new models and images? If light can be both wave and particle, surely that which St. Anselm called "a greater than which cannot be conceived" can be both personal and impersonal, infinite and finite, transcendent and immanent, static and dynamic, powerful yet vulnerable, perfect yet responsive.

Such an idea finds resistance among us because these other images have not been traditionally seen as applicable to our definition of God. However, I would contend we have not used all that is at our disposal to understand God. Can we revise our models and be faithful to that which we know and believe in? Can there be a paradoxical element of God that brings us to the door of mystery? Can we speak to the entirety of God in such a way that addresses both poles of God's reality? Can we use the discoveries of science to enlarge our conceptualizations of God? And more interestingly, does the Christian belief in the Trinity speak to the concerns we have raised?

Rethinking God

In the classical theist models of God that humankind has employed, God must be removed from the world, always seen as acting upon it, but not being acted upon. And yet this model differs markedly from our experience, especially in prayer. Many people pray believing that their prayers will have some impact upon the One to whom they are praying. This belief suggests that there is also a part of the tradition that does allow for God's intimate involvement in the world, being affected by it, possibly even growing with the experience.

Certainly, if we were to look at the biblical context, we would find there not one monolithic image of God, but a diverse set of images that reveal an increasing awareness of God's presence in the world in ways that do not fit earlier perspectives. This sense of vision is not just found in the tension between the Hebrew and Christian Scriptures; we even find tension within the textual and historical traditions of Judaism and Christianity.

A close reading of the prophets results in the realization that their vision of Yahweh was one that was moving from the tribal to the more universal. Likewise, in Christianity we find a growing awareness that God was not quite what previous models had allowed for. One has only to see how difficult it was for the earliest Christians to understand that the meaning of Jesus was universal in scope to get a sense of how hard it is to let go of those beliefs that keep us tethered to the past (Acts 10). New understandings of God are difficult to maintain in the face of broad acceptance of old models by the community of faith.

One of the models of God that is gathering much attention among those in the scientific community who are interested in exploring this connection between our ultimate symbol structure and our understanding of the cosmos comes to us through the work of people such as Alfred North Whitehead and Charles Hartshorne. These two and others, such as David Ray Griffith, suggest that a metaphysics of substance and perfection can be replaced by a metaphysics of process. One of the most powerful notions to emerge from this concept is that God's perfection does not have to be defined in terms of power or immutability. Instead, God is so much a part of all that is that God can respond to the world's suffering, its joys and sorrows, because God's moral constancy is unchanging.[5]

The concept that most encompasses the definition of God starts with the premise that because God is ultimate, all categories may be properly attributed to God. Starting with the primary dichotomy we have used, God is both personal and impersonal. Rather than either/or, the divine life incorporates both dimensions. Likewise, God is both infinite and finite, both transcendent and immanent, both eternal and temporal. The life of God encompasses all categories. God is not removed from the world, but immersed in it.

In this fashion, as long as God holds the world within Godself, then God has entered into the very life of all things. Every quark, every particle, every aspect of matter and energy is connected to God's desire and hope for the world. This point of view does not reduce the divine life, for God is not collapsed into the processes of the physical universe. Rather than a claim that mirrors pantheism, the belief that the things of the cosmos do not exist apart from God speaks to the presence of God in all things, but not exhausted by all things. This perspective combines elements of both theism and pantheism into a belief known as panentheism, not one or the other, but both/and, which seems to be for many a more accurate reflection of experience and tradition.

The belief that God is manifest in the energies of the world protects from religious projection. The God who is intimately involved in the processes of the world cannot be imprisoned in any one segment of the religious life of humankind, for the world is not the possession of anyone or anything. We all come to it as a gift. Panentheism also denotes the belief that the processes of life are not totally random and unknowing. There is still the idea of agency. Divine will and purpose do exist in the universe.

The difficulty for many persons is that their conceptualizations of a supreme being mean that someone is in control and will direct the final outcome. But the models or metaphors of God that are emerging suggest that while God does respond to the world, God does so perhaps in ways that do not seem readily apparent. God's involvement and response to the world are to be seen as an inseparable part of the world, but the divine life is not limited solely to external action upon the world.

It is difficult psychologically for those who have internalized the traditional images of God to entertain another image. But think for a moment what may happen if we do. If that which our language seeks to apprehend overcomes all dualisms, all separations, all attempts at definitive definition, then we are truly in relationship with a wondrous energy.

God, who creates and sustains, has created a world where freedom is an authentic dynamic of burgeoning life. The processes that are in play with the world's coming to be emerge from the Giver of all life. I do not mean the type of freedom that results from God's predetermining power. Rather I am speaking of a genuine openness whereby the future is truly open and we cannot guarantee which way it will go. In the being of life, is it the case that God lets things become what they will be? John Polkinghorne writes of such a world:

The gift of Love must be the gift of freedom, the gift of letting-be, and this can be expected to be true of all creatures to the extent that is appropriate to their proper character. It is in the nature of dense snow fields that they will sometimes slip with the destructive force of an avalanche. It is the nature of lions that they will seek prey. It is the nature of cells that they will mutate, sometimes producing new forms of life, sometimes grievous disabilities, sometimes cancers. It is the nature of humankind that sometimes people will act with selfless generosity but sometimes with murderous selfishness. That these things are so is not gratuitous or due to divine oversight or indifference. They are the necessary cost of a creation given by its Creator the freedom to be itself. Not all that happens is in accordance with God's will because God has stood back, making metaphysical room for creaturely action.[6]

For many of us this cannot be good news. We are not comfortable with the notion that God gives the world that kind of freedom. We are not filled with confidence that humankind has the power to determine the fate of the earth. In some deep part of ourselves we look at the destructive power we have amassed and believe that at the last minute God will step in and save us from ourselves, but this is whistling in the graveyard. The ideas we are about to explore go further than just the human world. Many who are reflecting upon the world today are suggesting that freedom extends to the more-than-human life as well. Not only humans, but animals, cells, even atoms have unpredictability as a constituent part of their lives.

In fact, this seems to be one of the most important shifts in our thinking about the world given the discoveries of science in the last century. Unpredictability seems to be an integral part of the world. We find it difficult to know in detail the future behavior of quantum systems, yet we know that events are not totally and absolutely random. An unstable atom's "future options converge to a certain portfolio of possibility called a 'strange attractor' and it is only this limited range of contingencies that will be explored by the system in an apparently haphazard fashion."[7]

This statement seems to offer clues to the type of world we appear to be dealing with, one in which freedom is a constituent part of everything, yet is exercised within boundaries that establish its limits. An atom's freedom is constrained by proximity to those conditions that limit its choices. Human freedom, seemingly so vast, is itself exercised within certain boundaries.

How Shall We Define God?

How do we hold these tensions in some unity? Because analogies and metaphors are the language we have at hand to try and grasp this continually elusive presence, one model that seems to be particularly fruitful is the image of the body's relationship to the mind or soul. In this way God is present in every moment of life because the universe is the body of God. God is present in every physical interaction and at each point in space and time. God is found in both the ordinary and extraordinary, for there is never a moment that is not known by God.

This image, of the universe as the body of God, is somewhat more organic than past images. One of those past images consists of the more mechanical model wherein the universe is like a giant and intricate mechanism and we discover how parts and wholes fit together. This approach is still used by some scientists who believe that by reducing things to their smallest parts, we will be able to understand how the whole functions. While this is a useful line of inquiry, others are suggesting that a more organic approach may also be helpful in understanding the universe.

The organic approach is meant to overcome the types of partial approaches that allow us to overlook what is actually going on around us. Seen in this sense, the world is not a series of random events, but everything is connected to everything else, each contributing to the processes that bring forth life. Using this image opens up ways of thinking about how things relate to one another, indeed, opens up the space to see the world as a series of relationships.

In this image the world is seen as functioning in such a way that all aspects are giving information to all other aspects of life. There is one gigantic circle of energy affecting atoms, molecules, cells, and universal systems. The causality chain runs in all directions, top down and bottom up, and any other direction we can conceive, all influencing the other. In a religious sense all things are seen as being in communion with one another.

This image has been met with some criticism, even by those who are interested in exploring new ways to understand God. One criticism is that while the universe does not look like a machine, it does not really look like an organism either. Thomas Tracy says the universe does not resemble a unified organic process, but seems more like a looser society of distinct agents.[8] It would seem to lack the coherence of our own bodies. John Polkinghorne asks, "To put the matter bluntly, if the world is God's body, where is God's nervous system within it?"[9]

The further criticism of this image comes from the fact that the way we are constituted by our bodies means that we are vulnerable to them, eventually losing consciousness in death. For some this image makes God too vulnerable to the world. Surely the God of Christian tradition cannot be in such a dicey place.

But in some ways this attitude misses the point. A metaphor is an attempt to link ideas by letting the likeness or analogy open the space to think new thoughts. Surely the psalmist who spoke of God as a rock was not attempting too close a connection. If a successful metaphor opens our minds to new and creative ways of thinking, should we not consider it? The notion of God's embodiment in the world is too valuable an insight to disregard completely.

Of course, one can take the path that God's embodiment in the world is of a different order than the rest of life. I may have some awareness of my thoughts and feelings, and even what is happening to my cellular life, but such awareness is always imperfect and limited. God's awareness is one of perfection. God's omniscience means that God is totally aware of all that happens, not limited in the same way we are. In such a manner, God does not need a nervous system.

The employment of this model, whatever its weaknesses, is meant to try and get at one way of conceptualizing the relationship between God and the world, and that is by using the notion of human agency. We must keep in mind, however, that as a metaphorical image, human agency is not a precise description, but an attempt to connect with new levels of understanding that cannot be attained in literal ways.

One of the strengths of this metaphor is that it does not separate the world and the being of God, but opens up fresh possibilities for seeing the sacred in all things, especially those things that we had previously disconnected from the life of God by the incorporation of the dualistic model of sacred/secular. God is much closer and for that very reason much more of a present reality than we may realize.

Some persons may fear that this metaphor really does reduce God's reality to the world and that the danger of pantheism is lurking in the shadows of this model. Because we have embraced the accepted models and metaphors of the tradition, this alternate way of thinking seems strange and unfamiliar. Better to live with the traditional model of Lord/subject, where the relationships between God and the world are seen in their proper order. To let go of the models we use seems to be a lack of faith, but in truth most people live an impoverished faith because they cannot let go of elemental images to contemplate new ones.

We do not reduce ourselves to our bodies, so why would we do this with the divine image? One of the most crucial and important ideas of Christian faith is that the totality of our identity is not to be found within our bodily life alone. There is that dimension of existence, call it spirit, soul, or even consciousness, that transcends bodily constraints.[10] This belief constitutes a fundamental reality of our lives in faith.

There are some who have so embraced the metaphors and narratives of separation found within Christian faith that they are unable to see the underlying unity of all that is with the being of God. Holding onto images of fallenness, or sin, they focus on those biblical passages that emphasize the separation of the world and God. They find comfort in the knowledge that while the temptations of the world, the flesh, and the devil surround them, they will emerge triumphant from these snares.

These are powerful images and difficult to let go of because they are metaphors that have ceased to be metaphors and are now literal truths, and to question them is to question the reality of God. It is more comforting to think of someone who is in charge, much like the young woman whom Soelle questioned. God reigns over the world and nothing happens without God's will being expressed. God is in control, and we can rest easy in that knowledge. This image of the body of God that is being suggested is too shaky for some. God is made much too vulnerable in this model. How can we even think in these terms? I get sick, cancer invades my body, eventually I will grow old and die. Surely you are not suggesting that I consider this image as any type of reality that constitutes God? Such an image makes God too dependent upon the world.

And yet is it not the case that the very core of Christianity is the embodiment of God in Jesus of Nazareth? Here God takes the ultimate risk, experiences the ultimate weakness, to place Godself in the hands of humanity with all our fears of difference, hatreds of various kinds, and anxiety of power.

One of the ironies is that, in the story of Jesus, humans take actions that seem to imply that we humans think we have the power of life and death over others, but we soon find this another illusion of our self-deceptions. The story of the resurrection speaks to the reality that we may try to kill God and God's messengers, but God will have the final word. This seems to indicate that God does make Godself vulnerable in the world, but that this vulnerability is found in the context of God's own hope for the world.

If this central story of Christian faith is extended, we are able to catch a glimpse of how the world as God's body could open us to new dimensions of our relationship with God. One of these new ways of seeing is found in the notion that there is a closeness and intimacy we have with God that escapes us most of the time. According to Sallie McFague,

> God's knowledge, action, and love are markedly different in the metaphor of the world as God's body. God knows the world immediately just as we know our bodies immediately. God could be said to be in touch with all parts of the world through interior understanding. Moreover, this knowledge is empathetic, intimate, sympathetic knowledge, closer to feeling than to rationality. It is knowledge "by acquaintance"; it is not "information about." Just as we are internally related to our bodies, so God is internally related to all that is—the most radically related relational Thou.[11]

Seen in this way, God's relation to the world is not one of radical transcendence, but of a transcendent immanence. God is more than the world, not absorbed in it, but the most fundamental reality constituting all that is. There is an immediacy to the relationship between God and the world that mirrors my immediacy to my own body. Just as the divine life encompasses both poles of the infinite/finite dichotomy, so it is with us. God chooses the weakness of finitude by virtue of relationship with creation and us.

Yet as long as that finite aspect remains, God does not relate to this world from a remote position, deciding who shall live and who shall die, which buildings will fall from the hurricane and which shall stand, where we shall be born and where we shall die. God does not work in an exterior way in the world, but in an interior one, being manifested in all the processes of life and death. The life of God is expressed in these energies of the cosmos and constituted within them, and as the book of Job seems to hint at, God struggles as well with the chaos.

It is for this reason that many people find this metaphor fruitful for theological exploration and spiritual reflection. New images of God emerge that point us in different directions than the ones we are so used to. These images not only help us out when we are thinking about the world of quantum physics, they have a pastoral side as well. Many today have given up faith in the God of the traditions they know. They yearn for something that rings truer than the God who is locked away in inaccessible transcendence, impassible and unaffected by our lives, predetermining for all times what is to come. When a child is born who suffers, they want to know that God is present with them in their room when the heart bears the weight of misfortune.

Can we say such a bold thing? Can we say that the God who is present in the forces of cosmic life, who brought all things into being, the vast array of interstellar galaxies and the lilies in my backyard, is present in the hospital room for the crying mother? Surely we have something more to offer than the cold comfort of the innocent suffering as the result of sin. Even more, can we say that God was present in the horrors of Auschwitz?

One answer comes from the writing of Elie Wiesel in the novel *Night,* when he writes of being in the concentration camps and having to watch a young child being hanged. As this atrocity was occurring, someone in the group forced to watch cried out, "Where is God now?" The reply came back from within Wiesel, "Where is He? Here He is—He is hanging here on this gallows. . . ."[12]

This can be a double-sided comment, of course, for Wiesel felt his faith had died in those camps and it would be difficult to retrieve a sense of God in the world. But if the comment could be seen as attending the death of God, it could also be seen in another way. God was there, suffering the pain and anguish of one who suffers innocently, because we have refused the invitation to be co-creators of life and are rather the authors of death. God is present in the world to such an extent that all its pain and suffering are absorbed in the divine life. God is not the tyrant who decides who is to live or die, who is to suffer and be blessed, God is not the omnipotent power dispensing grace to the chosen few. No, in the words of A. N. Whitehead, God is the "fellow sufferer who understands."

How can we make this claim when so much of the world argues against it? When persons such as Polkinghorne say that faith will have to address the "cruciform" shape of life, they are searching for the mystery of something profound, God's way in the world. We have traveled some distance from our initial questions and we have only begun the journey. In the contemporary situation is there any room for a reconsideration of one of the most powerful images of God, the Trinity, to deepen our spirits and enhance our faith?

Even though contemporary theology may entertain new models for our understanding God, perhaps one avenue to explore is to return to the traditional images of God found in the Trinity to ask if this concept does not in fact address the classical theist position and the contemporary situation as well. If we use all the resources of our tradition to interpret the world, we may find some spiritual discernment concerning the life of God in the world. Trinitarian development was aimed at overcoming the space between humankind and God, and should provide us with rich resources for thinking through how we might perceive the life of God in the world. Though

many today may still be attending the funeral of God, it is becoming harder
to maintain there is something in the casket.

NOTES

1. Dorothee Soelle, *Theology for Skeptics: Reflections on God* (Minneapolis: Fortress
Press, 1994), 13–14. I also refer the reader to A. N. Wilson's book, *God's Funeral* (W. W.
Norton: New York, 1999), for a historical treatment of the way in which the rise of
modernity, helped along by the work of Hume among others, led to the construction
of God's casket.

2. Fyodor Dostoyevsky, *The Brothers Karamozov* (trans. David McDuff; London:
Penguin Books, 1991), 281.

3. Clark Williamson posed this issue in his book on post-Holocaust theology by
using Will Greenberg's statement that we should make no theological assertion that
could not be made in the presence of burning children. Clark Williamson, *A Guest in
the House of Israel: Post-Holocaust Church Theology* (Louisville, Ky.: Westminster/John
Knox, 1993), 13. I first came across this statement in John B. Cobb and Clark H. Pinnock, eds., *Searching for an Adequate God: A Dialogue Between Process and Free Will
Theists* (Grand Rapids, Mich.: Eerdmans, 2000), 15–16.

4. See, for instance, Barbour's discussion of this in *Religion and Science,* 101–36.

5. An interesting exchange between those who consider themselves process theists
and those who consider themselves free will theists is found in Cobb and Pinnock,
Searching for an Adequate God. This exchange was in some respects brought about by
the publication of Pinnock's edited volume *The Openness of God.* This book and the
subsequent firestorm it provoked among the evangelical community is an example of
the way in which our investments in the images and theologies we have developed
become solidified into boundaries we feel cannot be transgressed and still remain
faithful to the Christian faith.

6. John Polkinghorne, *Belief in God,* 13.

7. Polkinghorne, *Belief in God,* 52.

8. Thomas Tracy, *God's Action and Embodiment* (Grand Rapids, Mich.: Eerdmans,
1984).

9. Polkinghorne, *Belief in God,* 57.

10. This of course opens a whole area of inquiry that won't be dealt with at this
point. Is the nature of consciousness such that it only exists within the workings of the
neural systems of the brain?

11. Sallie McFague, *Models of God: Theology for an Ecological, Nuclear Age* (Minneapolis: Fortress Press, 1987), 73. McFague has had enormous influence on the issue
of defining God with her numerous books in the last several years. She has written
extensively on this issue and in some ways has presented new challenges for contemporary theology to consider.

12. Elie Wiesel, *Night* (trans. Stella Rodway; New York: Bantam Books, 1982), 62.

4

THE CRUCIBLE
OF CREATION

Creation is the task of energy; it is for nature to beget.
—St. Gregory of Palamas

Chance alone is the source of every innovation,
of all creation in the biosphere.
—Jacques Monad

It is God who made the Pleiades and Orion, who turns the dawn
to dusk and day to darkest night . . . Yahweh is his name.
—Amos 5:8

As science and theology seek to give accounts of the "way things are," they both incorporate models and metaphors in order to extend our understanding. Yet, in the employment of these models and metaphors, there appears to be that element that functions as mystery, a door we can't seem to open. Nowhere does that mystery extend itself more than the notions of origin and beginnings. And nowhere does the great divide between science and religion seem to extend itself more than at this point of creation and evolution.

This divide, of course, works itself out on a cultural stage as scientists such as Richard Dawkins and E. O. Wilson offer the interpretation that the sheer processes of life indicate that biological evolution is an inherently meaningless process. They observe that the impersonal laws of the universe are so full of waste and suffering as to suggest that nothing either intelligent or very designing could be behind it. The story they tell shows blind chance, natural selection, and immense periods of time combining with "selfish" genes in a struggle for survival that is rather grim.

Stephen Jay Gould, while not as harsh as some, nonetheless registered his take on the whole issue: "Odd arrangements and funny solutions are the proof of evolution-paths that a sensible God would never tread but that a natural process, constrained by history follows perforce."[1] Willem Drees, among others, makes the point that the universe as we know it seems much larger than we need for our kind of life. The sheer size seems pointless and wasteful and suffers innumerable design flaws.[2] Thus, the voices of modernity weigh in with the best verdict their examination of the evidence can give them—the universe seems rather pointless.

If the processes of life are sufficiently explained from material causes, where is the need for a transcendent intelligence to act or intervene in evolution? If surviving organisms can adapt to the challenges of their environment, where is the need for agency? Any type of directive organization can be explained by this adaptive quality and the processes of nature.

These questions put us in touch with another mystery to consider, the mystery of how inchoate violence seems to be woven into the fabric of the universe. Viruses, meteors, galaxies that experience continuous explosions, and the formation of red giants and white dwarfs, of such things is the universe made. We stand at the door of mystery and wonder sometimes with heartbroken and anguished souls. What purpose must this death, this suffering, serve? We are not accustomed to death and do everything in our power to push it away.

Take, for example, the beautiful city of Reston, Virginia. Extensively planned as a model city for America's future, Reston seeks to address a host of concerns about community life. But in their quest for the perfect city, Reston's planners did not allow a funeral home or cemetery within the city limits. If you wanted to die you had to go to Herndon, Virginia. Death, for all its ubiquity, is still a taboo subject for many of us in American society. Yet, death is the overwhelming reality of nature.

We romanticize nature, talk about how much we love it, but we spend most of our life avoiding the real thing. Of course, we will drive along the Blue Ridge Parkway, get out of our SUVs or campers long enough to snap some pictures, or maybe even rough it and camp out. But what we experience is a sanitized version of nature.

Spend a few nights in the depths of the real thing and you quickly discover that nature is one vast killing ground, with powers and energies that cannot be tamed. Long-term exposure to nature will show you carcasses, shells of creatures decaying, flies, mosquitoes, predators of every kind. Once in the jungles of Bolivia I had the opportunity to visit with people who were resettled by the Bolivian government from the Andes Mountains to the jungle floor. Their lives were one of almost constant difficulty dealing with the snakes, diseases, insects, and animals that dominated the jungle. They were not prepared for the boreworms that started as parasites on their clothing and then wormed their way into their bodies and started to feed and grow once inside. Sores, wounds, and constant difficulty were a way of life. There was no romanticizing of nature here.

One person who has spent some time in nature and understands it is Annie Dillard. Her observations on an area close to where I grew up in Roanoke, Virginia, led to the book *Pilgrim at Tinker Creek*. Dillard would closely observe the land around her and had a firm handle on how things really worked in the world:

> He was a very small frog with wide, dull eyes. And just as I looked at him, he slowly crumpled and began to sag. . . . His skin emptied and drooped; his very skull seemed to collapse and settle like a kicked tent. . . . Soon, part of his skin, formless as a pricked balloon, lay in floating folds like bright scum on the top of the water: it was a monstrous and terrifying thing. I gaped bewildered, appalled. An oval shadow hung in the water behind the drained frog; then the shadow glided away. The frog skin bag started to sink.

As Dillard was watching this spectacle she was careful enough to notice that the frog had been attacked by a water skimmer, one that was a highly functional killer:

> It eats insects, tadpoles, fish and frogs. Its grasping forelegs are mighty and hook inward. It seizes a victim with these legs, hugs it tight, and paralyzes it with enzymes injected during a vicious bite. The one bite is the only bite it ever takes. Through the puncture shoot the poisons that dissolve the victim's muscles and bones and organs—all but the skin—and through it the giant water bug sucks out the victim's body, reduced to a juice.[3]

All things bright and beautiful indeed! How in the midst of this type of testimony do we affirm the benevolence or love of God toward the world? So many people are unable to reconcile the cunning devastation they see occurring in nature with the God who creates and sustains life that it becomes impossible for them to hold faith.

It offends people's sensibilities that nature seems to be so wasteful, destructive, and even cruel. Much of the writing that addresses this concern indicates that if we can conceive of a natural order that could be more efficient, then so could God:

> Whatever the God implied by evolutionary theory and the data of natural history may be like, He is not the Protestant God of waste not want not. He is also not a loving God who cares about His productions. He is not even the awful God portrayed in the book of Job. The God of the Galapagos is careless, wasteful, indifferent, almost diabolical. He is certainly not the sort of God to whom anyone would be inclined to pray.[4]

Much of the argument in contemporary terms revolves around the presuppositions of what we would do if we were God. Nature should actually be the way we would like it to be if there were an all-loving entity behind it. Matters could be so much more efficient and better constructed if God, as we conceptualize God to be, existed in just such a way. Perhaps it is the way that a certain cultural construct of God has become concretized and presupposed that is the problem. Metaphysical presuppositions about what God would actually be like drive the type of statements that we get from scientists like Richard Dawkins: "The universe we observe has precisely the properties we should expect if there is at bottom no design, no purpose, no evil and no good, nothing but pointless indifference."[5]

It is not only an assumed construct of God that informs our perspective; it is also a presupposition about nature that shapes us. If we believe nature is supposed to be perfect, harmonious, without stain of death, decay, or conflict, then we will have a difficult time reflecting on the God who suffers with the created order of the universe as it finds itself in a constant state of becoming. Paul Santmire asks:

> Is it spiritually realistic to aspire to encounter nature untamed, unpacified, and unromanticized, with all its ambiguities and its death-driven violence, as a gift from the giver of every good and

perfect gift, as a tabernacle of the most High, and thereby to be able to embrace nature spiritually, as a world charged with the glory of God, overflowing with blessings, beauty, and goodness?[6]

Can we ever learn to embrace the reality that we are on a pilgrimage toward death; that in some manner the entire cosmic dance of life is tending to this end? Difficult to entertain on its own terms, it is illumined for us by the narratives of a crucified and risen God who becomes "the firstborn of all creation." This truth does not sit well with a culture terrified of death. Nor does it sit well with a culture that has constructed an image of God in which God's presence is removed from the world. For when many persons think of God, they confine God to the spaces of the spirit, separating God from the world of matter. Our incipient and unaware Gnosticism has so removed God from this world (save, perhaps, for "sacred" space like the sacraments) that we no longer understand nature, with all its tragedy, as sacramental.

On the other side of the cultural divide there are those who argue that rather than randomness and destruction, what we have is the working out of rather elegant mathematical equations that point to some intelligent designer. Chief among the proponents of this argument is William A. Dembski, one of the primary voices in the intelligent design movement. His work appears on the pages of such publications as *The Chronicle of Higher Education,* as well as numerous articles and books, arguing for a specific approach to interpreting scientific data. The intelligent design movement hopes to overthrow the cultural legacy of Darwinism by providing what it hopes is a better model for understanding the processes of life and the universe.[7]

While the cultural battle rages and will be fought out in the schools of the United States for quite some time, I want to focus on something that I find more interesting. I am assuming that however much knowledge we acquire, the deep mysteries of existence will always be before us. These mysteries that emerge in the compositions of chemical, gas, order, and chaos will always leave us with questions. Why does matter form? From where can we get an account of consciousness that does justice to the depths of it? Why does human life even think in abstract terms such as value, beauty, and morality? Is the universe really pointless in the end? Why am I not able to know a thing as it really is?

I find myself poised on the edge of a mystery when I try to comprehend the apple I am holding in my hand. So simple a thing is filled with mystery in and of itself. I can perceive its color, I can feel its solidity, I can taste its sweetness, but in fact all those things in some regard are being manufac-

tured by my mind and the electrochemical processes that go into constituting my experience. Without the interplay of light energy upon the retinal
cones of my eye, there would be no color; without the surface cells of my
tastebuds to convert the particular molecular structure of the apple, I could
not taste. The matter I think I perceive of as so solid is in truth a veritable
beehive of actively buzzing, zooming particles that appear and disappear in
continual states of motion.

Reality, whatever it may consist of, is rooted in the mysterious. Consider
space and matter. The space between things is what makes it what it is to us.
Remove the space and you remove the reality we experience. Remove the
inner space from atoms and you find compactness so dense it is truly amazing. If the planet earth could be pulled together by gravity into the sort of
compactness that exists in a black hole, then it would occupy the space the
size of a child's marble.[8]

Why does reality as we presently understand it behave the way it does?
Science brings us to a door of a mystery that will remain ambiguous and
puzzling. And yet, even so, we are called to probe this mystery in ways that
stretch us and force us to contemplate the question of why the universe even
developed in such a way as to make intelligence possible.

Telling the Story

One of the ways that humans approached this mystery previous to the narratives that science offered us involved the use of creation stories. These stories served to place humankind and the rest of the creation in a larger
narrative context. Most of these stories involved some type of material. Dirt
is gathered up under the fingernails of a swimming creature and swells to
form land, water is the matrix from which life emerges, fire is created by the
act of sexual intercourse; many ways were found to narrate a mystery.[9]

The most telling part of these stories is not the details invoked about the
processes of creation, but is rather the intent of the Creator. These stories
reflect the context and communal assumptions of the culture in which they
emerge. Creation accounts differ depending on cultural (and climatic) loca-
tion. The identity of persons, their place in the world, the call to participate
in the worship or service of the Creator, the various roles assigned to gender, these are the underlying aspects in most creation stories. The narrative
places God and humans in relation to one another, often with imperatives
for how moral life is to be led.

This is true as well for biblical narratives of the creation. However, the interpretation of these accounts has sometimes led to a total dead end in the Christian tradition. The entirety of the biblical witness has not been allowed to fill out, deepen, and increase the texture of these stories. I will explain this in more detail presently, but for now let us think about the stories themselves.

All Christian theological reflection upon God as Creator arises from the stories of creation found in the Hebrew Bible. This much is fairly self-explanatory. Much of the tension today between the forces of creationism and evolution arises from the fact that for some it is difficult to believe that the Bible, for all its inspiration, is still a historical text, written in particular historical contexts, which cannot be ignored when seeking to interpret Scripture. Though the significance and meaning of the Bible extends from the historical context within which it was written, forming the type of narrative world that many persons assume as their working model for the relationship between God and the world, the original conditions under which these Scriptures were written should not be ignored in our search for new understandings.

This means that we cannot read the creation stories without an understanding of the circumstances in which they emerged. In the case of these accounts in Genesis, they must be read within the context of Israel's defining itself and its faith in contrast to the Babylonian creation accounts. We do not expect writers in the sixth century before the appearance of Christ to have a contemporary understanding of modern science. They were writing their own theology of nature to answer what they knew about the claims being made by the Babylonian creation accounts found in the *Enuma Elish*.[10]

In the priestly creation accounts, we have the response of Israel's belief in Yahweh in the context of the cosmogonies of Babylon. Israel, in looking back on its covenantal history with Yahweh, was seeking self-definition in the midst of a position of exile, but in the development of the biblical tradition the relation of the world to its Creator stands in contrast to these other stories. In this way one fact that does emerge from comparing the stories is that the world does not arise from violent conflict, such as we find in the struggle between Marduk and Tiamat, but from a gracious act of God. Creativity, not violence, is an expression of the being of God in these accounts.

Within this creativity some interesting aspects are folded into the story as it proceeds. Something new happens with each and every event. As each element of life is brought forth, it constitutes a new thing, not seen before. So, one might understand that God's creative acts in history bring forth new things. In this bringing forth life the Creator calls upon the earth to bring forth new things, plants and animals (Gen 1:11; 24). Thus God is not the only actor in this drama, nor the only one responsible for the creation. God's freedom issues in the world, which has a role in its own becoming. Matter mediates its own coming to be, whatever its ultimate dependency on its Creator.

A careful reading of the Genesis accounts allows for (and such has been the case since Augustine) a certain separation of the act of creation from the being of God. This separation becomes necessary in some senses so that creation can have a freedom that is not wholly determined by God. Unless God withdraws in a sense, creation is not independent to be what it will be. This is not just true for the creature created out of the dust of the earth; it is true for the dust itself.

Some interpreters see here God's creative love being rooted in the willingness to allow for a self-emptying or kenotic stance in the world. Thus the manifestation of God's power in the world is not through omnipotence as we think of it, but of the almighty power that is rooted in the vulnerability of self-giving. If the triune God is manifesting the creative energies, there is a truth that the entirety of the being of God is present in the creation from the beginning. At the center of God's being is the self-chosen path of suffering love.[11]

This understanding allows for the realization that the creation itself is not the Creator, which does not mean God's total absence from within the processes of creation. God struggles with, calls, persuades, and is manifest in the creation itself. God is the creator of all possibilities for life to explore as well as the boundaries within which potentialities will actually become reality. One such reality was the appearance of the human creature.

Many persons believe that the creation of the human is the crown of creation. Thus the purposes of God are fulfilled when the human is created. But in fact it is not the human creature that is the fulfillment of creation, it is God's Sabbath rest. The human in some measure shares with the rest of life the "breath of life" (Gen 1:30), but the human creature is self-conscious enough to have the privilege of understanding its dependency and need for relationship. This also means that the human creature has the joy of being able to respond to the Creator with gratitude.

But the appearance of the human raises the issue of responsibility as well. In these accounts humanity is set within the fabric of God's intention for creation. In fact, what really saves the creation accounts from animism is the notion that God's intentionality for relationship with the entirety of the created order will constitute the continuing story. This story is written from within the context of Israel trying to work out its sense of covenant with God, and this will entail, if nothing else, a history, a process.

Where does this process lead? Gerhard von Rad in his Genesis commentary suggests that the Sabbath day of rest actually constitutes God's future intention.[12] Jürgen Moltmann carries this suggestion forward by making the interesting observation that this original creation was almost effortless in the sense that God spoke and it was so, even with the attendant responsibilities given the created order. It was the ongoing process toward God's Sabbath of shalom that created so much agony. The struggle of Yahweh was not so much with the original creation itself, but with the human creature's response to it. For example, Isaiah has Yahweh saying, "You have burdened me with your sins, you have wearied me with your iniquities. But I will blot out your transgressions for my own sake and I will not remember your sins" (Isa 43:24).[13]

From the beginning the creation narratives were in themselves not pointing to a past completed action by God, but were rather oriented to a future. This future was indeed God's rest, but it was creation's rest at well. A biblical doctrine of creation must not concentrate solely on the first three chapters of Genesis, but consider the entirety of the biblical witness. Within the context of Israel's suffering exile, these accounts can be seen as pointing to the future, when God's shalom will be the one true reality of life.

Thus the creation is that which extends itself even to the end of time (Isa 65:17). Looked at in this way, creation encompasses the entirety of God's saving presence in the world. While the origins of God's creative act were important to establish the identity of life and what it is moving toward, they needed to be complemented by God's ongoing intention for the creation.

Seen in this light, the manifestations of life and death we see around us must be understood eschatologically. The life of the world today is made manifest in pulsars, quarks, odd particles, electromagnetic fields, human and more-than-human life. As creations of God these entities are not mute, blind forces without redemptive possibility. All systems of life are open to future possibilities, some of which are, as of yet, unknown.

The natural order is not inherently ill-designed, but it does function as parable and manifestation of the creative, sustaining, and redemptive energies of God. Thus, a comprehensive understanding of creation from a theological point of view only starts with the notion of the original creation. It will also be alert to the ongoing processes of existence as the continuing activity of God.

The tradition of Christianity has employed terms to speak to this point of view, arguing that the biblical trajectory of the narrative lends itself to understanding creation as *creatio originalis, creatio continua,* and *creatio nova*. Taken together, these concepts of original, continuing, and new creation address the whole of the biblical narrative and suggest that creation was not a once-and-for-all act, but an ongoing process leading to the establishment of God's purposes for the entire cosmos, whatever the human's role in this may be.[14]

And in this regard we find ourselves poised on the edge of another mystery. Christian faith asserts the belief that the world is the manifestation of the creative energies of God, who relates to this creation in a myriad number of ways. However, this assertion does not consist of accessible data to be read from the world itself. In fact, given the data we can see with our own eyes, we are more likely to find ourselves occupying the same ground as those who see the forces of death and destruction holding the firmer hand on the processes of life. We will have to journey deeper into the mystery to find our answers.

A New Story

Let us start our journey by considering a creation account that was offered by Arthur Peacocke, who retold the stories of beginnings in the following way:

> There was God. And God was All-That-Was. God's Love overflowed and God said, "Let Other be. And let it have the capacity to become what it might be, making it make itself—and let it explore its potentialities."
>
> And there was Other in God, a field of energy, vibrating energy—but no matter, space, time, or form. Obeying its given laws and with one intensely hot surge of energy—a hot big bang—this Other exploded as the Universe from a point twelve or so billion years ago in our time, thereby making space.
>
> Vibrating fundamental particles appeared, expanded and expanded, and cooled into clouds of gas, bathed in radiant light. Still the universe went on expanding and condensing into swirling whirlpools of matter and light—a billion galaxies.
>
> Five billion years ago, one star in one galaxy—our Sun—became surrounded by matter as planets. One of them was our Earth. On Earth, the assembly of atoms and the temperatures became just right to allow water and solid rock to form. Continents and mountains grew and in some deep wet crevice or pool, or deep in the sea, just over three billion years ago some

molecules became large and complex enough to make copies of themselves and become the first specks of life.

Life multiplied in the seas, diversifying and becoming more and more complex. Five hundred million years ago, creatures with solid skeletons—the vertebrates—appeared. Algae in the sea and green plants on land changed the atmosphere by making oxygen. Then three hundred million years ago, certain fish learned to crawl from the sea and live on the edge of land, breathing that oxygen from the air.

Now life burst forth into many forms—reptiles, mammals (and dinosaurs) on land—reptiles and birds in the air. Over millions of years these mammals developed complex brains that enabled them to learn. Among these were creatures who lived in trees. From these our first ancestors derived and then, only forty thousand years ago the first man and woman appeared. They began to know about themselves and what they were doing—they were not only conscious but were also self-conscious. The first word, the first laugh were heard. The first paintings were made. The first sense of a destiny beyond—with the first signs of hope, for these people buried their dead with ritual. The first prayers were made to the One who made All-That-Is and All-That-Is-Becoming—the first experiences of goodness, beauty and truth—but also of their opposites, for human beings were free.[15]

As a story this one has not acquired the same hold on people's imaginations as the traditional accounts that one might find in Genesis. However, there are elements of this story that do speak to the deep mystery of divine action and abiding life in the world.

Think first of the sheer energies that are involved in the formation of the universe. If accounts of our current investigations are correct, in a moment of vast power all matter, all dimension, all energy, all time exploded in a massive fireball, exceeding 1,000,000,000,000 degrees centigrade. As the first microseconds emerged and cooling took place, atoms began to form from subatomic particles, which were formed from the cooling of energy. The other invisible forces that constitute the very matrix within which all life emerges, gravity, strong and weak forces, electromagnetism, become operative.

And in the first moment the words of Genesis, where God says, "Let there be light," were paralleled by the profound presence of light.[16] As this process continued, electrons and other elementary particles also present (quarks, neutrinos, gluons, etc.) "would have collided constantly into each other at such speeds and temperatures that their mass would have immediately converted into the energy carrying photons."[17] As this dance of collision and energy continued— mass-carrying electrons, protons, neutrons, combining to form quarks, atoms capturing electrons, energy gravitating toward the formation of mass—all of these engaged in a process that can only be called wondrous—self-organization.[18]

Star formation alone gives rise to interesting thoughts. In the models of existence that we have now, we understand that in the first three minutes matter consisted of electrons, protons, and the nuclei of a few of the lighter elements, especially helium. After the temperature dropped came the formation of hydrogen and helium atoms. Matter was disturbed, and small concentrations of matter attracted more matter and began to cluster as the beginnings of galaxies.[19]

This leads to the fascinating phenomenon of self-organizing processes, "which begins without any direct outward influence and develops in chaotic fashion."[20] These processes in turn lead to huge clouds of hydrogen collapsing into a dense ball of gas (a process that takes millions of years), resulting in nuclear fusion. Throughout this process, energy is released and a star is born. Stars also die. When the available hydrogen in the core has been used, the energy production stops and the star continues its gravitational collapse.[21]

In this process stars return a large part of their matter to interstellar gas. But in this process the matter returned is no longer the original matter, but the enriched heavy elements such as carbon, oxygen, and phosphorous, resulting in the formation of iron. The stars of younger generations contain the contributions from old stars. The collapsing old star spins off material that leads to the emergence of new life. Our sun was dependent on this process and, what is even more fascinating, is that so are we. The carbon and oxygen in our bodies come from the helium combustion zone of an old star. Two silicon nuclei, found in a supernova explosion, become the iron in our blood's hemoglobin. The calcium in our teeth formed from the same processes, as did almost every chemical process in our body.[22]

When at funerals the minister intones that from dust we emerged and to dust we will return she is not necessarily thinking about the notion that we are in fact stardust, temporary participants in the formation of a universe containing energies that are nearly incomprehensible and, upon closer inspection, interconnected in the deepest of ways. Yet this is the truth of the matter.

Think for a moment about the path the universe took to bring us to contemplation about it. We have moved from a possible singularity to particles, electrons, leptons, protons—seemingly mindless matter has formed over time to release energies into the world that use the death and destruction of stars and galaxies to create new life and lead to the formation of a ball of chemicals that incorporates gravity to solidify eventually.

In the midst of these seemingly random forces we find conditions forming that allow for the emergence of life. The mass of an electron, the gravitational constant, total energy, electrical charge, the number of leptons, indeed, the very parameters of the universe, appear to have remained constant for more than fourteen billion years.[23]

Within this vast explosion of matter and energy we find the emergence of cells, organisms, DNA, strings of biological life that stagger, struggle, fall, and survive. From a beginning of a ball of gas we find the rich abundance of existence we see before us. The sheer ongoing complexities of life astound us. The very fact that in this complexity I would find beauty and joy also is cause for wonder.

Why does the universe from the earliest moments dance in such a way that novelty upon novelty emerges? Elementary particles partner up and continue the cosmic two-step, gases form and condense into galaxies, atomic fields interact and join together, as do molecular fields, leading to the creation of patterns that will result in the emergence of cells. And even more amazing, these forces have resulted in something I find beautiful.

I am looking out my window at the lovely green park across the street. I enjoy the leaves of the trees floating in a summer breeze. When I go over to the park, I sit in the shade and reflect deeply on the life I see in front of me, and in the midst of contemplation I find myself amazed that billions of years ago this was gas, without form, and yet containing even then the possibility of what I see in front of me. The intricate, creative development of photosynthesis leads to cyano-bacteria (prokaryotes). The inclusion of this bacteria into eukaryotic cells, resulting in brown, red, and green algae, leads to the rise of the green plants that so enrich my life.

What really stuns me is the reality that this complexity of organisms that I am beholding also rests upon mathematical equations. The pine cone I am looking at, the tree branches, the petals of the flowers beside my bench, the dahlia, all are sharing a mathematical pattern known as the Fibonacci sequence. This mathematical progression is found in much of nature and shows a distinct pattern and ordering to seemingly unconnected things.

In this seemingly random process we have the phenomena of such intricate precision. Take the question of why the number of particles at the big bang was slightly greater than the number of anti-particles. John Russell points out that without this initial imbalance, the material universe simply would not exist.

The number of particles left over, about 10^{-80}, determines the pace of the gravitational forces that give rise to life as we know it. The mass of the neutron, the particle that joins with the proton to form the nucleus of the atom, is "so finely constituted that a decrease of 0.2 percent of its actual value would cause the proton to decay (into a neutron) and atoms, the basis of existence, would never have formed."[24]

The other aspects of a fine tuning are understood as well. Take the expansion rate as one example. In commenting on this Steven Hawking states: "If the rate of expansion one second after the big bang had been smaller by even one part in a hundred thousand million it would have recollapsed before it reached its present size."[25] Ian Barbour points out conversely that if it had been greater by one part in a million the universe would have expanded too rapidly for stars or planets to form.[26]

We also find this fine-tuning in the strength of the nuclear forces. If the strong nuclear force had been weaker, we would not have had the complex evolution of hydrogen into helium. If the force had been slightly stronger, hydrogen would have converted totally into helium, not allowing for the emergence of carbon, oxygen, and nitrogen.[27]

In fact, if all the forces that presently conspire to bring forth life were minutely altered, such alteration would result in something very different from what we are able to observe and experience today. The statement is often made that we are carbon-based life forms, and so carbon is essential to our existence. As seen previously, carbon is initially synthesized within the vast furnaces of stars. All proteins, amino acids, vitamins, fats, and carbohydrates of the human body exist because carbon formed inside of stars.

This set of circumstances can be carried out even further, but it is enough at this point that we can echo the psalmist, who declares that we are "fearfully and wonderfully made"(Ps 139:14). Without the balance of precision, we would not even be present to contemplate life.

Why should the universe develop through these processes that allow for such complexity and self-organization? Why is the universe operating in such a way that life is possible? There has been a great deal of attention paid to these questions in the dialogue between religion and science. They are answered by what is usually referred to as the anthropic principle, but which has sometimes been called the biotic principle, for it is not just humans who participate with or benefit from the forces at work, it is all of life.

The anthropic principle raises the question of why the universe developed in just the way it did. The basic physical constants, such as the mass of protons, are not arbitrary qualities, according to this argument. If the electron were of the same mass as its sister particle the muon, the universe would consist of nothing but neutrons and neutrinos. Is such an outcome a matter of total chance?

While we must be careful about ascribing a direct line between natural phenomena and God, at the very least we can say that these many happy accidents or coincidences lead to a richness and diversity. Of course part of the problem for many is that these coincidences also form the environment for diseases and opportunistic parasites to grow and destroy life. The very fact that we are here is probably due to a catastrophic event initiated by a meteor slamming into the earth about sixty-five million years ago.[28]

To say that among the many possible universes consistent with Einstein's equations ours is unique in the way that the conditions for life arise is different than saying that human life was the sole purpose for the type of world we live in today. Phrasing things in terms of the biotic principle might allow for some humility regarding the Creator's purpose. The ideological employment of the anthropic principle to center all of life upon the human creature alone represents an imposition upon the rest of creation.

This does not mean that we should find ourselves without a sense of wonder and amazement at the vast array of forces that have brought us to this place. The very fact of self-consciousness and the intelligibility of the universe is enough to evoke feelings of awe in even the most austere of hearts. But to claim it is solely for our benefit is to deny God the pleasure and joy and entirety of all the creation. In fact, given human care of the earth and one another, we may represent more of a burden to God's enjoyment of what was once declared good.

The Stories We Tell

Having looked at a couple of the ways in which we tell our story, I believe care must be taken not to attach the big bang hypothesis of present cosmology too closely to the biblical narrative, or even to the traditional Christian theology of the *creatio ex nihilo*. This doctrine of creation out of nothing is a theological assertion that addresses God as the sole and transcendent Creator of all that is. It speaks to the dependency of the creation upon the life of God and claims that there is no Demiurge, no coexisting reality other than God that brings life into being. To contend that modern physics must confirm or support this theological assertion would be the type of move that makes unwarranted claims.

Mark William Worthing makes the point that while the classical doctrine of *creatio ex nihilo* may no longer be scientifically unintelligible, the same scientific arguments have been used to counter assertions of the Creator God. All these theories, from quantum wave fluctuation to big bang singularities, proceed just fine as explanatory categories without the use of a God hypothesis. On a purely scientific basis, the Creator becomes redundant.[29]

This is the type of understanding that constitutes another space between science and religion. From a theological perspective, the original grounding of the *creatio ex nihilo* was meant to point to the universe's dependence upon God and God's continuing relationship with that universe.

The universe is brought forth out of the fullness of God's own being and thus it becomes fertile ground to till in search of God's presence. While we would want to be careful about drawing too straight a line between natural phenomena and God, there is a space where people of faith can interpret the reality around us as space that is not devoid of a Creator. There is some justification for seeing the Creator as immersed both within the original and continuing conditions of the universe. In fact, the existence of a universe for us to contemplate demands it: "The challenge to theology is essentially this: If we confess a God who is beyond space and time yet created space and time, can we neglect to listen to what contemporary physicists are saying about the nature of space and time?"[30]

This listening does not have to assume an uncritical stance, but should open us up to new metaphors and a deeper sense of wonder about the mystery that rests at the heart of the universe. It may allow us to understand more deeply our story of God. In what way can this be done?

We have previously found that one of the deepest disagreements between science and theology is that theology asserts the belief that the world is the manifestation of the creative energies of God, who relates to the creation in various ways. But this assertion is not readily accessible from the data to be observed from the world itself. As we have seen at the beginning of this chapter, the data has led people to the opposite conclusion.

Yet, given what we are now considering, the physical processes that were present in the initial stages of the universe, we can take some preliminary steps in interpreting our story. We have already mentioned that the priestly biblical story of creation found in Gen 1:1–2:4 originates in a context of Babylonian culture. It was never meant to be a scientific doctrine, but a theological message for people in exile. In the backdrop of a culture where the connection of deity to the natural order resulted in various deities tied to natural forces, the narrative of Israel's transcendent One meant a reevaluation of the relationship between God and the world.

But the reception of this narrative in the tradition meant that an undue emphasis was placed on creation as a completed and final act. Because of this culturally mediated interpretation of the Genesis accounts, the belief in stability and unchangeableness as positive aspects of the universe meant that both God and the cosmos became viewed as inherently static entities. Even though the Greeks acknowledged the changeableness of the universe, they were hesitant to allow for change in the Source of the universe. Given the previously mentioned Hellenistic impact on Christian theology, it became difficult to imagine the possibilities of life as open emergence, oriented toward a future potential as part of the creation story.

Constancy was valued as a primary category of interpretation and yet this does injustice to the entirety of the biblical witness. The emphasis on creation as a finished act had profound consequences for how God was understood in the cosmos. One of the most compelling intersections of science and theology in the last couple of decades is the possibility that Christian faith can rediscover the God who, like the creation, is continually in motion. God in the biblical sense is the God who is always open to doing a new thing, especially in response to the human creature's decisions (Isa 43:19).

The biblical texts themselves place the stories of creation in the process of revision and innovation. Because the particular interpretation of those stories assumed such embeddedness in Christian tradition, those aspects of creation that point to the new arising out of what was already formed did not have as much influence on how we interpret the creation theologically.

If we were to embrace the notion that from the beginning the new was embedded within the old, waiting to be born, we might have another model to employ that would complement the *creatio ex nihilo*. This might also allow us the space to see that the Bible itself calls for a continual openness to new and fresh potential. It calls for openness to the future.

This theological perspective should not find purchase among many today because we now have the wonders of the quantum world to consider, or because we are uncovering with increasing speed the dynamics operative in chaos and complexity theory. Rather, the understanding of God the Creator can never stand apart from God the Redeemer and Sustainer. Openness to the future is to be seen in the entirety of God's desire for the world, which in turn is seen through the redemptive intent manifested, in part, in the narratives of Jesus of Nazareth.

Creation should never be seen by any Christian as merely an object, suitable for domination, abuse, or destruction. God's relationship within the world must not be conceived as a one-sided domination of spirit over matter, but because God-as-Trinity is intimately involved in the ongoing processes of the world, creation can be embraced as redemptive from the beginning.

A Christian doctrine of creation that does not view the world in the light of the suffering Messiah will not understand the very processes of life as being directed toward God's liberating wholeness for all life. Creation, in other words, is not focused and oriented on the past. Rather, it is moving forward to a future and its true destiny resides there in God's Sabbath rest.

A trinitarian understanding does in fact connect God to all that is, created, redeemed, and sustained. An encounter with nature is also an encounter with resurrection as much as an encounter with death. Especially in the realm of Christian belief, the pain of the universe should be viewed in the faith that embraces all that is as the manifestation of the One who will redeem all things.

If we grasp creation as encompassing the entirety of God's saving presence, then we truly can understand the world as the manifestation of the creative energies of the triune God. This data is not to be "read off" the natural world, but is seen in the light of the One who is immersed within it, seeking to call us to the future that God dreams. The implications of allowing this narrative to have a voice would be immense.

To begin, the oppositional position of creation and evolution (or intelligent design and evolution) would be a nonissue for persons of faith. Creation has tenuous connection with evolution because creation is a theological term that can embrace a variety of understandings about the processes of the world that have brought life into existence. We should have the ability to realize that all theories about the world's emerging are provisional drafts that can be superseded by the next rendition. This is not only good science, it is good theology.[31]

Creation, as a theological belief, implies that all of life emerges from and is found within the God from whom we live and move and have our being. In the discovery of life's mysteries in the ongoing creation, theology offers an interpretation that speaks to what we find. The deep belief that creation is not finished and has not reached an end is located within a biblical trajectory that moves toward the eschatological fulfillment of the life of God.

In this movement, though the human creature may assume a position of centrality, especially given the incarnation, humanity is not necessarily *the* central figure in the redemptive drama. The recovery of an eschatological perspective might also mean that our theology moves to a true theocentric perspective. This is ultimately about God's life and not ours. Taking this perspective into the core of our being might mean that an examination of our arrogance and hubris would be in order.

The attempt to read the text within the larger context of its origins also means that a literalistic reading of Genesis is unnecessary to the ongoing faith of the church. One of the perennial mistakes of the church has been tying the biblical narrative in a too-concrete way to transitory cultural expressions.

Of course, the charge can be laid at my feet that this is exactly what I am doing. Instead of seeking the causes of creation, I am using evolution as my grid to interpret God's action and relation to the world. I have simply substituted one theory for another. Does this not repeat the error of those who made God a mechanistic automaton who assumes deistic shape under influence of the Newtonian worldview?

I believe this critique can be addressed in a number of ways. First, there are truths that are with us still from Newton's discoveries. His understanding of the boundary conditions within which life comes to be still applies to our knowledge of the world today. Einsteinian physics did not completely overturn Newton, but rather extended and enlarged upon it. I suspect that in the field of evolutionary science we are going to have to revise our current understandings, especially as the role of adaptation is better understood. No matter how our revisions appear, however, I believe we will still find the notion that life is a process-oriented force to be a part of a fundamental reality.

I think much the same can be true of how we grasp the ongoing process of Christian tradition. We are not necessarily tied to the provisions of the past (would anyone still want to argue with Paul about the importance of circumcision?), though we are rooted in them, illumined by them, and should not forget that our identities are shaped by them. This does not mean that they might not stand for some revision. I am arguing for fresh dimensions of apprehending God because I believe our communal assumptions about God need to be rethought.[32]

The examination of our tradition does not have to result in compromise or dissolution. It may mean that we recover some things of importance that got lost along the way. While we possess the touchstones of Scripture and tradition as vital to our narrated identities as Christians, we should not fear an engagement with our faith that has the potential to enlarge and extend the tradition.

If we are rooted in our tradition, we can understand the triune God in a way that will enable us to interpret the knowledge we are receiving about the world. The way the Cappadocian tradition and subsequent orthodox theology developed, the Trinity operated as a boundary on all human attempts to define God in isolation from God's redemptive presence found in Jesus Christ. It served to protect from theological idolatry because it placed us in the realm of mystery.

Because the triune God is seen in ways that reflect relationality, God's presence can be expressed in the world in such a way that gnostic separation of the world and God should not be allowed to be a central part of Christian belief. The triune God indwells all things and thus space opens to show that all the processes of what we believe to constitute life are themselves the manifestations of God seeking to accomplish God's will. And this is true not just of the original creation, but of the continuing and new creation as well.

And this is where the rub truly comes in for the people mentioned at the beginning of this chapter. For what type of God are we dealing with that would allow such waste and suffering to define a world coming to be? If what we have been reflecting on to this point has any merit, then we can say that the biblical witness itself speaks to the realization that redemption involves the entirety of the created order.

While the way that life manifests itself is open to a number of different interpretations, many of them without religious or theological warrant, for the Christian who thinks through creation, the world revealed by science is not without theological significance, no matter how provisional and transitory this knowledge may become. Let us move to consider some of the ways we can interpret the world on the basis of belief in the triune God.

NOTES

1. Stephen Jay Gould, *The Panda's Thumb* (New York: W. W. Norton, 1980), 20.

2. Willem Drees, *Creation: From Nothing Until Now* (London: Routledge, 2002), 16.

3. Annie Dillard, *Pilgrim at Tinker Creek* (New York: Bantam Books, 1974), 6

4. David Hull, "The God of the Galapagos," *Nature* 352 (1991): 486.

5. Quoted in Gregg Easterbrook, "Science and God: A Warming Trend?" *Science* 277 (1997): 892. Cornelius Hunter has some interesting observations regarding the way in which the unspoken and unacknowledged metaphysical presuppositions about the action of God in the world drive particular scientific views of evolution in his book, *Darwin's God: Evolution and the Problem of Evil* (Grand Rapids, Mich.: Brazos Press, 2001).

6. H. Paul Santmire, *Nature Reborn: The Ecological and Cosmic Promise of Christian Theology* (Minneapolis: Fortress Press, 2000), 95. See also his *The Travail of Nature: The Ambiguous Ecological Promise of Christian Theology* (Minneapolis: Fortress Press, 1987).

7. See, for instance, Dembski's *Intelligent Design: The Bridge Between Science and Theology* (Downers Grove, Ill.: InterVarsity Press, 1999); and *The Design Inference: Eliminating Chance Through Small Probabilities* (Cambridge: Cambridge University Press, 1998). Another book that has received a lot of mention is Michael Behe, *Darwin's Black Box: The Biochemical Challenge to Evolution* (New York: Touchstone Books, 1998). For an interesting volume that looks at these and other approaches to this issue, see James B. Miller, ed., *An Evolving Dialogue: Theological and Scientific Perspectives on Evolution* (Harrisburg, Pa.: Trinity Press International, 2001).

8. Adam Ford, *Universe: God, Science and the Human Person* (Mystic, Conn.: Twenty-Third Publications, 1987), 17.

9. These in fact are actual creation accounts coming from a variety of sources, from Native American cultures to the *Kojiki* chronicles in Japanese religion, where Izanagi and Izanami, the creator couple of Japan, created elements of the world through sexual congress.

10. A really interesting treatment of this point of view, which incorporates postmodern themes and issues, is found in J. Richard Middleton and Brian J. Walsh, *Truth Is Stranger Than It Used to Be: Biblical Faith in a Postmodern Age* (Downers Grove, Ill.: InterVarsity Press, 1995), 108–43.

11. See, for example, Moltmann, *God in Creation,* 86ff.

12. Gerhard von Rad, *Genesis* (trans. John H. Marks; Philadelphia: Westminster Press, 1972), 59–61.

13. This is one of the reasons that Moltmann argues that God's Sabbath rest is to be found in the future and eschatological domain of God's unfolding relationship with humankind.

14. See, for example, Barth, *Doctrine of Creation,* CD III/1, 41. Moltmann incorporates this terminology in his understanding of the creation and it is found in numerous places.

15. Peacocke, *Paths from Science Towards God,* 1–2.

16. Sobosan, *Romancing the Universe,* 131. One of the best-known works about what the initial conditions of life might have been like is Steven Weinberg, *The First Three Minutes* (New York: Basic Books, 1977).

17. Ibid., 132.

18. Matter, as a form of energy, does seem to possess the capacity to be self-organizing given its atomic and molecular constituents: "Such self organization into spatial and temporal patterns has now been observed in hundreds of chemical, biochemical, and biological systems." Peacocke, *Paths from Science Towards God,* 69.

19. Drees, *Creation,* 27.

20. Arnold Benz, *The Future of the Universe* (New York: Continuum, 2000), 30.

21. Ibid.

22. Ibid.

23. Ibid.

24. Diarmuid O'Murchu, *Quantum Theology: Spiritual Implications of the New Physics* (New York: Crossroad, 2000), 99.

25. Steven Hawking, *A Brief History of Time* (New York: Bantam Books, 1988), 174.

26. Ian Barbour, *When Science Meets Religion: Enemies, Strangers, or Partners?* (San Francisco: HarperSanFrancisco, 2000), 57.

27. Ibid., 57ff. See also O'Murchu, *Quantum Theology,* 99.

28. William J. Stoeger, S.J., "Scientific Accounts of Ultimate Catastrophes in Our Life-Bearing Universe," *The End of the World and The Ends of God: Science and Theology on Eschatology* (ed. John Polkinghorne and Michael Welker; Harrisburg, Pa.: Trinity Press International, 2000), 19–28.

29. Mark William Worthing, *God, Creation, and Contemporary Physics* (Minneapolis: Fortress Press, 1995), 104–6.

30. Ibid., 107.

31. Moltmann, *God in Creation,* 196.

32. As one small example, take Augustine's understanding of time found in Book 11 of the *Confessions.* Here he treats time in such a way that God and creation stand at some distance from one another. Indeed, his entire theology is predicated on this basis. I have mentioned previously that this distancing was an important and necessary move to understand the freedom of the creation itself. But it was taken into the tradition so thoroughly that a strong emphasis on the distance of God and creation was the result. While one can certainly sympathize with the desire to maintain this distance, one can also ask if this distance doesn't prevent the immanence of God from assuming its rightful place. When Barth gives his stirring call for a recovery of "the infinite qualitative distinction" between God and the creation found in his commentary on Romans, we see the cultural context of nineteenth-century theology out of which that call emerges. But that can mean that God as "Wholly Other" can be too removed from us. Karl Barth, *The Epistle to the Romans* (trans. Edwyn C. Hoskyns; London: Oxford University Press, 1933), 10.

5

GOD *IS* IN THE DETAILS

Divinity is the enfolding and unfolding of everything that is.
Divinity is in all things in such a way
that all things are in divinity.
—Nicholas of Cusa

See! I am God. See! I am in everything. See! I never
lift my hand off my works, nor will I ever. See! I lead
everything toward the purpose for which I ordained it,
without beginning, by the same Power, Wisdom, and Love
by which I created it. How could anything be amiss?
—Julian of Norwich

Thou canst not stir a flower
Without troubling a star.
—Francis Thompson

In the year 1935, an experiment was introduced to the world by Albert Einstein and his Princeton colleagues, Boris Podolsky and Nathan Rosen, that became known as the EPR (Einstein-Podolsky-Rosen) experiment. Two fundamental assumptions were underlying the experiment: a sense of classical realism that individual particles possess definite properties even when no one is observing them, and the principle of locality, which suggests that no causal influence can be transmitted between two isolated systems at a speed faster than the speed of light.

Their experiment assumed a two-proton particle with zero spin splitting into proton A and proton B, with each proton going in different directions. The spin of proton A could have the possibility of spin in either direction, but proton B must have the opposite spin in order to equal the original zero spin of the original two-proton system.

According to the uncertainty principle of quantum theory, A and B have an equal probability of having either a left- or right-oriented spin and this spin is not determined until such time as it is observed or measured. The experiment argued that if A and B go in opposite directions until this measurement takes place, there is no possibility of instantaneous "communication" between the two. Yet quantum theory tells us that B must "know" in which direction to spin in order to balance the spin of A. Einstein and his colleagues argued against this type of instantaneous communication.

Later the physicist David Bohm proposed a simplified description of the EPR experiment that starts with a particle that isn't spinning. It separates into two particles and the halves speed off at forty-five degrees to either side of their parent's path with equal but opposite spins. At some distance the experimenter reverses the spin of one of them. According to quantum theory, the other half particle would have to reverse its spin.

This created a significant debate among physicists, but the experiment was still more of a thought puzzle until Alain Aspect and his Parisian colleagues confirmed quantum correlations over dimensions up to 85 feet and perhaps 110 feet. While still under great debate among physicists, it would appear that on some level the aim of this experiment, the principle of non-locality, is at least a theoretical option operative in some measure. The intuition that causal relations among things are not as linear or local as we understand them has given rise to much speculation about the universe.[1]

David Bohm believed that this conclusion is tentative confirmation for his theory that there is an underlying "wholeness" to the universe within the quantum physical systems. He used the term "implicate order" and argued that this underlying order functions as the primary ground for all reality, known or unknown. The explicit unfolded order that we observe and experience is the product of the former.

Bohm extended his understanding of this order by his conceptualization of holographic images. A hologram is created when a beam of laser light is partially reflected off a mirror and partially shines on an object. A camera is placed where the beam is reflected from the mirror and meets the light coming off the object. These two beams interfere and interact and the camera captures a photographic place of the pattern that forms. This plate is the hologram. After this is lit with another laser, you have an image of the object that has three dimensions.[2]

The curious thing is that if the photographic plate breaks, one need only shine the laser through a broken piece of the plate to make the whole image reappear. "Any part of a hologram contains information on the whole object because each portion of the interference pattern from the laser light carries information on the whole object."[3]

In Bohm's understanding, the total order of the universe is found in any part because the implicate order is present in all information exchanges within the universe, but this image is only provisional for our observations and can only deepen our sense of quantum mystery. Of course, a more ancient image of a similar dynamic is found in the biblical image of leaven, which, though a part, influences the resulting product (Matt 13:33; Gal 5:9).

Kevin Sharpe refers to this sense of implicate order by describing a device that is found in the British Museum. In this machine a spot of dye is slowly spun into glycerol until the spot disappears. When the machine reverses its spin, "the spot reappears almost to its original state."[4]

Sharpe uses this process to make an analogy about the enfolding and unfolding to describe a state where the glycerol enfolding the dye represents the underlying order of wholeness found in the universe and the movement or flux of this wholeness unfolds certain aspects that at times rise into relief—the spot reappears. Thus the unfolding also produces the explicate order.

There is some resistance to the implications that Bohm draws for a very specific set of circumstances and characteristics.[5] And while Bohm's theories may not reflect the opinion of most physicists, they do at least serve to point to an exploration among physicists to see the interconnectedness and contingency of matter and fresh thinking about how the universe functions.

Theology needs to be cautious in the ways we employ theories as metaphors for understanding, but even so, the notion of nonlocality does serve as interesting information for reflection upon a mysterious universe. At the very least, fresh insights concerning the way the world exists could enlarge our spiritual awareness that theological reflection cannot rest content on seeing God's relationship to the world primarily through an external or interventionist mode. Not only in the parts, but in the relationships among things, is the transcendent wholeness that sustains all existence found.

If we truly believe that God is the creator of "all things seen and unseen," we have a world to explore that is seemingly limitless. We will look at some of the implications of quantum and field theory in this chapter as metaphors and analogies for what we are discovering about the world. These figures of speech do not represent an unfaithful move to secularity, but offer avenues to deepen our awareness of the presence of God in the world. This may lead us to grasp that the God who sustains all of life does not necessarily do so from a position of absolute transcendence; rather, God may found be in the details.

Reality Isn't What It Used to Be

We have seen that the formation of our universe has emerged from a remarkable moment and has proceeded in a rather extraordinary fashion. The creativity of the universe has emerged in qualitatively novel and fresh dimensions of life. Not only have new structures come into being, they have, in turn, given rise to ever more unique expressions of life. For many scientists, qualitative development is a fundamental characteristic of the cosmos.[6]

For the past two centuries there has been growing discovery of the hidden structures the natural world processes. These discoveries have moved us from an understanding of the universe as a relatively stable place to an awareness of the universe as a relatively unstable place. All existence is in the process of becoming, and nature is involved in a unique history. Nature does not appear to be a closed system; it seems to be an open one.

Our perceptions are thus informed by the world that is being revealed to us. Of course, part of this story is the one told by quantum theory where names like Bohr, Planck, and Schrödinger offer interpretations of reality that speak to such phenomena as quanta, wave equation, and the often invoked principle of uncertainty attributed to Heisenberg.

What was before understood by us on the basis of Newtonian determinism, operating on some very specific ways of grasping the physical laws of the universe, has now become more elusive. The connections between cause and effect no longer seem determinative in a mechanistic way; rather, a change of metaphor is needed to explain it all. We now speak in probabilities because the "quantum atom is inaccessible to direct observation and unimaginable in terms of everyday properties; it cannot even be coherently described in terms of classical physical concepts such as space, time, and causality."[7]

When Werner Heisenberg formulated his uncertainty principle, he stated that the more accurately we determine the position of an electron or other particle, the less accurately we can determine its momentum. The reverse is also true. What emerged from ideas like this and others that followed is that perceptions of connectedness and causality cannot be expressed by concepts that would completely satisfy science. The deeper one looks into the universe, the more words fail, reason stands amazed, and we look for other forms of expression or language to express what it is we find. Sometimes this language comes from poetry or art, but other times it comes from a language that expresses its own sense of elegance, mathematics.

This notion of the open-endedness of the universe has been so untenable to some that they argue that the uncertainties proposed by quantum theory will yield to laws that will allow for exact prediction. This was the position that Einstein was taking when he stated "God does not play dice." Others argue that uncertainty comes from our permanent limitations on knowing the exact nature of the atomic world. The exactness is there, embedded so deep even our mathematical equations are not going to be able to uncover them.[8]

Finally, there are those who argue that indeterminacy is an objective characteristic of our world. While the possibilities for chance are always present, however, there do seem to be some constraints on the possibilities open to the entities we observe. The orbit of a particle is not entirely arbitrary because the possibility for chance is limited by Planck's constant.[9] While precision cannot necessarily be predicted, there are a range of options that would function as boundary conditions for future behaviors.

One of the difficulties that we run into is the notion that perhaps our own minds impose upon the world we observe the actualization of various possibilities. When physicists find the wave function collapsing to the value that is observed, they wonder how initially indeterminate results get fixed.

When several different possibilities narrow down to one upon observation, is it that all the possibilities present to our perceptions bring the reality of the one into being? Are we left with the notion that we occupy an observer-created universe? This is the position that some have taken and there may be a partial truth to this. Our observation both changes things and can never totally grasp the reality present to us. And yet there is a reality that continues on without us nonetheless.

The very fact that we are participants in this reality and that this participation has causal influence on what goes on to some extent has led some persons to use the category of relationship as a means of illumining what happens in the world. Using the category of relationship also opens up discussion about the interaction of life in ways that are acquiring new attention.

One of these is the move away from the reductionist model, which explains the whole solely on the basis of its parts alone. The structures the individual components construct carry as much explanatory importance as the parts themselves. As observations of the atomic and molecular fields have suggested: "The natural and human sciences give us more and more a picture of the world as consisting of complex hierarchies—as series of levels of organization of matter in which each successive member of the series is a whole constituted of parts preceding it in the series."[10]

In the physical processes that are in play, the whole cannot necessarily be explained by definition of the parts alone. The whole system seems to be irreducible to its parts. The entire system functions in such a way that the systemic behavior cannot be explained on the basis of whatever we understand about the constituent components. This is what we have pointed to by looking at the EPR experiment and its subsequent investigation: "Quantum states exhibit a surprisingly integrationist view of the relationship of systems which have once interacted with each other, however widely they may subsequently separate."[11]

We are now immersed in an ongoing complex of relationships that define us even as we in some measure define them. These relationships defy a simple causal analysis, because the entirety of a thing simply cannot be reduced. The whole of a person cannot be reduced to what is happening in the various parts or systems at work. Though the DNA can be analyzed, mapped, and manipulated, though biological functions can be described in minute detail, and even though we can describe the molecular level of the workings of the brain, there is still on some level going to be the mystery.

The biological processes of the body may enable us to describe the chemical interactions that arise with feelings of attraction or sexual arousal, but they cannot begin to account for what becomes manifest within the community of life that forms between two persons when they are able to move through life's joys and sufferings to find an intimacy that gives them an almost mystical sense of connection. Nor can it entirely account for the love that exists within communities of persons who are not together based on physiological attraction, but on the basis of a commitment to God.

There can be detailed explanations for the operations of the universe, but the contemplation of the night sky or the morning sunrise still leads us to territory that becomes difficult to articulate. It is a movement of something in us that seems too deep for expression. Many of us have felt in this moment a profound feeling of gratitude for being present, and participation in life is the most satisfactory response. Maybe we can explain physically what is happening to us, but our sense of being in the world pulls us to the deep waters of contemplation. *We are a part of this amazing universe!*

Through all the work done on the functioning of the brain, we now recognize that properties not found in the components of the brain emerge from the ways those elements constitute themselves. Though mental states are dependent and contingent upon lower-level events, it is a difficult move to reduce mental states, consciousness, to those events alone.

The basic processes of nature appear to be relatively simple, but the move to the next step reveals a complexity that becomes extremely difficult to trace back to basic physical causes. The universe appears to allow for the development of highly complex connections that for us have manifested the beauty, elegance, and even purposefulness we discern around us. The very fact that we are here is a mystery worth entertaining.

Certainly notions of causality that have been tenaciously clung to should undergo revision. This model of the whole behaving in such a way that the systemic behavior of physical processes cannot be reduced to its constituent parts has also led us to understand that at the level of systems we find emergent properties that express novelty and new experiences. Galaxies come and go, species die and new ones emerge, life explores and expresses itself in new ways.

This can sometimes be hard to wrap our heads around, this notion that all existence constitutes in itself a systemic reality. No longer understood under the influence of mechanistic models, we find a picture emerging of a cosmos engaged in a dance of constantly flowing information. In this dance there sometimes seem to be no discernible steps to us, or much in the way of a point.

This constant flow of energy is the one overriding characteristic that informs and forms all of life. It is the ocean in which we swim and it forms the matrix within which all of life's possibilities come to actualization. When discussions about this life proceed, they do so in the acute realization that forces minute and cosmic, known and unknown, are interacting, humming with activity.

A Passion Play

This open universe is a participatory system that depends upon vast exchanges of information and communication to extend itself at every level, and in these exchanges new levels of organization have manifested themselves: "It would seem that the universe contains within itself the trend towards the universal symbiosis of all systems of life and matter, by virtue of 'the sympathy of all things' for one another."[12]

The question before us as persons of faith is how do these forces speak to the belief in the triune God? If we are not careful, we will interpret God in the world as so amorphous that God becomes defined solely in terms of the world process. However, if we remove God too far from the processes of life, we end up with a remoteness that does not do justice to the biblical witness.

One approach is to describe God as the lure that draws us ever closer to the will of God for the world, and there can be some truth to this.[13] But does it not ultimately end up in abstraction? How would we define this will in the first place? On the basis of the evidence of nature alone we would be hard pressed to imagine what that might be exactly. And yet, taking the reality around us as a clue, we do find a system aligned for growing communication and response to information. We find microsystems that draw from and contribute to the larger structures present in life.

If God is seen as the lure that draws the world to divinity, it must be the case that God is the transcendent wholeness upon which the rest of the universe depends. Response to this wholeness leads to a fullness of life, but the question must be asked, can this lure be resisted? Can the very processes of creation resist the call of God to enter the dance of plentitude and growth? Does the Creator experience the contradiction of the creation?

Christian theology also opens up the possibility that God not only creates the potentialities, but also infuses these with the presence of the Holy Spirit and thus is presenting the creative potential before us in the universe. While it is a painful thought to entertain, sometimes the new creations emerge from the suffering and passing away of the old. This process of loss is an aspect of life that is so difficult for us to become accustomed to. However, it is an inescapable part of the processes that brought us here, and God is present even here, on the borders of decay and disappearance.

The theologian can understand and interpret these vast energies oscillating throughout the universe as the manifestations of the energies of God. The universe is not without sacramental significance on its own. Creativity is what brings actualities into being, and chance and necessity appear to represent boundary conditions within which life explores the creative potentialities. The One who creates, who is creating and has desire for the universe, also embodies and incarnates within the world to sustain the ongoing processes of creation. In this immersion into the world the Holy Spirit is continually responding to the cosmic journey that life is taking.

We have previously maintained that the original creative action of God in bringing forth the universe is due to the free decision of God. However, we must be alert to the realization that from the beginning we find a creation in flux with informing processes that bring forth emerging properties. These systems exhibit amazing new levels of complexity that could not necessarily be predicted.[14]

In mysterious paths where shadowy reality rests hidden from us, the universe as a system seems to exercise its own freedom in becoming. It chooses certain paths, some of which lead to fertile expressions of life and others which lead to extinction: "The pathetic element in nature is seen in faith to be at the deepest logical level the pathos in God. . . . The secret of life is seen now to lie not so much in hereditary molecules, not so much in the natural selection and the survival of the fittest, not so much in life's information, cybernetic learning. The secret of life is that it is a passion play."[15]

And it is this sense of passion that sometimes gets lost from our discussions. The notion that in the processes of existence we find a sense of suffering love is beyond the "space between" that we have previously invoked. From the scenes relayed from the Hubble telescope or in our electron microscopes, we find something we did not anticipate. It is not the passive apathy of a deity who remains in remote transcendence, but the eros of God we discover. More than some of our imaginations can hold, we find our world grasped by the great mystery before us.

Here is where a certain caution should be noted concerning our reflection upon the universe. While we have been exploring the possibility of new metaphors to serve as descriptive tools for Christian tradition, we realize that culturally dominant metaphors have historically been used to address the ways we model God.

The use of the machine, for instance, whether it is a clock or a computer, has been used to tease out the implications of order and regularity found in the previous models operative in worldview construction. As the emerging sciences of mathematics held sway, the world became understood in more quantifiable categories. This was the starting place of the modern approach of reductionism, wherein each particle of a thing is its own reason for being, its own nature.

The continuation of this process whereby nature was broken down into autonomous particles contributed to the mechanistic metaphors of theology and developing science. But perhaps more importantly, this view of the world issued in certain technologies and our notions of power.

As science compartmentalized and reduced nature to bits and pieces, the possible interconnections of parts and wholes were ignored. The fact that the reason for things may rest in a larger framework than individual cogs in a machine seemed low on the list of interpretations of life. This led to the development of technologies that became technologies of control and dominance, not cooperation. We have the power to split the atom, and now we also have the power of DNA coding. We will not only understand, we will improve on what we have been given.

Through a long process we have divested nature of its ability to enchant us and have instead made of it an object of our control and dominance. This objectification of nature was not without its beneficial side, for much came to human life because of it. But great fear and frustration also came into the world. Since the atom was split, the world has lived with a deeper sense of dread and fear.

Undeniable, however, is that this technological manipulation has led to a loss of the sacred, of human accountability to the Creator. Our desire for mastery of the world emerged in no small part from our increasing ability to have technical mastery over it. This in turn has served the purpose of disconnecting us from the world of nature.

Because our technologies have exerted such a powerful influence over us, it is important to subject our use of those metaphors to reflection upon God's relationship to the world found in the biblical narrative and the traditions arising from them. Even as we have been arguing for revision of a certain understanding of God, we should still be cognizant of the dangers.

As one small example, our technology has recently led us to an understanding of the sender-receiver view of the information exchanges found within nature, which, in turn, raises certain issues about how information is passed and how micro and macro systems interact. But when we start to examine the interactions of parts and whole, perhaps we should think in terms deeper than mere communication. To fill out the concepts we are now considering, we should think in terms of communion when we consider the processes known and unknown to us by which the universe comes to be. This move to think in terms of communion opens up the way to think in terms that manifest deeper connections.

Given what has just been said about the passion of God, it is not knowledge as such that should root our potential metaphors, but the transformation of our knowledge into compassion. If our knowledge is leading us to seek yet more mastery and dominance over the natural order, perhaps we should step back. If, however, we were to internalize the sense that God does in fact experience the creation, we would find a profound space for our reflection that at the heart of the world beats a heart of grace. How, though, can we see the forces of life as sacramental, as vehicles of grace?

Fields of Dreams

It is difficult to think of forces as such as being vehicles of grace. Usually we associate grace with personal interaction. However, if we think about the forces that are present in the sustaining of life as part of God's sustaining presence in the world, then it is not too difficult to understand God's grace being manifested in them. Given the issues of nonlocality and holism raised so far, can we find a legitimate place in nature for seeing God's sustaining presence?

One such place that some theologians have explored is the area of field theory. Presently physicists talk about four main fields, usually referred to as gravity, weak, strong, and electromagnetic fields. While there is much dispute among scientists working in the area of field theory, there is a common notion that fields constitute nonmaterial regions of influence. Interestingly, the "seminal form of modern field theories can be traced back to the Stoic doctrine of the divine *pneuma* (spirit) which has been identified as the direct predecessor of the field concept in modern physics."[16]

This sense of force is profoundly influential in all of matter. The gravitational field is omnipresent and in a sense omnipowerful in its influence in the universe. The other three constitute a ubiquitous presence in the world as well, but some persons focus on the electromagnetic field as so pervasive as to stand as the strongest candidate for possible analogues for describing God's presence.[17]

Through the pioneering work of James Clerk Maxwell and the extension of his work by other such as Richard Feynman, Julian Schwinger, Shinichiro Tomonaga, and Freeman Dyson, who formulated the theory of quantum electrodynamics (QED), our understanding of this force has yielded much knowledge. The concepts surrounding the theory of quantum electrodynamics showed that electromagnetic force between electrically charged particles is carried by unobservable photons. These shadow or virtual photons stand in contrast to real photons of visible light. These shadow photons are not mere conjecture because in experiments they "kick back" when measured: "Shadow photons kick back by interfering with the photons we see and therefore shadow photons exist."[18]

In the electromagnetic force, the necessary component of life is found. Without it the molecular structure that makes possible all biology and chemistry would not be available for the furtherance of life. The electromagnetic field "makes it possible for bacteria, the smallest living cells, to exhibit purposeful mobility, coherent collective action, and remarkable sophistication in their growth and survival."[19] If we extrapolate to larger systems, we find our most intricate interaction with matter to be the electromagnetic interaction.

Without the presence of this force or field of influence, all things presently holding together would collapse. If I put the apple I held in my hand in the previous chapter on the table, it would fall through the table as the table itself would fall through the floor and so on. This force is the primal reality of the world we experience. All knowledge of the other three forces comes from electromagnetic "sensors." Electromagnetic radiation is the door through which we peer at the vast history of the cosmos and is important for sight.[20] Upon closer inspection of some of the most minute and complex theories of existence, we find "we and all apparently material earthly objects are a part of a vast ocean of essentially nonmaterial space energized by an innumerable multitude of virtual electromagnetic phenomena."[21]

This phenomenon offers us the lens with which to see the world in ways that were not accessible before. Measurements of the quantum world have proceeded on the basis of electrodynamic means. The evolutionary process from the earliest assembly of molecules to the existence of human beings is accomplished by the "incessant probing and testing by a multitude of exquisitely sensitive 'electrodynamic photon messengers.'"[22] These photons serve as the means of experimentation and search for higher level complexity and organization: "Thus the construction of a gene, consisting of beautifully symmetric double helix DNA molecules, which in turn exhibit vastly varying arrangements of nucleotides, has been effected by multitudes of subtle electromagnetic interactions."[23]

Electromagnetic interaction, and its corresponding field, functions for Lawrence Fagg as a meaningful physical analogue to God's immanence. This does not mean that God is the electromagnetic field itself, only that the connections and fresh perspectives that it offers us serve as an analogue for God's presence.

We could certainly say it is ubiquitous and all-pervasive. But it can also help us think about analogous sensitivities from subtle to intense that are operative in the ongoing processes of life. There are ways in which heightened sensitivity to electromagnetic fields is expressed in the material world with the appearance of matter or concentrations of energy. The ongoing explorations of life and the emergence of new properties result not just from cosmic explosions, but also from cellular choice.

Light as electromagnetic radiation offers us a new aspect of metaphorical consideration for the entirety of creation because light has been a consistent metaphor in the biblical narratives as well. Light serves to open our minds and hearts to the realization that, despite these biblical metaphors, Christianity has been primarily a faith rooted in hearing. The Word of God is testified to, preached about, spoken of, and so on. Perhaps it is time to supplement, not supplant, that image with the metaphor of seeing.

Though much of the reality of electromagnetic radiation is hidden from our eyes, it is what enables our sight. Despite the limitations of empirical observation, it is quite possible that if the tradition of Christianity were to embrace not only a verbal tradition, but also one of sight, it could become visionary. A theology of seeing is as important as one of hearing.

Field theory may be an analogical and provisional approach, to be held lightly, but it has been explored by other theologians as a model for understanding the effects of God's presence in the world. As such it presents us with one model for our understanding God's sustenance of creation through the Holy Spirit.[24] Fields emerged from the earliest stages of creation to provide the conditions for self-organization and sources of creativity. Without acquiring the type of precise definitions we referred to earlier, life as we know it would not be this continuous dance of exploration.

Once again, the electromagnetic field is not to be seen as God, but certainly the analogical use of fields would allow for another notion of God's sustaining Holy Spirit in the world. Some have even thought of fields as being "*horizons of belonging,* creating a relational matrix for creative possibilities."[25] Fields form the boundaries of home, where things make themselves and where God dreams the possibilities for the creation emerging from God's creative energies.

Out of the Chaos

Such a perspective opens a space for us to understand a dimension of existence that offers fresh visions of the Holy Spirit. For much of Christian tradition we have understood God as a subject acting upon the universe as an object. This results in a separation between God and the created order that is seen as a necessary aspect of differentiation. While maintaining the otherness of God (indeed God maintains within God's triune identity otherness), fields do allow us the realization of a unity that transcends all dualisms to imbue the internal character of the world with a consciousness with which it responds.

The spiritual dimension of the universe is not to be isolated in particular moments (though certain moments may well manifest a greater sensitivity to God's presence), times, or places, but is everywhere at all times working to make itself known. This spiritual dimension, understood by Christians historically as the Father, Son, and Holy Spirit, is the ground within which all unfolds and is connected.

The recognition of God's continuing creation means God is not absent from the creative processes in play, nor is God to be found solely in the establishing of the basic forces and parameters that allowed existence to flourish.

God is so connected to the life that is coming to be that divine presence immerses itself in the world, though it is not exhausted by it. This divine presence is as all-pervasive as electromagnetic reality, responding to and interacting with all of life in order to bring about the rest of God's shalom.

While we may possess a partial understanding of this recognition, the fact is that we are so embedded within these movements of becoming that we are simply unable to offer an account of the whole thing. The tension inherent in this partiality is shared by all human participants and points us once again to the realm of mystery. We simply cannot step out of all this to grasp what is going on in its entirety, and why it is the way it is.

Part of the problem we face is that we are able to see that what we are speaking of causes chaos as well as order in the cosmos. Indeed, we are quite cognizant of the destructive powers that oscillate throughout the cosmos, thus creating chaos. When we use the term chaos here, it is not in the contemporary scientific model, which we shall turn to in a minute, but chaos in the ancient Greek sense of indicating the confusion and disarray present in the universe.

The notion of chaos is a part of some of the creation stories of the world. Chaos is the primal condition from which the universe arose, and overcoming chaos was the first creative act to restore order. In Taoism, for example, all was initially chaotic until the first movement of order emerged in the complementary opposites of yin and yang. Once this fundamental division of opposites (hot/cold, light/dark/, positive/negative, and so on) occurred, then some sense of order was established in the universe. This order represents the Tao, or the Path or Way. Follow this, stay in harmony with it, and you will live in harmony with yourself, others, and nature. If you do not respect the balance and you do not honor the path, your relationships with all things will yield disharmony. This is just one example of a narrative dealing with the chaos.

Chaos seems to be a constitutive part of the universe. Consider one event that occurred as I wrote this chapter: the sun unleashed a torque of flame that stretched hundreds of millions of miles. Fortunately, earth wasn't in the way. If it had been, power outages, communications failures, and birth defects from the radiation would have been only some of the results.

When we cast a long hard look at the realities of life, we do see that chaos and catastrophe are woven into the fabric of the universe. What are we to make of these various catastrophes? Is it possible to say yes to this order of life? Is there a faith strong enough to see in exploding galaxies and collapsing stars energies at play that can even remotely be understood as benevolent? How is God's redemptive will manifest in such a situation?

In the scientific model of chaos, of course, the term is not seen as applying solely to destructive powers and conditions of disarray. The term is used in ways that point to the investigations upon behavior of systems and patterns of organization that exhibit themselves in nature.

One of the best-known examples is termed the "butterfly effect," which states that the earth's weather systems are so sensitive to small disturbances that a butterfly flapping its wings in a canyon in Peru could have consequences halfway around the world in the form of a thunderstorm moving through Japan. This idea has entered the consciousness of the public in ways as diverse as the Honda commercial of a few years ago that encouraged viewers to buy a Honda because you never know when and why bad weather will strike, to television shows with episodes entitled "Chaos Theory." All this serves to show how familiar this theoretical map has become.

The chaos mentioned in this theory, of course, does not point to an absence of order and the presence of complete disorder. Instead, it shows how supposed chaotic flux actually follows rather precise patterning. When the numbers are run, we find incredible precision behind the various phenomena studied.

Consider the work of Mitchell Feigenbaum, whose study of chaotic systems revealed interesting properties that seem to rest hidden in nature. In the study of systems such as dripping taps or pulsating stars, researchers encountered a situation where the solution curve breaks into two different directions, a phenomenon known as a bifurcation. On the first break, the curve can take on two values and will move between the two. However, in this oscillation more separation or bifurcation can occur, leading to what is known as a bifurcation tree. This rate of dividing or branching out gets faster and faster until an infinity of possible branches is reached. This is the point at which the term chaos enters the picture.

There is a critical moment in this process for the onset of chaotic behavior where the value at which chaotic behavior begins is a precise mathematical designation of 3.5699. When the gaps between successive branching become closer, the gap is slightly less than one-quarter of the previous one, a ratio tending to a fixed value of 1\4.669201. In addition, Feigenbaum "also noticed that the rate of shrinkage between the prongs on the bifurcation tree is also close to a standard two-fifths of the previous one and calculated to the numerical value of 1\2.5029."[26]

The discovery of these ratios led to the concept of the Feigenbaum constants, numbers that recur in different contexts: 4.669201 and 2.5029 seem to be fundamental constants of nature, just like the Fibonacci sequence we mentioned earlier. While chaos theory has drawn our attention to the systemic laws and nature of the universe and the extraordinary implications that an underlying order sustains systems seemingly in random flux, we are still left with some uncertainty.

In discussing this inherent uncertainty at play in physical systems, John Polkinghorne uses the illustration of air in a room. The air molecules collide with each other along the model of billiard balls. In 10^{-10} seconds, each molecule has had fifty collisions with its neighbors. He asks how accurately must circumstances "be known initially if one is to calculate with tolerable accuracy 10^{-10} seconds later whether a particular molecule is moving towards or away from the brick wall?"[27]

While the billiard ball collision may be a perfectly determined event, any variation, no matter how small, results in an inability to predict future behavior of this system. Thus, the failure to calculate the effect of an electron on the other side of the observable universe interacting with the air in the room through its gravitational effect will result in an uncertainty about the behavior of the billiard ball. So, infinitesimally small uncertainty concerning initial conditions can lead to enormous uncertainties in predicting the subsequent behavior of systems.

And yet, one of the most amazing results of our understanding is that systems behave in a mathematically precise way. There are even repetitions of geometrical patterns that reveal fascinating complexities embedded within physical systems. Known as fractals, these patterns reveal themselves in computer simulations that use algorithms and mathematical procedures to translate data into geometric forms. These mathematical relations reveal the potential of nature to acquire great symmetry within itself.[28]

The discussion of chaos theory usually leads to the mention of complexity theory as well. The physicist Ilya Prigogene and his colleagues studied the behavior of dissipative systems far from equilibrium. In their study the realization emerged that unstable systems will yield to a new level of collective order and stability will reappear. The disorder of chaos leads to new order at a higher level than previously, with new forms of complexity. Randomness, which seems to be an inherently destructive force when the word chaos is used historically, is seen to yield new possibilities, novel expressions of life, and increasing diversity.

The conditions for the furthering of creation seem to emerge in the images of underlying order, even mathematical precision, which allow the boundary conditions for the exploration and experimentation by nature itself. We cannot predict the outcomes because, even as order seems to be foundationally constant, so do chance and freedom. The dance of life consists in the existence of possibility and potential, and disorder seems to be the ground from which new life arises.

The difficulty for us is that as part of this disorder we must face the reality that so much dies. Without death, there would not be life. Without the death of stars, we would not be here. Without the possible experience of an asteroid slamming into earth 65 million years ago, we would not have the life we do now. Even though we may realize this truth, it provides nothing other than cold comfort. On the face of it, this truth does not seem to provide much pastoral comfort either. When we consider the questions raised earlier about the violence of the universe, we find ourselves feeling a little like the biblical character of Job found in Hebrew Scripture.

In this story, which has been misread by countless persons over the ages, Job has launched an extreme protest against God for his suffering. The original story consisting of the first two chapters and the epilogue at the end tell the story of an innocent man who suffers because Yahweh enters into a wager with a character called the Adversary. Seen more as a prosecuting attorney than what we have today, this character accuses Job of serving God for personal gain and prosperity.

At the end of the first two chapters we find Job suffering patiently, not protesting his fate, but in the third chapter something happens that causes Job to curse the day he was born. There follows one of the most interesting pieces of theodicy ever published as the author(s) explores religious answers to the deep questions of human existence. All the usual answers are brought forth and found wanting. Job has not sinned, God does not just punish the wicked and reward the righteous; sometimes God punishes the righteous as well.

As he spews out his frustration, Job calls upon Yahweh to give account for the ordering of the world. And Yahweh puts in an appearance, but it is not quite what Job had in mind. When Yahweh shows up he takes no responsibility for having entered into the initial wager. He does not seek to comfort Job. Rather, Yahweh speaks and questions Job, asking where he was at the dawning of creation. Where was he when the foundations of the world were laid (Job 38:4–11)? Where was he when life was created and given its own path to follow? Does Job struggle with the Leviathan (41:1–8) or the Behemoth (40: 15–24)? Can he bind the chains of the Pleiades or loose the cords of Orion? Yahweh lays out before Job the entirety of creation and asks Job essentially how he thinks he has the right to question God.

Job is overwhelmed by this response from Yahweh and in the end capitulates with the words "I had heard of you with my ears, but now I see you face to face." Is this an answer that can satisfy our protests against the destruction at work in the world? Does not this represent one of our greatest fears, that God will not love, much less be accountable to, the creation in any way?

We will come back to this theme later, but I would like to suggest that perhaps we find in this answer of Job something less than unconditional surrender and a caving in to the overwhelming superiority of God. In what is less a surrender than a recognition, Job has moved from hearing to seeing. This is why a theology of seeing can lead us to new depths of faith.

Clearly, seeing truly does not mean romanticizing nature with some naïve sentimentalism about "Mother Nature." Nature bites back. Nature has forces that are beyond our control and issue in death. I have had numerous occasions over the last several years to visit Hawaii's Volcanoes National Park. I have watched lava flow into the ocean, destroying everything in its path. Nothing can withstand its immense heat and destructive powers. Trees, houses, cars, roads, lava will take it all as it moves inexorably toward the ocean. After it cools, it leaves a landscape of blank desolation that appears as if nothing could ever grow there again.

Still, I have stood upon field after field of this geological formation and observed a piece of greenery here, a flower flourishing there. I have marveled at the mystery before me—out of death and destruction comes life. The lava that flowed into the sea is creating more land. Every day on this planet more land and more life is coming forth. The knowledge that the land I am standing on was one day not there, and from rock and desolation gave forth life, is enough to fill me with wonder.

The destruction of life does not mean the disappearance of life because life supposedly lost to the destructive powers of nature makes its reappearance. Even more important, I am aware of the mystery that leads me out of myself and my self-centeredness toward that which I cannot even begin to comprehend. There is something redemptive happening within these vast forces at play, something redemptive in the fields and electrons of existence, something infinitely sensitive to the least fluctuation, and something that patiently responds to the exploring of life.

Quantum perspective and acknowledgment of quantum reality as we presently understand it takes the chaos of the Leviathan and creates a new order, a new level of life from the old. The *creatio originalis* forms the conditions for the *creatio continua*. If we can imagine God in continual communion with creation through the subtleties of nonlocality or holism, we can discern an imagination that is rich with possibilities for the future. Even though we may be able to see more, however, there is still the issue of suffering to keep in front of us, for some of us may not be happy with Job's response and may want more. Perhaps we are ready to ask if God shares in any way the sufferings of the creation.

NOTES

1. This experiment is found in a number of places, but see Mark Worthing, *God, Creation and Contemporary Physics* (Minneapolis: Fortress Press, 1995); and Kevin Sharpe, *Sleuthing the Divine: The Nexus of Science and Spirit* (Minneapolis: Fortress Press, 2001). For a nontheological treatment of this experiment, see James T. Cushing, *Philosophical Concepts in Physics: The Historical Relation between Philosophy and Scientific Theories* (Cambridge: Cambridge University Press, 1998), 317–30. This book will be especially interesting to those who have a physics background, because the discussion is extremely technical and offers numerous equations.

2. Sharpe, *Sleuthing the Divine*, 20–21.

3. Ibid., 21.

4. Ibid., 23.

5. For example, John Polkinghorne, "The Quantum World," in *Physics, Philosophy, and Theology* (ed. R. Russell, W. Stoeger, and G. Coyne; Vatican City: Vatican Observatory, 1988).

6. See Benz, *The Future of the Universe*, 34.

7. Barbour, *When Science Meets Religion*, 67.

8. Ibid.

9. Benz, *The Future of the Universe*, 37.

10. Peacocke, *Paths from Science towards God*, 48.

11. John Polkinghorne, *The Quantum World* (London: Penguin Books, 1986), 79–80.

12. Moltmann, *God in Creation*, 205.

13. This imagery figures prominently in process theologies such as those found in Whitehead and Hartshorne. See, for example, Lewis Ford, *The Lure of God: A Biblical Background for Process Theism* (Philadelphia: Fortress Press, 1978); or Norman Pittenger, *The Lure of Divine Love: Human Experiences and Christian Faith* (Cleveland: Pilgrim Press, 1979).

14. Peacocke, *Paths from Science towards God*, 46–47.

15. Holmes Ralston III, "Does Nature Need to Be Redeemed?" *Zygon* 29 (June 1994): 205–29.

16. Worthing, *God, Creation and Contemporary Physics*, 117. For an extended treatment, see pages 117–24.

17. Theologians such as Wolfhart Pannenberg are especially interested in field theory. One proponent is Lawrence W. Fagg, who has written *Electromagnetism and the Sacred: At the Frontier of Spirit and Matter* (New York: Continuum, 1999). See also Fagg's "Sacred Indwelling and the Electromagnetic Undercurrent in Nature: A Physicist's Perspective," *Zygon* 37, no. 2 (June 2002): 473–90.

18. David Deutsch, *The Fabric of Reality* (New York: Penguin, 1997), 88.

19. Fagg, "Sacred Indwelling," 477.

20. Ibid.

21. Ibid., 478.

22. Ibid., 483.

23. Ibid., 484.

24. See, for instance, Thomas F. Torrance's treatment in *Space, Time, and Incarnation* (London: Oxford University Press, 1969), 70ff.; Wolfhart Pannenberg, "The Doctrine of Creation and Modern Science," *Zygon* 23, no. 1 (March 1988); O'Murchu, *Quantum Theology.* There has been considerable disagreement on the legitimacy of this move; however, as an analogical and metaphorical aid to our understanding, we do observe the impact of fields in all that is. See Worthing, *God and Contemporary Physics,* 117–24.

25. O'Murchu, *Quantum Theology,* 68.

26. Mitchell Feigenbaum, "Quantative Universality of a Class of Nonlinear Transformations," *Journal of Statistical Physics* 19 (1978): 25–52. Quoted in O'Murchu, *Quantum Theology,* 128.

27. John Polkinghorne, *Science and Theology: An Introduction* (Minneapolis: Fortress Press, 1998), 41–42.

28. For a fascinating study of fractals, look at the work of Benoit B. Mandelbrot and his book, *The Fractal Geometry of Nature* (San Francisco: W. H. Freeman & Co., 1977).

6

DANCING
IN THE SHADOWS

The great accumulation of understanding
as to how the physical world behaves
only convinces one that the universe has no meaning.
—Richard Feynman

To see a World in a Grain of Sand
And a Heaven in a Wild Flower,
Hold Infinity in the palm of your hand
And Eternity in an hour.
—William Blake

When we look at the natural world today it is hard sometimes to see anything that reminds us of a God who loves the creation. We alluded earlier to the objection lifted up by observers of the natural order that there seems to be too much suffering involved in the processes of life to warrant any belief in a divine design. The same forces at work in star formation also are in play with the emergence of cellular life, and thus blind dumb luck of opportunistic organisms results in the fecundity of life within which we find ourselves. This sense of randomness and destruction does present one of the greatest challenges to traditional faith, to the point where it has broken some who have sought to work out why a

seemingly benevolent God has ordered the world to contain such indis-
criminate acts of violence. In his book *God After Darwin,* John Haught
refers to such a person who was a former member of the Christian clergy.
Echoing Annie Dillard, this man asked:

> Could an Almighty God of love have designed, foreseen,
> planned and created a system whose law is a ruthless struggle
> for existence in an overcrowded world? Could an omnipotent,
> omniscient, and omnibenevolent God have devised with such
> cold-blooded competition of beast with beast, beast with man,
> man with man, species with species, in which the clever, the
> cunning, and the cruel survive?
>
> How could a loving God have planned a cruel system in
> which sensitive living creatures must either eat other sensitive
> living creatures or be eaten themselves, thereby causing untold
> suffering among these creatures? Would a benevolent God have
> created animals to devour others when he could have designed
> them all as vegetarians? What kind of deity would have designed
> the beaks which rip sensitive flesh? God would intend every leaf,
> blade of grass, and drop of water to be a battle ground in which
> living organisms pursue, capture, kill, and eat one another?
> What God would design creatures who prey upon one another
> and, at the same time, instill into such creatures a capacity for
> intense pain and suffering?[1]

Putting aside for the moment the realization that perhaps a presupposed
metaphysical assumption about how God is supposed to behave does in fact
control this response to God's supposed providential care of the world, we
are still left with the brute facts as the skeptic states them. In the universe as
it is known to us there is much that is destructive and seemingly filled with
violence. The creation suffers.

In large structures such as those we find in physics or biology, death itself
is as important as life. How do new things come into being? Usually through
the decay of what was before. Self-strengthening processes are nonlinear
and decay triggers the energy flows that bring forth new life.

The story that we have been telling so far forms a chain or web of events
that leads to and beyond us. The atoms in our bodies did not spontaneously
arise, but they stem from earlier processes. Think, for instance, of the chain
that leads "from the formation of hydrogen nuclei, the protons, of clusters
of galaxies and individual galaxies to early massive stars, which have pro-

duced the elements heavier than oxygen, then on to the condensation of dust particles until the formation of planets."[2]

Without this chain there would be no human being, and this chain has led to the emergence and the development of consciousness. In this journey matter has developed the capacity to self-organize in intricate relation and communication within the totality of its being. In the previous chapter we were given the theory for why we find chemical, biochemical, biological, and all physical systems in various forms of stability and flux, eventually leading to increasing complexity and a new level of order. Referring to processes such as this, Arthur Peacocke makes the observation that one of the propensities of evolution is that, given enough time, "a complex organism with consciousness, self-consciousness, and social and cultural organization (the basis for the existence of 'persons') would be likely eventually to evolve on any planet amenable to the emergence of living organisms."[3]

And yet in that process we have a story told to us through the fossil record of untold number of species that have come and gone, sometimes, from all we can gather, through horrible catastrophes. Even if we maintain that life does not emerge purely by chance, it does further itself by the creativity it possesses to adapt and survive, sometimes by preying upon the weak. This is the part that is so difficult for us to accept; death and suffering seem to be built into the path that leads to us. Our existence has been and continues to be contingent upon the suffering and death of other living beings, many of whom possess exquisite feelings.

This is a difficult story to accept, but it is at least an aspect of the reality present to us that we cannot deny. There have been a number of ways of explaining this inescapable fact of life. Some of the religious responses to this story state that it was the fall of the human creature that brought this curse upon the entirety of the created order. What we are experiencing is the direct result of the human decision to disobey God. However, there are problems with this interpretation, as we will see.

The nonreligious story that is most familiar to us is the one that started with Charles Darwin who, in 1859, published his seminal masterpiece *On the Origin of Species*. In this text he painted a portrait of life coming to be that spoke of the competition for survival. Through subsequent appropriation of Darwin's work, words such as "natural selection" and "survival of the fittest" became part of the narrative furniture with which modernity decorated its living spaces.

Further chapters in this story were contributed by the work in genetics that showed how the dynamics of mutation and the combination of units of heredity (genes) from two parents were sources of variation.[4] As the story developed and discoveries revealed hidden genetic complexities such as DNA, or the ways in which environment can trigger changes in physical systems, another chapter was written. A synthesis of "neo-Darwinism" arose to help solidify the contours of this narrative. One aspect of these new contours of interpretation was the seemingly logical acceptance that materialist causes were sufficient grounds for understanding the processes that brought forth life.

This new synthesis has not been entirely smooth and without controversy. It proceeded and still moves in fits and starts. Some scientists have proposed models to try and account for the changes they see in the fossil records and have drawn the fire of other colleagues. One of the most controversial of these theories was the idea of *punctuated equilibrium,* first proposed by Stephen Jay Gould and Niles Eldridge, which postulated that long periods of stability were interrupted by brief periods of amazing change. Looking at the fossil records showed long periods of time with very little change, interspersed with rapid bursts of activity, leading them to argue that alterations in developmental sequences produced major structural changes. This idea raises the question of how change takes place at all and under what conditions it may happen.[5]

Other biologists turned their attention to such phenomena as how organisms selected certain paths to follow when interacting with their environment. How these interactions of genes and environment operated in the evolutionary process became one of the big mysteries to try and understand. We are still trying to understand the mechanisms present that move the natural world along. There is much debate in the scientific community about evolutionary processes and a certain caution should be exercised about the precise mechanisms operative. However, it would not be an unwarranted claim to say that we may discover that a synergism of cooperative adaptation will most accurately be found to portray the coming to be of life.

It is this version of the story that school children in Western culture learn as they are growing up. In turn, the story we learn as children certainly has implications for how we understand the notion of God to play a role. For some it obviously meant that every pious illusion about God's "plan" had to be jettisoned as the relic of an outdated, outmoded mythology, no longer useful to modern humankind and its search for answers about how the world comes to be. Richard Dawkins and a number of other vocal colleagues have argued that biological evolution has to be seen honestly for what it is, an inherently meaningless process.[6]

Daniel Dennett, of course, is one of the most ardent and passionate defenders of the notion that Darwin had made belief in the benevolence of God a difficult proposition to maintain in the face of all the evidence. But he is only one of many who argue that life explained on its own terms is the impersonal working out of blind and random forces that experiment and eventually destroy or prey upon one another in order to survive.

One wonders, exactly, when the metaphysical assumption is made on the basis of studying the processes of life, if the universe is inherently meaningless. Is this an entirely dispassionate analysis? Is there a certain image of God that the critics have in mind that drives their judgments that life is ruthless indifference? Is this warranted as a scientific finding, or does it reflect the prejudices and predispositions of those who make the assessment? Nothing in the science itself can actually lead us to make the statement that the universe's story is necessarily one of pitiless forces and dumb luck.

Certainly it would be realistic to argue that if a certain image of God is being held as the presuppositional ground for the assessment, this would move us beyond the inquiries of the various disciplines. If the image of God held was informed by the classical theist position that defines God on the basis of philosophical abstractions such as omnipotence, omniscience, impassability, immutability, and infinity, then the ordering of nature would be a problem.

When looking at the world as we know it, there is a chaotic messiness to nature that seems to be at odds with the great designing God who is in control of all things that happen and does not allow anything to happen that is not divinely willed. If we possess an image of God's life that establishes the acceptable bounds under which God may interact with the world, then we will be bound by that image.

Sometimes the objection to theistic belief is voiced in the complaints that if we were God, we would do things a little better because we are better able to engineer the world. If we are able to see the various design flaws, than surely an omnipotent creator could have done a better job. Thus Steve Jones, in speaking of the eye, argues that good design would have meant that photoreceptor cells, which detect incoming rays of light, would have the detectors at the front rather than at the back of the cell. This example, among others, was used to argue that complex organs are "not the work of some great composer but of an insensible drudge: an instrument, like all others, built by a tinkerer (i.e., the evolutionary process) rather than by a trained engineer."[7]

So, the issue of what type of metaphysical assumptions are in play when we make such judgments on the basis of scientific inquiry should be explored. We should look at statements like this with a suspicion about what stands in the background that would allow for such a conclusion. Theologically speaking, if the models of God we internalized from the traditions of classical theism and deism (which are the current working models for most Christians) are our operative understandings, then Dawkins, Dennett, and like-minded souls may have a legitimate critique. It would be hard to imagine not joining them in protest against God.

Do theories of evolution shape what we will allow God to be? Or are these theories shaped by a prior assumption about God? Cornelius Hunter argues that this is the case. Evolution has been shaped as much by a metaphysical assumption as it has by the physical evidence itself: "Evolution is deeply wedded to its metaphysical presuppositions. A particular doctrine of God is a prerequisite for evolution's success. It is a theological view that preceded evolution historically and became the metaphysical landscape on which the theory was constructed."[8]

The question, however, is whether this is the only perspective we have from which to understand the world we are seeking to know. Even if we cannot agree entirely with Hunter, we can at least grasp that background assumptions do influence how we interpret the data. This much cannot be denied. Given the uncovering of this unspoken assumption about metaphysical commitment, we are faced with the puzzling mystery we have been contemplating. Life comes from death and suffering, and these serve as the partial conditions for adaptive change. Whether or not a certain formulation of the theory of evolution informs this reality, it is an undeniable fact of what we see in front of us every single day at the lake, mountain, or out our back door. How does this reality become the arena for the manifestation of God's mercy?

How Do We Listen to the World?

Previously we have seen that in the vast forces at play in the ongoing processes of life certain dynamics are operative in the outworking of those forces that portray a creation in flux. Moving from lower levels to higher levels of organization, moving from less to more complex levels of life, we find matter and energy engaged in a dance between law and chance with possibilities being explored and chosen as areas for the furtherance of life.

The influence of lower-level structures on higher-level ordered systems and top-down causality on lower-level systems suggests intricate and nonlinear interactions that make information sharing and communication possible among all orders of life. Cells, molecules, bodies, galaxies, all are continuously responding to the environment around them and patterning themselves accordingly.

In our present day we are coming to understand communication as quantified bits of information that are coded and uncoded by sender and receiver. Lately the notion of instruction that is of intense concern and interest to us is computer binary code.[9] Ian Barbour understands information as an ordered pattern that is one among many possible sequences or states of a system, say DNA or binary digits.[10] Communication of information occurs when one system responds to another and selects to receive what the other brings to it. Usually this takes place within a certain context. Depending on the discipline that interprets this exchange, communication means that information takes on distinctive patterns. From the human sciences to the mathematical ones, information and its processing proceed to a variety of ends. At bottom, however, we must say that information is embedded within nature and, in ways that are still completely unknown to us, pattern the coming to be of life.

In some ways the term information functions as a metaphor for the realization that what is going on in nature is not merely the exchange of matter and energy; messages form in the usual physical processes of life that regulate order and define the world as we know it. The informational component escapes purely mechanical and material explanation. Information "quietly orders things while itself remaining irreducible to the massive and energetic constituents that preoccupy conventional science."[11]

Do we stand at the intersections of mystery and information? Does deep thinking about this subject offer us any sense about how the God we worship, the Creator of "all things visible and invisible," is the sustaining life and goal of existence? By way of illustration, consider the story of the red knot bird. Chet Raymo tells us of this species in his book *Skeptics and True Believers: The Exhilarating Connection between Science and Religion*. His is the story of the red knot juvenile and a rather remarkable journey. The red knot is a type of sandpiper that twice a year appears on the eastern shores of the United States. The appearance of red knots on these shores occurs in the context of a eighteen thousand-mile yearly journey from the tip of South America to the northlands of Canada and back again. As a part of this journey, the birds stop along the way in the Delaware Bay area and Cape Cod.

When they are in the southern hemisphere, they feed at the beaches of Tierra del Fuego, renewing their bodily ability to make the trip northward sometime in February. On the northward journey they know exactly where to find food, and sometime around mid-May they arrive on the marshy shores of the Delaware Bay area. Their arrival there just happens to coincide with the laying of millions of eggs by horseshoe crabs.

The birds stay for a few weeks enjoying a vast supply of food from these eggs, by some estimates as much as thirty-five thousand eggs for a single bird. Fat and presumably happy, they continue north until they arrive at their Canadian home where they mate and breed, each female red knot laying four eggs. The babies when hatched quickly prepare themselves for flight, and in mid-July the female adults leave their young to make the long trip home. The males stay around for a few more weeks and in mid-August they also leave the fledglings as they head down south. The juveniles are left to fend for themselves until late August, early September, when they too begin the nine thousand-mile journey to the south.

What follows is for Raymo an astonishing and wondrous thing—the young red knots, numbering in the thousands and "*without adult guides or prior experience,* find their way along the migration route."[12] Along the way those birds stop at feeding grounds where they know they will find food and eventually join their parents on the beaches of Tierra del Fuego for the southern summer.

These birds have been studied, banded, and tracked by ornithologists, so they know this in fact happens, but the question is how? How do uninstructed, unguided birds navigate that journey and survive? What allows for what can only be looked at as an occasion of wonder? Is this the place to look for divine providence? If we were to include genetic inheritance as part of divine providence, then, yes, the hand of God is found here. From a single fertilized cell, that cell must contain vast amounts of information, "the biological equivalent of a set of charts, a compass or sextant, and maybe even something akin to a satellite navigation system."[13]

We keep digging into how this happens because we are curious, but what we eventually realize is that this entire journey is written into a molecule of DNA. The red knot's maps and navigational manuals are written in a chemical language of only four letters. As a foundational example of the type of information we are reflecting upon, DNA is one of the most exquisite.

Most of us are aware that deoxyribonucleic acid is a long molecule stretched out in a chain of nucleotides. The chain links are constituted like letters in a sentence and DNA codes tell our bodies what to do. Hair, eyes, features, in some ways the outlines of our very identities are encoded here. The primary alphabet that makes up the DNA code is A, T, C, and G, which are nucleotides. They are found in pairs facing each other, A plus T, or C plus G, no other combinations. These four acid bases are what code and shape living beings. In the expression of the DNA in a growing embryo, the linear message of the DNA molecule produces a linear protein chain that leads to structure, which leads to function: "A very complex set of genetic regulatory programs with activators and repressors switches the activity of gene systems on and off so that the right kind of cell is produced at the right place and at the right time in the growing embryo and in the continuing functioning of the organism."[14]

This process of information gathering and selection is in interaction with its environment in extraordinarily subtle ways. While relying on the laws of chemistry, DNA will nonetheless act in ways that allow for openness and indeterminacy, resulting in the nucleotides ATCG being arranged in any possible number of configurations within certain constraints. These configurations lead as well to higher order systems.

In each cell of the red knot's body, an arm's length of DNA makes it possible for a bird to fly nine thousand miles on a journey it has never taken, stopping at specific places where there will be ample food, and eventually arriving at a destination it has never seen. In its vast volumes of code sequences, DNA is hardwired to allow for something that can only be observed with wonder and amazement.

As mentioned before, on one level the DNA is understood to function according to chemical laws. However, when unpacked to a greater degree, the deep mystery of cellular life becomes apparent. A short strand of DNA is able to reproduce itself when the double helix "staircase" unzips down the middle. Each of these halves takes chemical components from the surrounding matrix and proceeds to build a full strand. Yet the complexity of this seemingly simple event is rather astonishing. The DNA found in a single human cell would reach from fingertip to fingertip of outstretched arms. There are billions of cells in the human body, with enough strands of DNA to stretch out to the sun and back a dozen times. The activity of replication itself is occurring at hundreds or thousands of sites, and billions of chemical units in the DNA must be copied exactly, exactly once, no more, no less. Any mistake can be damaging or fatal.[15]

This activity is not a static transfer, for it is a continuing whirling dervish of activity. What appears under an electron microscope as a tangled strand of fishing wire is "a pulsating, undulating, farrago of threads, feathers, knobs, and whiskers, a microscopic lace maker frenetically making a lace called life."[16]

In this process something is happening that is difficult to reduce to strictly deterministic chemical processes. The indeterminate number of arrangements possible implies that the informational ordering and complexity that incorporates such phenomena as memory, interaction and adaptation to environment, and selectivity and perception escapes purely chemical explanation. The chemical laws are the grounds upon which this information is being communicated, but the openness and developmental processes at play indicate a communication of information that cannot be predetermined solely on the laws of physics or chemistry.

Information as such cannot be atomized but takes place within the web of environment and response to it. The information being exchanged between lower-level cellular life and the more complex levels of higher-order organisms occurs not in violation of nature or its laws, but in response to its larger context:[17]

> In the case of DNA, too, the meaning of the part depends on larger wholes. Control sequences (operons) regulate whole blocks of activities. Recognition codes provide responses to particular molecular structures. . . . In each case the patterns among components at one level set boundary conditions for activities at lower levels. The patterns in the DNA do not violate the laws of physics and chemistry, but they could never be deduced from those laws. . . . The meaning of the parts is determined relationally by their participation in larger wholes.[18]

What does all this informational ordering lead to, what is the point of it all? It is undeniable that it leads to increasing complexity, but this movement also points to a certain sense of hierarchy. This is a word that has received fairly negative connotations in recent years because of its identification with a patriarchal system that defined hierarchy in terms that pointed to maleness as the height of ascending order. Not just in monotheism, but even in religious structures such as Confucianism, we find an ordering of the world that privileges the male as the final sense of authority.

For this reason the word itself has acquired such suspicion that it is difficult to see how it might be helpful to us in thinking about God's relationship with the creation. The contemporary theologian might be more inclined to speak of growing circles of influences, or relationships, or even complexity, anything to indicate a leveling of distinctions so no one stands as superior to another. The great Chain of Being that led to such ordering of the world in the past is seen as the outmoded relic of a bygone age.

John Haught points out that the notion of hierarchy is a term that needs to be recovered, for it speaks to something very vital about our understanding of the world. He reminds us that the word comes to us from two Greek roots, *hier*, meaning sacred, and *arche*, meaning origin. In this sense, hierarchy helps us to hold onto the conviction that at bottom the reality we are related to is really about God. It is of sacred origin and therefore shares in some deep way an identity with the Creator.[19]

Haught goes on to argue that this concept does not allow for a rigorous reduction of life and mind to matter. Some dimensions of reality are more comprehensive and reflective of higher order. We have levels of reality enfolded into one another that defy reductionist explanation, and hierarchies are unavoidable. They do not have to be assigned the connotations that past interpretations have given them. Life consists of multilevel systems. Think of the structuring found in quark, nucleus, atom, molecule, macromolecule, organelle, cell organ, organism, and ecosystem, or the neural hierarchy of molecule, synapse, neuron, neural network, brain, body. How do these entities order themselves into forms of coherence and mutual interdependence?[20]

What accounts for that movement from a paramecium searching for food to a red knot sandpiper born with navigational abilities that astonish the mind? Even more, what allows for the growth of an organism that is able to express the symbolic communication of abstract concepts such as speech, art, and even mathematics, one of our greatest maps of the universe? It is the activity and presence of information that embeds itself within the natural order as possibility and potential.

This information is seen by some as a continual communication occurring within all forms of life, where lower-level forms of life are influencing higher-levels forms of life and these levels fold back in some way to influence lower levels. It is Arthur Peacocke who has used the terms "top down" and "bottom up" causalities to indicate the influences of the various systems on each other. It is true that the particular does in fact influence the action and process of more complex systems, but it is also true that the more comprehensive systems influence the smaller systems. Nothing involved in the interaction remains unchanged. How this works is one of the most interesting puzzles that is being explored by thinkers from a host of disciplines, from information systems and technology to philosophy.[21]

Of course, part of the difficulty inherent in this inquiry arises from the background assumptions that investigators bring to the task of understanding the forces at work in world forming. If we are like some persons who are shaped by a profound belief that mechanistic models are descriptive of reality, we may tend toward mechanistic explanations. If we are inclined toward a belief that all higher-order levels of organic functioning are explained by the particular and discrete pieces present for our observation, such that the ultimate level of explanation will be found within those irreducible aspects, this belief would probably rule out the notion that information exchanges exhibit a subtle and irreducible aspect from the whole to the part.

If we think the interpretation of these processes and the energy that is being exchanged among them simply cannot be flattened out to the impersonal working out of natural processes, we will be more inclined to think about how hierarchies function to structure life. As we saw previously, the attempt to explain on the basis of each particle carrying within it the reason for its being can lead to explanatory closure that invests all interpretative power in terms of efficient or material causality.

This move to efficient and material causality as adequate explanation has not been without its consequences. One of the directions in which it took us was the banishment of deeper cosmologies of the type that might be seen when nature is understood as having its origins rooted in the sacred. When efficient causality is enthroned as the truly rational and scientific approach to grasping our world, the sacred is vacated from the world. The fact that deeper purposes may rest within nature, even amid all the predation, opportunism, and struggle, is lost to us as God becomes defined on the terms of what we think it is fit for God to be.[22]

When we turn to the metaphor or dynamics of information, I do not want to suggest that the sacred returns (in the sense of epistemological verification), because there will always be other explanations that do not necessitate the existence of any supreme being. But the reality of information flows does allow for the consideration of metaphors and ideas that may help us grasp divine presence in ways that were difficult to understand previously.

Our understanding of the phenomena of nature cannot be satisfactorily explained on the particulars alone, but on the entirety of the structures present to us: "Information 'works' we can say at the very least, only by *comprehensively* integrating particulars (atoms, molecules, cells, bits and bytes) into coherent wholes. Thus, any attempt to specify the comprehensive function of informational patterns in terms appropriate only to the comprehended particulars themselves is logically self-contradictory."[23]

Information is both stored and communicated among biological processes at all levels. It serves to integrate and order those processes and is embedded within the natural order. It is dynamic and relational and leads to certain metaphysical questions. Is the patterning we experience merely the order our minds impose on purely blind and random forces? Why do the hierarchies of life order themselves in such a way that greater complexity results, and more sensitive and informed modes of life emerge? Why does life continuously engage in a communication that gathers itself into more comprehensive wholes, which in turn fold back into other aspects of life? Information is so enmeshed in a world coming to be that we have to allow for the sense of mystery that rests at the heart of the matter. Is this the way God involves Godself in evolutionary history?

When we think about information in this way, we start to enter into the territory of thinking about consciousness and intention. At least in the way the world works, we see the possibility that consciousness is not reducible to constituent parts. In human consciousness, for instance, it is very difficult for scientists to understand the totality of consciousness, even though explication occurs at certain levels for some operations of the brain.

This is an instance where we are able to see the notion of top-down and bottom-up causality at work. It is a given that various constituents of the body are operative in the processes of brain functioning. This is an undeniable aspect of who we are. Yet the knowledge that we have of the various systems that are interacting to allow for the emergence of thought cannot totally explain the processes of consciousness that allow for an influence on systems of the body as a whole.

Some of these influences are in some measure unconscious to us. Breathing, heartbeat, and other functions occur on unconscious levels. Consider, for example, certain forms of healing. If I cut myself, I don't will my finger to heal. However, my body starts the process of cell regeneration and renewal that leads to the cut healing itself.

Other forms of consciousness issue in more intentional aspects. I decide to choose one form of action over another. I follow a creative impulse, or I decide to be lazy and not discipline myself enough to respond to the gentle urging within me to write, paint, compose, or even play. The point is that something is happening from within me that is in communion with all physical processes as I experience them.[24] This place within is where God is understood to be acting to influence the world. Some recent thinkers have suggested that this is where we find God's ability to express divine intention. On the analogy of mind/body unity, we find a space for connection between the mental and the physical, but even deeper, the connection between the spiritual and the physical.[25]

The tradition has a place for this in its understanding of Jesus as the Logos of God (John 1:1–14). In Greek understanding, the *logos* was the principle of rationality that had ordered the world. The Logos was seen in John's gospel as the principle by which creation came to be. The connection between creation and order is present here. The Logos creates and patterns both the world and through its rationality our comprehension of it.

The Logos points to the importance of language and communication. In communication, words are sometimes exchanged, but these words are themselves a form of organizing the self and its relations with existence. Language does in some senses work to establish our windows on the world. In the mystery of spoken communication, we sometimes actually stumble upon understanding and comprehension. We find, to our surprise, that the universe is intelligible. As Einstein reportedly remarked, "The eternal mystery of the world is its comprehensibility."[26]

This sense of deep rationality in the world, operating in conditions that can at best be called fragmentary, leads us to the type of ground that mystics held when in moments of deep awareness they perceived the underlying connectedness of simply everything. In this I must confess that though I am seeking to tease out the implications of inaccessible light through Scripture, tradition, and science, all our concepts will have to be held provisionally.

Whistling in the Dark?

So, we are still left with some questions about what all of this might mean. Does life have a point? Is life as random as it seems? The processes of life that emerge in such disarray lead us to answer yes as easily to one question as the other. Some would privilege the nontheistic answer on the basis that what the universe displays is not an inherent rationality, but a system of cruelty.

I have just suggested that information is a necessary ground for the emergence of life and that the hierarchical patterning of life leads to higher ordered systems. The paradox or mystery before us is that this ordering in fact leads to greater forms of sensitivity to the pain and suffering of life.

Consider the development of biological systems. The more advanced the nerve and brain structures, for example, the more advanced the consciousness. This does not mean that more-than-human life does not possess feelings or emotions, but it can be argued that the more advanced the sensitivity to pain, the better the chance for survival. The greater the ability to know pain, the more alert we are to danger. Yet this very aspect of life creates the conditions for great suffering. The more intense the subjective dimension is, the more the potential for suffering. This sensitivity does not just encompass responses to purely physical events, but rather it emerges in the type of self-consciousness that informs the whole area of feelings.

When we look at life, can we conceive of the journey of billions of years that has brought us to this point in time as a movement toward increasing sensitivity to divine becoming? At first glance such a question sounds a little ridiculous. But if we let the idea sit with us for a while theologically, we could say that the movement of the world leads to an increase in sensitivity to suffering that could well be reflective of God's own suffering in the creation.

Is it such a stretch to say that whatever the image of God that is supposed to constitute human distinction, it is our capacity to feel not only physical but emotional pain that situates us in a different category of awareness concerning the world? Questions of this sort lead us to consider the purpose of evolution in new ways and bring out the central place of the gospel narratives for our consideration.

We have explored some of the wonders of the richness and amazing intricacies of life and we have seen that a story exists to narrate our place within it that seeks to replace the various religious interpretations. This story of blind, pitiless indifference is not the only avenue of interpretation that can be legitimately applied. Purely from a scientific point of view, there should be the recognition that opportunism and survival of "selfish" genes constitute a part of the story. However, in the levels of communication that are taking place, we are finding not only competition but cooperation and synergy of systems that occur with the passing of the old and the emerging of the new. Sometimes life may be, dare we say, willingly given up so that new life might emerge. We find ourselves within the mystery of the tragic.

The unbelievably rich tapestry of existence that has journeyed from matter to consciousness, the life that has emerged in ways that fill us with wonder and awe, giving us such great delight, is not without its more puzzling and darker side. Is it all meaningless, or worse, the work of a sadistic or semi-omnipotent God who is powerless to overcome the darkness?

Many responses have emerged from the Christian perspective to try and acquit God of responsibility for this great degree of suffering the world experiences. We have seen how ideas like omnipotence and omniscience have led to difficulties in trying to understand the mystery of divine life. These ideas and others from our tradition have also offered an interpretation of life. God's ultimate design was one of perfection, but our response to it was imperfect, so suffering was in some ways contingent upon humankind's inability to choose well.

We find here the echoes of one of the primal narratives of the Jewish and Christian traditions, the story of the fall of the human creature into disobedience. We will have opportunity to reflect on this later, but for now let us simply say that to some people, this story line possesses great explanatory power for the suffering and evil with which we are faced. The utter ubiquity of this suffering must emerge from humankind's inability to have faith in God.

The story we have been telling, however, does not begin with a primeval fall; rather it begins with the triune God. It is in this context that we should pose our questions about suffering. I have already suggested that reflection on God the Creator and God the Holy Spirit as the sustainer of all life as we know it forces us to reject a gnostic separation of matter and spirit.

God's very being, while separate, is still found within all things as the sustaining power of God's Holy Spirit. If the means of the continuing creation are those such as we find in the ongoing evolution and emergence of life then we have an open window through which to see something extremely vital about God's action in the world. God is in, with, and under the very unfolding processes of life. In the world of creaturely becoming God is not absent but present to its every moment, experiencing and responding in patterns of communication to the emerging diversity and richness of life.

What was once inconceivable to those like Athanasius has become cause for amazement and gratitude among us. God suffers in the coming to be of life. It is not just the humanity of Jesus that suffers on the cross, but the divinity of God as well, and not just there, but in all of life. The crucifixion was the historical manifestation of the inner life of God. If life is leading to the increasing sensitivity to suffering then we should not rule out that this reflects in some mysterious measure God's great capacity for suffering within the world itself.

This notion is not based on the desire solely to vindicate God to the world, but emerges from the revelation that God is not only Creator and Sustainer but is also the Son who willingly gave himself for the world. Divine suffering for the redemption of the world stands at the heart of the Christian story. What is perhaps new is a belief we have not always possessed historically; God's suffering, found in Christ, should be extended to the eternal life of the triune God. In this way crucifixion may well be an internal, eternal reality of God's sensitivity to the creation.[27]

God does not limit God's relationship to the world in a one-sided dimension of remote transcendence. God as triune desires and seeks relationship with all of creation. A Christian understanding of this relationship must be set within the context of Jesus, the Messiah and Redeemer of the world. Seen in this light, creation itself has been on pilgrimage from the very start.

This ongoing process has not been without risk. Especially if we understand God as immersed in the processes of life, we find an enormous mystery. God who creates all creative potentialities is rooted as well within them, struggling and responding to their choices. God has not attained the Sabbath rest. The great mystery is that these creative processes have led at least to the appearance of a creature who exercises vast freedom, more often than not in direct contradiction to the Creator. God not only suffers the contradictions that may be found in open systems of biological life, God also suffers the internal pain of neglect, abandonment, and outright rejection. The Hosea narrative mentioned in chapter 2 captures this with an intimacy that is profoundly moving, if sexist. The Gospels and subsequent Scripture show that God makes Godself vulnerable to the world by self-limitation and divine emptying *(kenosis).*

The emotional life and pathos of God is a central aspect of the biblical narratives. Time and again God calls persons to relationship only to be ignored, neglected, or willingly rejected. In those stories we find the expressions where God is truly grieved over the creature's unwillingness to enter into relationship (Matt 23:37–39). The realization that God's response to humankind was one of heartbreak should lead us to reconsider how we understand the divine life. This vulnerability of God to the creation was not without a point, though, for God with infinite patience never lets go of God's people.

Science, of course, cannot accept this particular notion (although scientists can) anymore than it should proclaim that the universe has no meaning. Both ideas are metaphysical interpretations of matter and as such cannot be privileged solely on the basis of science having a certain type of authority in the modern world. Having said this, however, Christian faith can see science as offering us understandings of the world that allow for fresh insight into the triune God. The biblical witness does not conceive of the impersonal working out of forces, but of a movement of promise and blessing. Creation is not inherently wasteful; it is inherently redemptive.

The new thing that God promises in Hebrew Scripture points to God's response to the creation. Even when creation exercises its prerogative to break covenant with God, the response is salvation and faithfulness in the midst of rejection: "The inexhaustive creative power of God in history makes itself known first of all in the inexhaustibility of the power of his suffering."[28] It is this ability to embrace suffering that rests at the root of God's creative activity in its original, continuing, and anticipated dimensions.

It is this suffering that allows God to maintain communication, relationship, and even communion with those ongoing energies of existence that have broken off communication. We have seen in the cosmic story that billions of years have brought us to this point by open possibility, emergence, new creation, and fresh directions: "Through his inexhaustible capacity for suffering and readiness for suffering, God then also creates quite specific chances for liberation from isolation, and quite specific chances for the evolution of the various and open life systems."[29]

In the evolving processes of the cosmos, we see ultimately something that preserves life. We see the preservation of life by electromagnetism or gravity. We find the ongoing sustenance of life in cells that emerge into new forms of life, even while some pass away. In the journey to where we are, which has not been a straight line by any means, we have found a life that responds to existence with creativity and innovation. God the Spirit, not some amorphous spirit of God, is situated both within the life that has arisen from the passing of the old, but also within that which has passed away. In this passing the conditions are created for the emergence of the new. Nothing is lost to God and nothing that passes away is truly lost.

This is difficult for us to see owing to our captivity to certain assumptions about the being of God in the world. In fact, it may be a point of irony that those who believe the strongest in God as defined by the traditions of classical theism and those who reject the notions of larger purpose in the world actually occupy the same space. Both inherently see God in ways that would remove divine action to either outside intervention or nonexistence, respectively.

Many times our rejection of God comes from an inadequate or immature rendering of God as the great Being who determines simply everything that happens, much like the woman whom Dorothee Soelle encountered earlier. The belief in God that many hold today could lead the honest and thoughtful person to no other consideration than atheism. The critique of those such as Freud and Nietzsche carries weight for us. What we see too much of in the world is the God of our projections, the cultural constructions of a God we have smoothly domesticated for our own purposes.

Mention should be made that God is not the only belief in which humanity has invested its fears, anxieties, dreams, and hopes. We have also done this with nature. We have personified it, interpreted it, and painted the picture we wanted to see on it in any number of ways. It has been variously seen by us as benign, ruthless, nurturing, and pointless. Nature is not a truly objective fact; it is a reality we interpret to ourselves.

Isn't all theology essentially a futile attempt to describe what rests outside our grasp? Aren't all religious narratives ultimately the expression of ethnocentric tribes or communities seeking to sequester God as a private province of their own? Aren't all interpretations of the world ultimately avenues to expression of selfishness? If we take an honest look at a world of such religious conflict, disbelief may appear to be the only response that has any integrity.

This is an unavoidable dilemma in the contemporary world and we must always seek to be vigilant to the hidden assumptions that go into our interpretations of the world. What is being offered here and numerous other places is the argument that what we see happening in the universe, the ways we presently understand and interpret it, are not necessarily oppositional to Christian faith itself, though they may well be in conflict with culturally shaped beliefs in God that in themselves are not germane to Christian faith.

In Jewish and Christian Scriptures the foundational belief presented is that God's redemptive action is found within the world as we know it. Creation is the context for the unfolding of God's purpose found in covenant, promise, and redemption. The part we will presently consider is the belief that this redemption is not merely directed toward the human, but to the entirety of creation, which also awaits God's Sabbath rest and the peace, the shalom, of God.

God Is an Event

Christian faith has always understood itself as rooted in an event rather than a doctrine. The appearance of Jesus of Nazareth is the decisive moment for Christian faith and holds the key for all Christian interpretation of the world. The narratives and subsequent renderings of this life shape the core beliefs of Christians. These beliefs may assume a variety of shapes; however, for Christianity, Jesus constitutes the singular moment of Christian identity and carries original significance. All Christian understanding of God orients itself around this central figure. All speculation concerning God and God's relation with the world finds concrete expression in Jesus Christ and the community founded in his name.

There are many things to discover there. Jesus' use of parables, his way of incorporating the world around him to point to the deeper significance of life, and his deep appreciation for the natural order reveal to us that Jesus sees the world as holding the potential to reveal the life of God to us. In his mind, birds, flowers, seeds, sand, sea, humans all serve the purpose of opening us to something about our world that we have a hard time getting directly from the matter of the thing itself—at the heart of the universe beats a heart of love and passion for life. Passion joins Logos to form the home in which we all live, move, and have our being.

In the life and teachings of Jesus we find a commitment to proclaiming God's reign that understands it as including healing (Matt 9:18–22), sight to the blind (Matt 9:27–32), and deliverance from forces and compulsions that are deemed demonic (Matt 8:28–32). There is a strong element of social justice in the accounts of this ministry (Luke 6:20–45), and deep concern with how persons order their lives with God and one another. Jesus proclaims a way of God's intention for the world that calls for a reorientation of life away from the acquisition of power and wealth to healing and inclusion. He offers a view of love that transcends all religious claims to parochialism.

Moreover, this love is not defined in ways that we anticipate. For love does not express itself through power, but through humility and the willingness to suffer. In this embodiment, God manifests Godself in a way that does not overwhelm human subjectivity or decision. The cross stands as testimony that God risks absence in order to allow things to become. Suffering love does not seek to force the world or us to be what it desires, but it does offer visions and hopes for the creation to respond to. In the movement of life God does become absent enough from creation to let it become, but this absence is not a total absence. God's continual response to the ongoing emergence of life is grasped by faith as the immanent connection found in the relationship of all things.

Is it compromising Christian faith to suggest that the ongoing communication among cell and organism, environment and mind, photon A and B, ultimately does have a point? God's power is not manifest so much as the intelligent designer, working out a mechanism to perfection, or the omnipotent ruler in control of everything, because if this is the case then God has indeed failed miserably. Is it faithful to the biblical witness and Christian tradition to discern God as the influencer of a life coming to be? In the intensification of the inner life found in the ordering of the universe we also find another realm of mystery—we have the power to respond to or reject suffering love.

The Christian belief in the incarnation speaks to the profound mystery that God truly seeks embodiment. This sense of embodiment should be seen as the goal of the divine will. The human creature is that with whom

God grounds communication and witness to God's desire for union with the creation. In so doing there are implications concerning the creation.

One of these implications is that the incarnation stands in some measure as a historically rooted reality of the gulf between what God's intention and hope is for human life and our failure to live into and honor that hope. The gap between the life and teachings of Jesus and the subsequent history of the church reveals distortions within human life that can only be called tragic.

Some of these distortions are readily apparent when we look at the vast sweep of human history and our inability to build a world, or even a community, that manifests God's peace. This inability is all the more heartbreaking when we realize that those who call themselves religious have especially failed to understand the deep connectedness of our lives not only within the human community, but within the entirety of the created order. Our relationship with earth and water, with animal and air, has been broken by our willingness to exploit and allow selfishness to be our guiding principle for how we live.

Our continuing exclusions of humanity on the basis of political or social structures are but negations of the belief that ultimately God chooses human flesh to communicate that no unbridgeable gulf exists between God and the creation. God willingly chooses immersion and identity with the world through the Father, Son, and Spirit in order to redeem and reconcile all things to God (2 Cor 5:17–19). This immersion is located distinctly and rooted in temporal conditions in a concrete particularity and a finite and vulnerable expression, the human creature. In this sense, what is seen as the impersonal working out of natural forces does form the ground for a personal expression and reality.

All discussion about the ways in which God's being is unfolded, expressed, and embodied in creation must include at some level the realization that God's creative energies express themselves in terms of vulnerability, self-giving love, and powerlessness. Reflection upon the life of God in the world cannot take place in abstraction from this singular reality of Jesus Christ. The appearance of Jesus in the domain of nature roots the mystery of God. This event does not overwhelm or dominate, but offers us a vision of God's intention for the world.

Central to this vision is the appearance of the new in the midst of the old. This is seen most intensely in the stories of the resurrection found in the gospel accounts. These accounts proclaim that something new has entered the world and the world is changed by it. The events of Good Friday and Easter are the narrated spaces where Christianity states that we have the possibility of new relation not just with God, but with the world. Here is something new where death and decay are not the final word. There is birth and new life in the midst of the old.

There have been and still are a number of approaches to take in the interpretation of this event. The resurrection stories themselves imply a transformation of the world of energy and matter into something new. Paul speaks of different types of flesh in 1 Cor 15. One approach has tended to objectify this event in ways that lead to thoughts about the resuscitation of a dead body. Another approach has suggested that the resurrection of Jesus was a vital aspect of the disciple's inner world and thus is a subjective awareness that Jesus was not truly dead at all, but lives on in the heart of his followers. Surely those closest to Jesus were the ones most affected by the resurrection.

If we turn totally to the subjective account of these narratives, we must inquire as to whether a certain idea about what science "allows" from the natural order constrains and even intimidates Christians from other understandings. At the same time, it is difficult to specify exactly what the objectivity of the event entailed. We simply don't have accounts of a resuscitated human body in the recording of how this event influenced the earliest witnesses to this moment. Certainly we have to account for the type of hope that transmutes a community of grief into a belief that their savior, contrary to all evidence, lives.

While the details of that event remain inaccessible to us, we do find here a pattern that would establish Christian belief in the world. In this regard perhaps we can see this event in ways that fill out and deepen the subjective/objective categories. According to Jürgen Moltmann:

> The resurrection of Jesus witnesses to the assertion of God's unconditional creativity over against the exhausted possibilities of created matter to maintain its life. The new life that is granted to the dead Jesus by God is discontinuous with his life before the death on the cross in the sense that the risen Jesus is not the reanimated Jesus. Yet it is continuous with God's unconditionally creative relationship to creation.[30]

Continuity with God is maintained even through the discontinuity of death, but even though this occurs within the natural order, it is not rooted totally in it. It is rooted in God's love, which responds to Jesus with the formation of a new order of life. On the outer boundaries of life, where death intrudes and chaos reigns, we find God creating new possibilities at the edge of disorder. Life responds to God's call in an entirely new way. Perhaps matter and energy will be translated into a new complexity, a higher order of life that sees hope, and not pointless indifference, as the final word.

Jesus' story is the story of God's life in the world and signals that God wills to have a relationship with us that not even death can negate. This resulted in the great hope of Paul and subsequent Christianity. This hope does not rest on apparent renderings of life found in an educated pessimism. It allows for the emergence of novelty into the world.

This hope must walk through shadows and darkness, must struggle with death, chaos, Auschwitz. I have found after visits to Dachau and elsewhere that there is a certain haunting to spaces in the world that is palpable and real. We cannot ignore this darkness or shadow, for hope would then be an empty optimism built on transitory feelings, or cultural expressions that we are getting better and better. This is not the hope engendered by the biblical witness and the reality of the triune God.

This hope builds habitations within the darkness of the world in order to proclaim the new world that has been inaugurated in God the Son. This hope is not, nor should it be, contingent upon the circumstances of the moment, no matter how dark it seems. In the resurrection narratives and in the processes of life, we know that on the edges of chaos the new is waiting to be born. The novelty waiting to emerge is the unexpected and unanticipated reality of divine love and grace.

This is not a cheap grace, for the securing of new life is never accomplished without great suffering and pain. This is how things make themselves, and in some way unfathomable to us, this is how God makes Godself. If the triune God were at a distance from the struggle of a world coming to be, we should raise our voices in protest to the tyrant God. But the Christian story sets the stage for a deeper understanding of God's involvement with the world. Immersed in the very movement of life itself, responding to the choices creation makes, suffering the pain of loss, and celebrating the joy of new creation, God calls us to the creation of a new future. We turn now to a consideration of the contours of this future and its hope for all creation.

NOTES

1. A. J. Mattill Jr., *The Seven Mighty Blows to Traditional Beliefs* (2d ed.; Gordo, Ala.: Flatwoods Press, 1995), 32. Quoted from John F. Haught, *God After Darwin: A Theology of Evolution* (Boulder, Colo.: Westview Press, 2000), 21.

2. Benz, *The Future of the Universe*, 105.

3. Peacocke, *Paths from Science Towards God,* 82.

4. Barbour, *When Science Meets Religion,* 91.

5. See, for example, Niles Eldridge, *Time Frames: The Rethinking of Darwinian Evolution and the Theory of Punctuated Equilibria* (London: Heinemann, 1986); Niles Eldridge and Stephen Jay Gould, "Punctuated Equilibrium Prevails," *Nature* 332 (1988): 211–12.

6. Just a few of the most referred to books are Daniel Dennett, *Darwin's Dangerous Idea: Evolution and the Meaning of Life* (New York: Simon & Schuster, 1995); Dawkins, *The Blind Watchmaker* and his *Climbing Mount Improbable* (New York: W. W. Norton, 1996). There are numerous others by a multitude of authors.

7. Steve Jones, *Darwin's Ghost* (New York: Random House, 2000), 130–31. This illustration was taken from Hunter, *Darwin's God,* 83.

8. Hunter, *Darwin's God,* 159.

9. A recent work by James E. Hutchingson, *Pandemonium Tremendum: Chaos and Mystery in the Life of God* (Cleveland: Pilgrim Press, 2001), argues that the computer has profound significance for theology and has raised deep concerns for the intersection of religion and science.

10. Barbour, *Religion and Science,* 227–30.

11. Haught, *God After Darwin,* 71.

12. Chet Raymo, *Skeptics and True Believers: The Exhilarating Connection between Science and Religion* (Toronto: Doubleday Canada Limited, 1998), 22. The emphasis is Raymo's.

13. Ibid., 23.

14. Barbour, *When Science Meets Religion,* 106.

15. Raymo, *Skeptics and True Believers,* 29.

16. Ibid.

17. See Barbour, *Religion and Science,* 227–33; and Haught, *God After Darwin,* 72–73.

18. Barbour, *Religion and Science,* 229. Peacocke says about the same processes that "this occurs also in the much more complex, and only partly understood, systems of genes switching on and off and their interplay with cell metabolism and specific protein production in the development of biological forms. The parts would not behave as observed if they were not parts of that particular system (the whole). The state of the system-as-a-whole is influencing (i.e., acting like a cause on) what the parts, the constituents actually do." Peacocke, *Paths from Science Towards God,* 52.

19. Haught, *God After Darwin,* 69.

20. Barbour, *When Science Meets Religion,* 106–16.

21. See, for example, Arthur Peacocke, *Theology for a Scientific Age* (Minneapolis: Fortress Press, 1993).

22. One of the great ironies of this move is that we move into the space vacated and so become the creator gods of a new world. More often than not, because there will inevitably be some hubris concerning our abilities, we will be led into a technological manipulation of nature that leads to a particular worldview that carries its own dangers. We think that if we can do it, we must, and more often than not we have, with mixed results.

23. Haught, *God After Darwin,* 75.

24. Philip Clayton has an interesting take on this point in his book *God and Contemporary Science,* 101ff. In a very careful and comprehensive study of the field, he lays out a very sophisticated argument for his understanding of panentheism. While my work here cannot go into the depth of his, I am grateful for his framing of the questions concerning the action of God. I have a preference for speaking of the presence of God, but I suspect this is not far from what he has in mind.

25. Ibid. The connection between matter and mental states is becoming a commonplace point of recent discussions in the religion and science interaction and will yield increasing work in the coming years.

26. Albert Einstein, *The Quotable Einstein* (ed. Alice Calaprice; Princeton, N.J.: Princeton University Press, 1996).

27. Moltmann is not the only one who says this; so does Haught, *God After Darwin,* 47.

28. Moltmann, *God in Creation,* 210.

29. Ibid., 211.

30. Moltmann, "Is There Life After Death?" in Polkinghorne and Welker, *The End of the World and the Ends of God,* 115.

7

BETWEEN THE ALREADY
AND THE NOT YET

*God is constantly speaking only one thing. God's speaking
is one thing. In this one utterance God speaks the Son
and at the same time the Holy Spirit and all creatures.*
—Meister Eckhart

*The cosmos is fundamentally and primarily living. . . .
Christ, through his Incarnation is internal to the world . . .
rooted in the world, even in the very heart of the tiniest atom. . . .
Nothing seems to me more vital, from the point of
view of human energy, than the appearance and eventually
the systematic cultivation of such a "cosmic sense."*
—Teilhard de Chardin

I am presently sitting out on my deck enjoying the warm afternoon sun. As I contemplate the future, I am thinking of this ball of fire. Generally believed to be about 5 billion years old, the sun is probably more than halfway through its life span. The vast forces of nuclear fusion within this mass cause atoms to slam together with a force that is hardly to be imagined, eventually creating photons, which carry to me what I experience as light and heat. Eventually the massive energies at play will cause the sun to balloon into a red giant star, extending beyond the earth's orbit and leading to our certain disintegration. The sun itself will collapse into a "white dwarf" and over billions of years become a cold, lifeless lump. This is the way the world ends, not with a bang, but a whimper. The future does not seem promising.

And yet we are fascinated with the future. We have entire industries constructed around the future. Academics have studied it, superstitious persons have consulted fortunetellers or astrologers to know it, and we make movies and endlessly speculate about it. The future is territory that will always remain to be explored because it will always be coming to meet us. In all our endeavors we are actually trying to control the future. If we can possess knowledge about how it will go, or how we can force it in our direction, we will be able to control it. This is true of many Christian approaches to the future, especially those found in its most popular forms.

The last time I looked, one of the most popular series of books on the bestseller list were the books in the Left Behind series. Authored by Tim LaHaye and Jerry Jenkins, these books are a reflection of the type of eschatology that offers as little hope for the world as the sun flaming out. They stand in a tradition that in recent years was rejuvenated by the appearance of Hal Lindsey's *The Late Great Planet Earth.* This tradition, with a historical background that extends back to the Plymouth Brethren and John Nelson Darby, and later, the Scofield Reference Bible, uses current events to translate the apocalyptic imagery of the Bible. Trafficking in sometimes lurid depictions of good versus evil, the series has been embraced by no small number of Christians, not as a guilty pleasure, but as potentially accurate portrayals of the final conflict between the forces of darkness and the forces of light.

In these renderings there is a certain amount of acceptance of events, since they are believed to be happening according to the plan of God's will. In other visions of God and the future, the religious negation of hope leads to the pursuit of fanatical visions and goals, often accompanied by destruction and the myth of redemptive violence. Once the old order has been overthrown, a new and more harmonious life can arise.

Often these types of visions are rooted not in a meaningful hope or desire for community, but in a desire for power cloaked with the cape of a selfishly constructed deity. Love is not the fruit of these pursuits; rather, control is. The dysfunction of these approaches is often manifested in dichotomies between the saved and the unsaved, the chosen and the infidels, hell and heaven.

Their secular counterparts can be seen in the interpretations of the world that speak about a "clash of civilizations," or analysis of present world conflicts in terms of good versus evil, with each side believing that it is on the side of the angels and that the other is on the side of the evildo-ers. As exciting as this may be for those whose lives acquire higher mean-ing by this apocalyptic imagery, I would counter that these types of eschatologies in both their religious and secular variations are extremely damaging to a Christian sense of hope, which should root the Christian response to the world today.

Eschatology, the study of the last things, is capturing the attention of many today in the science and religion discussion because it focuses atten-tion on a vital dimension of both the natural order and faith's response to it. Much of the reason for this renewed interest rests in a recovery of the reality of hope and the realization that hope is necessary for the further-ance of both science and faith. Reflection upon the eventual death of this planet or the presence of death in the cosmos would not seem to be solid ground for hope. But is our struggle with the created order grounds solely for pessimism along the lines encountered earlier, or can it engender hope among us as well?

I do not mean to indicate by this that hope stands as some naïve sense of optimism that refuses to take account of the realities present before us, because optimism has become somewhat a devalued term in culture. Opti-mism can be the overly unrealistic expectation that "in every day, in every way, we are getting better and better." This goes beyond even the blind opti-mism that attaches itself to evolution as one vast upward progression.

Authentic hope should be framed by an accurate and realistic appraisal of our circumstances. A realistic assessment of the situation does not have to lead to paralysis; rather, it should issue in action that leads to the hoped for resolution.[1] In this sense, hope is not necessarily a manifestation of the "can-do" spirit so engrained in the American ethos. Hope moves along the borders of reality and anticipation and never allows itself to become defined solely by the present realities. It is in engagement with reality that hope finds concrete expression.

We have been exploring the mystery of a number of these realities from the viewpoint of scientific inquiry and at the end of the last chapter we came face to face with that ultimate reality that defies all interpretations of hope—death. In the face of death, hope becomes difficult, for the grief is so overwhelming that we do feel paralyzed and powerless. It is the ultimate horizon of the future we cannot control, no matter how much we try. Beyond this barrier we cannot see and imagination takes over. We fear it because we don't wish to engage in vain hopes or childish fantasies. And yet the most difficult realization is that death and loss stand as the twin pillars marking the space between which we must all journey. That the centrality of the Christian story resides in the overcoming of these terrors is a remarkable occasion of hopefulness, not just in our individual lives, but for a world coming to be.

Christianity has always understood itself as standing within the inauguration of a new order of life. The way of God has already been manifest through Jesus of Nazareth, so Christianity lives in the space of the "already" of God. The biblical witness seems to indicate that Christ's resurrection is the primal moment from which the new creation takes shape. However, we await with the anticipation born of hope the future "not yet" of unrealized possibility and God's continued involvement toward God's future.

In the last few chapters I have sought to paint a picture of a universe that is still in the process of becoming. Even for those who would tend toward a creationist or intelligent design model, the reality of change as inherent in the ongoing processes of life is hard to deny. Open to new possibilities, responding in ways that amaze us even as we lack precise comprehension of what we are experiencing, we find a future that rests before us.

This is not a future determined down to the finest detail by either matter or God, but one shaped and structured by boundary conditions that allow for the creative interplay of forces both cosmic and biological. There are conditions that structure these processes, but they do not prevent some freedom from being exerted among and within living systems. Chance is embedded within the physical processes of the universe.

Such a perspective does not rest easily with those who hold a firm faith in causality in either the scientific or theological arenas. We, like Einstein, prefer our reality neat and orderly. Many of us hope that once we have discovered the parameters that structure what we are interpreting as chance, we will have a more accurate picture of what is happening in the universe. Likewise, in theology, some are far more comfortable with a God who is in absolute control and will direct all events according to divine purpose. Nothing, we are told, happens without God making it or allowing it to be. All things happen for a reason, we tell ourselves.

What science and theology are both saying to us is that this is a narrowing down of the world, a shaving off of life. We will have to think about ways of understanding God's providence in a world that has the potential to surprise us, shock us, delight us, and perhaps sometimes confuse and break us. This is a mystery difficult to entertain, because we don't normally use these types of categories to describe what is happening to us as we behold the night sky, or sit by the hospital bed of our beloved child as she is wracked by an invasive force doing physical and psychic harm. How do we find the space for hope in the latter and yet realize that the same processes are at work in the former?

It is the same hope that sees in the resurrection accounts the narration of an event indicating that God is creating the new ever again from that which dies. One of the crucial distinctions I have been probing in this text, however, is the one that grasps that God does not kill to make the new; rather, God suffers death in order for the new to manifest itself. At the center of the Christian story is the infinite mystery of a God who gives the utmost to a creation coming to be. This giving leads to the Christian doctrine of grace, which claims that God so loves the world, fully and unconditionally, that God holds nothing back from it. Father, Son, and Holy Spirit are fully immersed in creation as source, origin, and sustaining power. Not exhausted by the creation, this love does not absorb or annihilate the creation, but brings it to be through love and compassion.

We are good at comprehending this grace in an individual way ("I once was lost, but now am found"), but very seldom do we extend this in a corporate way to the entire created order. It is too difficult to contemplate for many that God may be allowing the universe to be what it will through all the messiness and chaos we experience. It is a scandal too horrible for many and so the vast portion of Christianity struggles in disbelief at this notion. Is there anything within the tradition of Christianity itself that might enable us to entertain the notion that we live in a situation that sees God's vulnerability to the universe as an occasion of hope?

A Tale of Two Stories

As has been stated previously, most of us are not consciously aware of the ways in which the mental landscape we exist within has been the result of thousands of years of enculturation and narrative structuring. Our language structures the reality many of us accept and the concepts we use to further make sense of the world. A significant part of this structuring emerged from the interpretation of Christianity we discussed earlier. Through long and involved historical processes, we came to believe in a certain interpretative trajectory that defined God and God's action in the world that rooted itself in terms of power and the past—God's power, and our past.

The interpretation of this story narrated a plot line where the world was created in a state of perfection and became fallen because the human creature misused the freedom bestowed on it. The human being has suffered an exile from the Creator that has tainted both the creature and the natural order. Of central importance for us is that the original perfection rests in a past we can never recover.

The subsequent tradition that arose around this rendering of the story issued in such ideas as original sin and the inherent fallenness of the world order. This tradition lent itself to interpretations of the world that viewed the meanderings of nature as attempts to return to a perfection resting in Eden. Our suspicions of nature are shaped in no small part, whether we are conscious of it or not, by the contours of this story.

Interpreted in this fashion, Christianity has constructed a story that speaks to the loss of original perfection and therefore nature is not necessarily seen as that which is accomplishing the purpose of God. Seen in this light, the notions of chaotic systems or even entropy are manifestations of a disordering within the created order. This is a creation subject to decay (Rom 8:21). Certainly this perspective was part of the patristic tradition. There the notion of sin was seen in the disordering of the cosmos, which needed the redemption of God to reestablish its original perfection.[2] In this line of thinking, the types of difficulties we have addressed earlier regarding the suffering of the universe are to be interpreted as part of a fallen creation. All physical processes found in life and discovered by the sciences are the continued straying away from an original perfection.

It is hard to deny the appeal of this story. We have grown so used to it in some shape, even if we reject it out of hand, that it becomes difficult to let go of it in order to consider a different story. Christianity must acknowledge that whatever sin is, there is an ontological dimension of disorder that takes us beyond the category of moral acts alone. We have to account for the very processes that bring death into the picture. We also have to own up to the failure of the human creature to live into and honor what it knows to be the best of who we are. We should realize that all too often we have made ourselves the central concern of the cosmos, but we are not at the center of the story, God is.

Is there a way we can understand the ontological depths of the dis-ease known as sin and yet see it with the lenses of hope? Is there something in the Christian tradition that might offer revelation to us about the world and God's relationship with it? I have maintained that we do find possibilities for this in trinitarian understanding, but I also believe that neglected aspects of the tradition offer us resources for fresh insight into our common story. This possibility comes to us through a much earlier voice than that of

Augustine, who has exercised so much formative influence. A reading of Irenaeus of Lyons might offer us a way of seeing our lives in God in ways that are consonant with the world as we experience it.

Very little is known of Irenaeus's life, although he tells us he heard Polycarp preach. He traveled to Gaul as part of a missionary impulse of the church, and eventually contested the Valentinian gnostics and their intricate spirituality, leading to the writing of *Against Heresies.* There is no evidence that he lived longer than 198, although there is an uncertain tradition that he lived until 202–3.[3]

In Irenaeus we find an interpretation of the Christian narrative that may warrant our consideration for the theological approach we have been considering. It is difficult for some to see any coherence in his theology and many commentators point to his fluctuations as evidence that he is hard to distill. When one considers the intricate and labyrinth-like dimensions of his thought, all one has to do is consider that to which Irenaeus is responding. It is more of a jungle than his thought is; however, there are some who find a remarkable coherence in his thinking.[4]

His entire thought centered itself around God and his reading of what he understood to be the Scriptures, though his canon was different because it had not yet been fixed by the church. For him only God is; everything else is in a state of becoming. This becoming in the accepted telling of the Christian story is the reason for pessimism, because this becoming is oriented toward corruption and not completion. In Augustine's mind, even given human rationality and the vestiges of the Trinity found within the created order, the movement in the creation is still away from the creator's intent. In Irenaeus's mind the very creatureliness of the human being means that it is in its nature to become and change. Humanity was created with the possibility of an unending progression and development toward God.[5] Our very nature is oriented to growth and development. "For He formed him for growth and increase," and we receive "advance and increasment towards God."[6]

The central focus of Irenaeus's response to the Valentinian gnostics was God's economy of redemption. He was provoked significantly by their excessive spirituality, which, like all Gnosticism, negated the very physical, material aspects of life as being capable of bearing the reality of God to us. Irenaeus, in contrast, rooted his theology of redemption deeply in the material dimensions of human existence, in no small measure as seen by his depiction of humanity as the mud people, formed from the mud by the hands of God.[7] In his reading, Adam is the modeling of God's creative energies, formed from the mud, and breathed upon by the spirit. Though real persons to Irenaeus, Adam and Eve are also symbols of deep universal significance.

Augustine read this story in a far more literal way and ultimately rooted the reality of the story in the past. This reality entails helplessness on our part to change the consequences of the original transgression. The unfolding of the cosmos in history and within time finds its meaning wrapped up in this primal neglect of God's command. Christ becomes the intervention of God into human history, discontinuous with the past, not in the natural order, but in Jesus' willingness to follow God's will. This creates a bifurcation tree all of its own. One path leads to Adam and death, the other path leads to Christ and life. In Augustine's mind God exercised control over this dichotomy, with the factor of individual predestination being a crucial element.

Irenaeus's understanding is somewhat different. We do have the freedom to choose our path. Though there is always going to be discontinuity between God and humanity, there is not the total sense of separation, for the economy of God is the history of humankind, indeed, of the entire cosmos. God fashions the earth creature from mud after the pattern of the body of Christ. The image of God is not just internal disposition toward rationality or something else, it is the very body shaped after the pattern of the body of the incarnate God.[8]

Adam is not created perfect, but created in the image of God. The mud creature was intended to come into the likeness of God at the end of a process of development. The fulfillment of this development in the economy of God means that we, and by extension, all of life, are still a work in progress: "The image of God given in creation is the beginning of the process of growing like God."[9]

Change and development constitute the underlying reality of God, but this process of change is not oriented to nothingness or decay; it has a purpose, for we needed vast amounts of time to become accustomed to bearing the life of God, which is what we were created for: "Humankind needed to grow accustomed to bearing divinity and God had to grow accustomed to dwelling in humankind."[10] This is an amazing thought, not much embraced in contemporary Christian faith. The vast amount of time we have been developing has been time for God and us to make habitation with one another.

The disruption of this development came with our refusal to exercise the same patience God showed in allowing time to work this out. According to Irenaeus, we grasped for this similitude to God too quickly. Adam reached for that which, while his, was his in God's time and intention. Sin is shown in the desire to take one's development into one's hands, outside of God's own timing. If we allow God to fashion us according to God's creative desire, allowing ourselves to maintain the "moisture" in the mud where we will have softness of heart, we will be shaped to completion in God's timing.[11] "If, then, you are God's workmanship, await the hand of your Maker whose *creation is being carried out.*"[12]

We have a destiny Irenaeus asserts and that destiny is to become the image and likeness of God (Rom 8:28–30). This predestination does not determine for human beings their fate, but the primal choice not to listen to God, to grasp with impatience God's ongoing process of accustoming, means we have lost the true sense of identity we should possess both about ourselves and the rest of the earth. We may possess intelligence and freedom, but we are blind to their true source.

Here we have the notion that the mud creature and the creation itself are not a finished product, but the very means by which God is continually creating. Humankind was not created perfect, but was necessarily imperfect from the beginning with the potential to grow to perfection, which entails our transformation by the glory of God.[13] Our spiritual immaturity and refusal to accept God's desire and timing means we choose wrongly, with sometimes evil results. No growth will occur for those who refuse to participate in God's summons to the earth creature. However, those who do choose to respect God's ordering will find a new orientation to life in all its manifestations.[14]

Jesus becomes the inauguration of a new and revived humanity that will find its consummation in the future. Christ stands as the corrected humanity and as one who is open, accustomed to God in the fullest sense, patient, not grasping after Godhood (Phil 2:5–11). The incarnation marks a new stage in this process because in Christ we have a soul and body who is willing to embrace God's spirit to the fullest. What was before lost because it was too intense for human life, the Word of God, becomes secure in Jesus of Nazareth, who was "The Word of God who dwelt in man, and became the Son of Man that He might accustom man to receive God and God to dwell in man, according to the good pleasure of the Father."[15]

Though there is an undeniable discontinuity here, it is more an anticipation of the new that is to come, the completion of the creation where the processes of development are the means by which God makes all things new. All of this is a unified piece, unbroken even by our refusal to accept our true identity or accept with patience God's own timing. The Trinity, while complex, is the reality of God that nourishes the growth toward completion because creation and redemption alike are manifestations of the Creator and Redeemer, mediated to the creature through the Holy Spirit.[16]

This entire process is oriented toward one goal, the notion of the great exchange. God becomes human in Christ that we might become divine. And it happens in the unfolding processes of a world that is coming to be. We are in ceaseless motion toward God, though we do resist. It may well be that here we have the map of territory that would be fruitful to explore in articulating faith for the present day. As Eric Osborn puts it, "His [Irenaeus's] account of the incarnation and human nature, of church and tradition, of history and salvation and the forces of renewal illuminates the wonder of human development. His sense of human evolution has made Christianity more credible in a scientific age."[17]

Thus we have two stories to consider as we reflect upon how we discern and interpret what is taking place in the world. The one story takes us to the tragedy of all existence where perfection was lost and the garden rests in the inaccessible past, shut off to us in exile by the cherubim with flaming swords guarding the gates of entry.

The other story leads us to the future. It too speaks of a loss, but at our own hands. We were created to grow into God, to become home for the glory, even though we come from the mud. Destined for maturity and relationship, we grasped after our inheritance too quickly. The hope of our lives rests in the future, the incarnation being the first step where we find that humanity is capable of carrying God. Even though this may not be worked out temporally, we find the resurrection from the dead being the space where we also will be able to carry God.[18]

Perhaps the most significant part of this story is the statement that we need so much time to become "accustomed" to God. This is where theology can truly open our hearts to something profoundly mysterious about the universe. The heart of God is learned no other way than by time and change. Our willingness to be patient and allow ourselves to become accustomed to God often occurs within our willingness to suffer change, loss, and pain. This is the way of the universe in all its manifestations. It is also the way of God.

The exchanges between divinity and humanity that Irenaeus and others explore direct us to the space not of power or knowledge, but suffering love. It is in our embrace of the sufferings of others, our willingness to become present to them, to fight for them, to see the commonality of all life that allows us to grow into God. But in that growing we find ourselves manifesting the presence of God in the world in a way that allows for the possibility of authentic communion with divine life.

That we are impatient even in our spiritual development speaks more to the choices of Adam than it does to the life of Christ. All quick and easy avenues to a richer, fuller, and deeper spiritual life are shortcuts that will lead to dead ends and cul-de-sacs. The accustoming of ourselves to God is a process that is ever ongoing and ever drawing us toward the heart of grace, if we have the sensitivity for it. This movement is never without suffering, and thus we should consider that at the heart of the universe in all its manifestations, suffering patient love maintains itself in a continual calling of creation to become. The creature and creation respond to the invitation to communion in such a way that the life of God itself becomes richer and more deeply textured within our awareness of the true reality.

Just as it is God's capacity for suffering that sustains the natural order, it is our capacity for suffering that allows for our participation in God's life and a growing into the depths of this life. Some will read this with suspicion and wonder if this is not just another call to become willing victims of those forces that seek to kill and destroy. Why should we be willing to suffer, some will ask, and who are you to demand that my life in God leads to suffering? This sounds like another call to be happy in the "bitter here and now" while we await the "sweet by and by." This is the argument of those who seek to oppress and maintain the status quo of power.

The paradox of faith does not mean that a willingness to suffer entails helplessness and acquiescence in the face of forces of evil. The refusal to flee suffering means a spiritually acute response to oppression in the world because we have allowed ourselves the space to participate in God's suffering. Having felt the depths of God's sufferings means resistance to all forms of violence and deceit that issue from humankind's continued blindness to its one true source. Christians must realize their primary commitments are to God's grace for all life in the world. This commitment alone will offer the resources for Christians to resist appeals from particular social or political constructions of reality to assume absolute claim over the life of the believer.

This means we will not become defined by the terms of reality forced on us by those who oppose the life of God. Those who enter fully into the life of God will speak truths about the ways we should treat the earth and the inhabitants of it. Violence as a means of power and domination will be called what it is, sinful. The exploitation of the earth and its resources by the rich at the expense of the poor will be called what it is, oppression. Those who accustom themselves to the triune life will become destabilizing forces in the world because they will tell the truth. Their identities will not be formed by appeals to transitory artifices such as nationalism, political manipulation, or wealth.

It is those who enter into relationship with God through the vision of a new creation who will embrace the life of God no matter how much this leads us to those who suffer. It is precisely this space, the willingness to exist in relationship with God and the world, distinct and yet connected, that carries the potential to transform and renew the creation within which we all live, move, and have our being.

Back to the Future

We are now in a position to consider the future as a category of hope and not despair. The thought that the processes of nature might actually have a future orientation is not a particularly new one, especially since this is rooted in the biblical witness. The entire narrative movement of the canon speaks to the reality of fulfillment. God is going to do a new thing (Isa 65:17). Jesus proclaims he is the fulfillment of the law and the prophets, indeed, the very fulfillment of the reign of God (Matt 16:13–19; Mark 1:15; Luke 4:16–21). In this regard he was the future made present. Paul writes about the future redemption of creation itself (Rom 8:18–25), and he strongly indicates in his writings that the future would be a time of deliverance and blessing. Another very profound expression of this is found in Col 1:15–20:

> He [Jesus] is the image of the invisible God, the firstborn of all creation; for in him all things in heaven and on the earth were created, things visible and invisible, whether thrones or dominions or rulers or powers—all things have been created through him and for him. He himself is before all things, and in him all things hold together. He is the head of the body, the church; he is the beginning, the firstborn from the dead, so that he might come to have first place in everything. For in him all the fullness of God was pleased to dwell, and through him to reconcile to himself all things, whether on earth or in heaven, making peace by the blood of his cross.

This is the vision we need to cultivate in deeper ways. This is the vision that orients us to the future and hope. In many respects this future remains hidden from us, but the destiny of the world rests in the promise of God and the reality of Christ as the fulfillment of all creation. Despite appearances to the contrary, all the chaos of life we see placed before us is to be seen ultimately from God's perspective and not ours.

All Christian understandings of God's creative action must assume the new creation. In the order of time this action of God must be seen as sustaining presence, allowing all things to become what they will, but seen from the position of the Son all things will be redeemed and reconciled. It is not only in the preservation of the world that we find the work of the triune God; it is the very preparation of creation for completion and fulfillment.[19]

We find the created order being the place where the future is present to us if we have the ears and eyes to hear and see. Jesus in his parables is always challenging his hearers to consider the possibility of seeing God in a new way through the very living of life. He seeks to open his hearers to the presence of the reign of God in their midst by the use of novelty and the upsetting of social constructions of God prevalent at the time. In these parables we see the anticipation of a new future (Luke 12:35–40; 14:15–24), where a new order and way of seeing things emerges (Matt 20:1–16).

If we extend this to our previous discussions, it becomes a reality that we cannot ignore. Everything in the created order is moving to a future that is, while uncertain and by no means secure, to be hoped for with the eyes of faith. The novelty of emergence is not blind, pitiless nature, but the ongoing relationship between God and the created order God has brought into being. In the Irenaean model of God's creative intention, the sense of becoming is oriented toward the future and not the past in order that the redemption of creation might come to be.

It is a difficult move to make, this turning toward the future. Both science and theology are conditioned by their received and ongoing traditions to think in terms of the past. Whether through causal efficacy in science or the model of lost perfection found in theology, we tend to invest ourselves in comfortable interpretations. Certainly this constitutes another space between science and theology, for science does not necessarily make space for the ongoing processes of impersonal forces unfolding in mathematical simplicity and contingency to be interpreted with categories of future or hope.[20] This type of teleology is simply not a meaningful scientific category.

But surely Christianity should not reject the possibility that what we understand as the physical forces in play are oriented to the future:

> But, if, on the other hand, we understand that universe itself as involved in an irreversible history and in the course of evolu-

tion, then we are interpreting it as an open system. In this case an entropy may be demonstrable in individual systems and processes, but it does not apply to the whole. We must then, however, assume that the universe itself has a transcendent encompassing milieu with which it is in communication, and a transcendent future into which it is evolving.[21]

When we look at something like nature's contingency, this feature may be seen as random, accidental, or chance occurrences happening over long stretches of time. What if, however, we were to look at those processes on the understanding that they represent nature's fundamental openness to new creation still in the making? Not a mindless determination on the basis of chemistry, physics, or biology alone, but an exploration of potential and promise?[22]

Moreover, this is an exploration in which God is responding to the choices and decisions made. To see nature as being shaped by an informational pattern hidden from causal explanation in science requires a paradigm shift that allows for the freedom of God to be within the world in ways that transcend even our imagination, but "theologically speaking, we may surmise that evolution occurs at all only because in some analogous sense all of nature is being addressed by the future we call God."[23]

The shape of this future from the perspective of the Christian faith does not come from the unfolding of past causal events that might lead to a predictive end; rather, the future portends the arrival of something entirely new. This flies in the face of many popular eschatologies, but it is faithful to the biblical witness that addresses the redemption and reconciliation of all things, "whether on earth or in heaven."[24] In this sense Christ has always been "before" us, the vision we apprehend as God's intention for the creation and the human creature.

We are also able to take account of the type of cosmic redemption we find in the biblical texts. We are given visions of a new heaven and a new earth, we are told that the whole creation has been in struggle awaiting the day when it will be set free (Rom 8:19–21). This power of the future is not solely the concern of our individual lives, but is the hope of the entirety of creation as well. It is the lion and the lamb together (Isa 11:6–16; 65:25). It is God's Sabbath rest. In the tension between the already and the not yet we find hopeful expectation, even in the midst of our suffering. We find a reality that allows us to see with the eyes of faith that what presently appears as chaos is the ordering of God who is to come and who is now present. In the midst of the original and continuing creation there is a new creation being born, not just within our hearts, but in the very cosmos itself.

More than a capitulation to some neo-Darwinian interpretative scheme of nature, it moves beyond both traditions of science and classical theism to suggest that what we find all around us in the enormous energies at play in physical processes is life responding to the call of God. Our participation in these processes shares all the contingencies and sufferings of the present world order, but we are also able to embrace the deep hope that through this becoming we are becoming more accustomed to God, who is creating space within us for the divine life. For us to see this vision truly, we may need to embrace new stories, but they were always there, and they have always been true.

This does point to the space between science and theology because faith will find in the midst of chaos God's future being created. This ineffable sense of hope constitutes a foundational response to the world of matter and energy. This hope cannot possibly situate itself in the realm of a completed creation, or worse, a lost perfection. Instead, this hope claims the future as a promise, even among much suffering, for it realizes that God is suffering as well. Our participation in God's suffering is not cause for despair, but reverence, which is not a space between, for many share this space when they consider the universe. This deep sense many feel at being in the presence of the sacred intuits an awareness that the universe does not just exist as a stage for this slight human drama, but possesses the destiny of redemption for all creation. God has more at stake than we realize.

NOTES

1. Fraser Watts has some interesting ideas in this regard in his essay "Subjective and Objective Hope: Propositional and Attitudinal Aspects of Eschatology." He treats the issue of hope and argues that hope occupies a space between optimism and trust that encompasses both, but this never leads to inactivity. Polkinghorne and Welker, *The End of the World, the Ends of God*, 47–60.

2. See, for example, H. E. W. Turner, *The Patristic Doctrine of Redemption: A Study of the Development of Doctrine during the First Five Centuries* (London: Mowbray, 1952). Alister McGrath also points out that Thomas Torrance argues that the universe has fallen into disorder, which he connects to the thermodynamical idea of entropy, necessitating a "redemption from disorder." McGrath, *Nature* (vol. 1 of *A Scientific Theology*; Grand Rapids, Mich.: Eerdmans, 2001).

3. Irenaeus is a fascinating subject and this short treatment does not do justice to the complexity of his thought, though I hope it does bring forth themes that are ger-

mane to the present subject. Some of the most accessible texts for the interested reader are Denis Minns, O.P., *Irenaeus* (Washington, D.C.: Georgetown University Press, 2001); Robert M. Grant, *Irenaeus of Lyons* (Cambridge: Cambridge University Press, 2001); and Mary Ann Donovan, *One Right Reading: A Guide to Irenaeus* (Collegeville, Minn.: Liturgical Press, 1997). For English translations of *Against Heresies,* consult "The Writings of Irenaeus," in *The Ante-Nicene Fathers* (ed. James Donaldson and Alexander Roberts; American reprint of the Edinburgh edition; Grand Rapids, Mich.: Eerdmans, 1973); or a more recent translation, *Against the Heresies, I* (trans. and annot. Dominic Unger, O.F.M., with further revision by John J. Dillon; Ancient Christian Writers 55; New York: Paulist Press, 1992).

4. The entire text by Osborn is an attempt to show that Irenaeus has a deep coherence in his theology by virtue of his concentration upon God's work in the salvation of the world. Eric Osborn, *Irenaeus of Lyons* (Cambridge: Cambridge University Press, 2001).

5. Minns, *Irenaeus,* 68–69.

6. *Against Heresies,* 4.11.2.

7. *Against Heresies,* 5.14.2. This notion of the people formed from the mud is one of central importance in Irenaeus and is most interesting to contemplate with what we know of how human life emerges on this planet.

8. Minns, *Irenaeus,* 60.

9. Osborn, *Irenaeus of Lyons,* 16.

10. *Against Heresies,* 3.20.2. This particular translation is by Osborn, who develops this notion of the accustoming of God and humankind to one another, showing it as an extensive theme in Irenaeus. Osborn, *Irenaeus of Lyons,* 80–85.

11. *Against Heresies,* 4.39.2.

12. *Against Heresies,* 4.39.2–3, emphasis mine.

13. *Against Heresies,* 4.38.3–4.

14. *Against Heresies,* 4.39.1.

15. *Against Heresies,* 3.20.2.

16. *Against Heresies,* 5.18.2.

17. Osborn, *Irenaeus of Lyons,* 86. I would probably take issue with this statement in some ways because it implies that science must be the arbiter for what makes Christianity credible, but the quote does point to the idea that Irenaeus, writing in the second century, offers us insight into the economy of God found within the unfolding of the creation itself. It certainly does point us toward the future rather than the past.

18. *Against Heresies,* 5.8.1.

19. Moltmann, *God in Creation,* 209. This is not only the conceptual world found in Moltmann, but in many contemporary theologians such as Wolfhart Pannenberg, Miroslav Volf, and Ted Peters; and many others read the biblical witness to speak to this anticipation. Most notably, this orientation to the future is found in the theology of Teilhard de Chardin and his entire life.

20. Haught, *God After Darwin,* 95.

21. Moltmann, *God in Creation,* 204.

22. It is this notion that stands at the center of John Haught's project in *God After Darwin*. His entire orientation is toward a metaphysics of the future in which God is the future continually coming toward us. "It should not be too hard for us to appreciate, therefore, why a religion that encourages its devotees to wait in patient hope for the fulfillment of life and history will interpret ultimate reality, or God, as coming toward the present, and continually creating the world, from the sphere of the future 'not yet'" (91).

23. Haught, *God After Darwin*, 99.

24. Ted Peters uses the distinction of *futurum* and *adventus;* the former meaning sees the future as actualizing a potential already present, the latter as addressing the appearance of something entirely new, an act of divine grace whereby creation undergoes a genuine renewal. He also uses a third term, *venturum*, borrowed, which speaks to the reality that the coming future has an impact upon us before its full advent. The future has already made an impact informing the present. *God—The World's Future*, 308–9.

8

THE MYSTERY OF
RESISTANCE

*The creation of the world is not only a process
which moves from God to humanity. God demands newness
from humanity; God awaits the works of human freedom.*
—Nicolas Berdyaev

We are drowning in information, while starving for wisdom.
—E. O. Wilson

We have spent the last few chapters exploring a different model of the triune God and I have offered a vision of God's life in the world that is meant to offer grounds for a deep hope. To be captured by this vision means a new way of seeing nature that carries profound consequences. No longer can we allow ourselves to be carried along by the same delusions that so structure the world around us. The person who sees life and the natural order as inherently holy will have a radically different orientation to the world. The very miracle of being, of participating in life, will enable us to grasp that the being of God is embedded within life in a profoundly mysterious way. Whatever we do to the earth, we do to the God who creates and sustains it. This sight frees us to see the various bondages and illusions under which we live.

It also allows us to see that our individual redemption, while crucial for our ability to live redeemed lives within temporal time, is inseparable from the liberation of creation. In the Bible the final movement of God is not the salvation of human beings, but the redemption of the entirety of creation for God's Sabbath rest. Both Christian and Jewish Scriptures speak to this ultimate liberation of all of life and its being taken up into God.

In the story we are told from science, which uses its own language to describe how things will be in the future, a connection exists that can offer us wisdom and insight. We are ultimately dependent upon the processes that have brought us here, forces physical in nature. We are the product of star formation and cellular exploration. The scientific rendering of our dependence is striking, but truly difficult for us to grasp in an existential way. Being so numbed by our various pursuits, be they war, power, or the shopping mall, we find ourselves blinded by that which seeks to keep our attention focused on the fleeting and transitory.

We alluded earlier to the fact that the sciences have led us, among other things, to the vacating of sacredness from the earth. Emptied of sacred significance, nature really does become nothing other than an empty vessel into which we pour all our ambitions, greed, and desires. Rather than viewing nature as a gift, we construct a world in which violence and power seemingly play the truly efficacious shaping roles.

All religious imagery is being abolished under the whip hand of a thirst for profit and exploitation. Concepts such as sacred time or sacred space are being destroyed by the onslaught of our desire for power to define the boundaries of what is acceptable and what is not. The very rhythms of our lives before God have been vitiated by the vortex of consumption. The image of the world that many now hold is not the creation of a gracious God, but a vast global shopping mall, which has its own way of defining the relationship between humankind and the created order:

> This globalization includes human organs, sex objects, and experimental research animals. It does even more than that. It redefines the relation between nature and humankind: from dependency to disposition, from attachments to the rhythms of life to escaping the natural rhythms of life, from relationship with every creature to absolute rule over them, from the very ability itself to enter into relation to having virtual reality making that ability superfluous.[1]

There have been in recent years a number of responses to this type of devaluing life, save for its economic and political significance. One idea that has emerged in the science and religion discussion is the idea of the "created co-creator," which is most often associated with the name of Philip Hefner. This notion is one of the most interesting intersections between the worlds of science and religion in recent years.[2] Essentially, Hefner takes as his starting premise that "the evolving world process is actually a process of responding and adapting to God. God has created a process that is woven on the loom of adapting to its creator. This adapting is what constitutes the basic character of the world process."[3]

This sense of adaptation gives Hefner the ground from which to spin out ideas that are important to his thinking, even as they were to Herbert Spencer in the nineteenth century. One of these is that we are no longer in the purely biological stage of evolution. We have shifted to a new place where we must now consider the role of cultural evolution as well. Both culture and biology are part of the cosmic processes at play. This process has brought into the world something unique: "The *created co-creator* refers to the emergence of a creature, *Homo sapiens*, (1) who on the one hand is thoroughly a creature of nature and its processes of evolution—hence the term *created*—and (2) who at the same time is created by those very processes as a creature of freedom."[4]

This freedom exists in the context of our living in a world that forces our choices and where culture structures the stories that justify those choices. The "created" aspect addresses our genetic and biological dependence upon the forces that have brought us to this moment, but the "co-creator" stands as that which in some measure transcends our genetic determinations. Culture construction, while linked to our genetic coding and central nervous system, transcends those lower-level components by the exercise of freedom and decision.

There is a real sense in which the culture we construct will have significant impact on genetic adaptability. The relationship can be somewhat complex. For instance, this week the newspapers contained stories about the growing problem of obesity in America. Have humans evolved to crave fatty foods because they were scarce in the past, or has increasing reliance upon fat in industrialized societies, especially fast and processed foods, led to our addiction to these foods? One undeniable result is the increase in obesity and related problems such as heart disease.[5]

This cultural impact can be extended further than most of us realize. We know that bird populations are being affected by trends in global warming. Pied flycatchers, like red knot sandpipers, time their spring migration to their breeding grounds based on day length. Because of the effects of global warming, however, insects, their main food source, appear earlier in the season than they used to. The timing is now off and many birds are too late to coincide with the cycles of their food source.[6]

It would appear that our construction of culture is resulting in a world that is being extraordinarily changed by attenuations of physical systems that we are causing in the world. We have only spoken of the biological factors, but what of the larger factors such as war or development of land or crop engineering? Who knows what the effects on microbes and diseases have been with our attempts to produce enough for a rapidly expanding planet? Hefner does see that culture formation presents us with formidable challenges: "The challenge that faces our cultural construction is to fashion a system of information that interfaces with our world as meticulously and as adequately as our physico-biogenetic systems do."[7]

I wrote earlier of our technological habits of life. We must face the fact that our technology has now formed a net that has enveloped us all, and in some degree, has separated us from the world of nature. All the essentials we use in life—food, clothing, shelter, heat, and birth—are largely controlled by our technologies. Think of a world without coal, oil, gas, chemical fertilizers, electricity, crop engineering, even water, and the vast delivery systems to bring them to our homes. What would our lives look like if we were responsible for our own food, water, and shelter? However we view culture, our rational and technical control of the world have been no small elements in co-creating this present world. Hefner's observations have empirical evidence. We are creating the world every day.

A number of writers in the not too distant past explored whether this was an entirely good thing for humanity. Jacques Ellul in his *The Technological Society* was a harbinger to writers such as Neil Postman. Though technology has enhanced the quality of our lives, it has also emptied our culture of substance and wisdom. Because we have banished the notion of deeper cosmologies from our cultural constructions, it seems that what we have constructed takes its orders from our technical abilities: "Technopoly is a state of culture. It is also a state of mind. It consists in the deification of technology, which means that the culture seeks its own authorization in technology, and takes its orders from technology. This requires development of a new social order, of necessity leads to the rapid dissolution of much that is associated with traditional beliefs."[8] How do we reconcile this warning with the concept of the created co-creator?

In his treatment of human life in theoretical terms Hefner argues that his concept allows us to be the agency for the birthing of the future within evolutionary history. Theologically this leads him to suggest that *"Homo sapiens is God's created co-creator, whose purpose is the 'stretching/enabling' of the systems of nature so that they can participate in God's purposes in the mode of freedom, for which the paradigm is Jesus Christ, both in respect to his life and his understanding of the world as God's creation."*[9]

He makes this theological claim on the basis that nature itself has brought us to this moment by the transcendence of matter in the human creature who exercises significant freedom within the created order.[10] This claim is not discontinuous with the notion of intentionality within nature; rather, the appearance of the human creature signals nature's participation in freedom and transcendence. Metaphorically, humankind serves as sign that nature itself has exercised its intention within God's purpose by bringing us forth. We, in turn, are a window onto the processes of the world.[11]

Creation in this reading is the free action of God, but it is also conditioned ultimately by the character of God, who contains both freedom and intentionality, and even more importantly, love: "God's nature conditions the nature of creation."[12] If human life exists as the particular expression of natural complexity, then Jesus stands as the prime expression of God's intention for human life. In Jesus we find the paradigm of the created co-creator. The one who, being fully human and yet truly God, is dependent upon biological processes, yet exercises his freedom in a total orientation and obedience to God's call of life:

> Jesus Christ becomes the central event for understanding what it means for humans to be God's proposal for the future of the evolutionary process. In freedom—a freedom that has been bequeathed to our race from the aeons of previous physical and biological and culture development —we have the option to live now according to what has been set forth by Jesus as God's ultimate purpose: the renewal and perfection of all creation.[13]

This is a profound vision and one that carries intense emotional impact. While Hefner does not wish this to be an anthropocentric vision because he seems to be a theocentric thinker, the human creature does have a destiny and purpose within the created order that transcends the rest of the creation. We are, therefore, creatures of deep responsibility and enormous power. We do now possess the power to destroy much of life on earth through our technologies of war. Even more, we have the power to determine the future of life through our biological technologies.

But I think we also possess something else equally wondrous; we have the ability to love and to love in a way not necessarily rooted in genetic survival. We have been graced with the love that transcends cultural and biological evolution, a love that does not love just family, kin, tribe, but loves even the enemy. This is not a dynamic rooted in "selfish" genes, but in a transcendence to higher levels of complexity, able to embrace the entirety of life not for what it gives us, but on the grounds of gratitude.

In some ways this is the vision that was spoken of earlier regarding Job. Our reading of that story sees Job as moving to a depth of understanding in the struggle with God that he could not have obtained any other way. Moving from hearing about to seeing is a theological metaphor for the realization that no matter how hard it is to see, life is a gift. Even in our suffering we have the opportunity to transcend it with the realization that we are loved and accepted.

Because Hefner's vision is so compelling and even pastoral, it becomes all the more difficult to raise objections to it; however, there does seem to be a problem. While we can agree with him on the vision of a new humanity, informed by the vision of God in Christ, the reality of the world looks much different. The directional trajectory of evolution has indeed brought us to the place of world making, and we should take our powers very seriously in this regard.

We must ask, however, what kind of world are we co-creating? What have we accomplished with our technology and cultural construction? What are the uses of our sciences and knowledge, both historically and in the present moment? What are the powers to which we have attached ourselves in the present order, and how does the use of violence sustain these orders? Is it altruism, faith, or profit that drives the engine of the modern world? Why have science and technology been put to the service of political and military structures since the beginning of cultures and societies? The truth must be faced that our growing technological prowess has issued in more sophisticated means of carnage. Our record at taking our divine mandate seriously is dismal; neither have we allowed sufficient room for the mandate to grow among us.

We seem all too accommodated to a world of violence where our desire to kill, eliminate, and destroy those who are threats to us issues in glib and seemingly necessary justifications for our creation of the cultures of death. The structural powers that we have created do not have God as the partner of fashioning a new earth. Economics, politics, religion, and science might as well be the four horsemen of the Apocalypse for all the death, suffering, and destruction that have been unleashed upon the earth in their names.

How can we reconcile the vision of created co-creator with this destruction? This is perhaps the area where dialogue between science and religion finds its greatest difficulty. Christian theology narrates the reality that the creature contradicts the creation and the Creator by our unwillingness to acknowledge our dependence upon and gratitude to the Creator. Now we must entertain the mystery of the human distortion of creation known to Christians as sin.[14]

Speculation concerning sin has been an ongoing aspect of Christian self-definition since its beginning, but we now have a different layer of inquiry to deal with. How does a natural process, rooted in genetic, biological, and physical means, result in such an archaic notion as sin? While this word and the concepts attendant to it seem outdated, there are some undeniable realities present for us to wrestle with.

In our interpretations of life most of us are inattentive to the ways we move through the world. We are most often unaware of those forces inside of us that create havoc with our lives. The very best aspects of our lives, minds and hearts, can often become twisted by power, ambition, and worst of all, a distorted sense of love. We seem marked by an indelible sense of self-incurvature that forgets our commonality with all earthly and cosmic life.

We end up defining ourselves on the basis of transitory moments and our identities become shaped more by nation, tribe, ethnicity, gender, economic status, or prestige than by our identity as co-creator with God of a world coming to be. Personal identity, expressed in solidarity with all of the creation, is lost as we become a bundle of competing selves. We may appear on the one hand to be self-making, self-creating creatures, but too often we seem fragmented and weakened, caught in compulsions we don't even comprehend.

It is because of these compulsions that we forget what Hefner would argue is our identity as created co-creator. Captured by this gravity, we also lose the freedom to be able to understand ourselves. We do not even possess enough freedom to tell the truth about ourselves and our self-absorbing obsessions. The incoherent selves that compete within us for supremacy render us incapable of a liberating, self-transcending knowledge. These are the tensions that render us incapable of seeing with authentic sight our true situation. This self-incurvature is what needs redemption.

Some have addressed this tension between what we aspire to and what we create as the gap between the ideal and the real or the sacred and profane. Others have used the words of natural selection and biological determinism.

Whatever category we use, we find ourselves confronting an aspect of human existence that works against the very future that we envision as the one co-created with God.

In the vision of co-creating, the future should be marked by the understanding that the entirety of all life shares commonality within God because God creates all that exists. Though this is a simple theological statement, it appears impossible for us to realize its implications. When we reflect upon the deeper aspects of what this might mean for our planet, we wonder exactly why it is that creatures of such freedom seem to be so willing to destroy and exclude others. This is one of the struggles that gave rise to science in the first place.

Historically it was the appeal to the rationality engendered by science that led many to embrace it as a way of knowing devoid of the passions that were ripping apart Europe in the religious conflicts after the Reformation. Here was a place where the best of humanity could flourish and truly fulfill the promise of a paradise on earth. Science was a place where God could be removed from all national and tribal claims and the commonality of all things could be respected. It would be a discipline that would eventually eradicate the violence and destruction found in human life. The vast promise of science for many has been and continues to be a means of inquiry into the world that should humble us and cause us to cast about for new languages to speak of the mysteriousness of the universe without the need for domination.

That it cannot do so now is more testimony to the social dominance and power that has been executed in the name of progress, and thus science, like religion, needs to be viewed with some suspicion. With the rise of technocracies and the desire for power being manifested by the attendant technologies that are shaping the world, we have ample evidence of need for a theological critique of our ability.

Modernity has brought a narration to the interpretation of the world that views life on its own terms, far removed from any need for a creator. In this narration we are more accidental dance of the molecules than human beings created for the purposes of co-creation. Seen as a result of purely physical processes, we are more apt to be viewed as material to be manipulated and transformed through technologies and techniques. While serving humankind in significant ways, science, too, has been part of modernity's narrative: "The 'new science' was therefore, from the outset, preoccupied with narratives about the transformation of nature. However, these were no longer myths of magical action which could only be symbolically represented in ritual. Instead, they could be literally repeated under the proper conditions, artificially re-provided."[15]

Science, like theology, issues in certain habits of thought that go a long way to constructing the world in which we live. Science can form the limitations around what we believe is plausible and even moral, offering us accounts of the world that have quite specific consequences. Every artifact of culture that emerges from our constructions has the power to shape us, even to the point of dictating the type of world we will construct. Science, as a part of this culture creation, "alters and delimits just what we try to do, just as thinking of the cosmos as a big machine spawned many actual terrestrial machines."[16]

The contemporary account of the world that most of us operate under gives us a picture of the world rooted in the dynamic of cause and effect, and in the understanding of these factors, a mastery over life. The emergence of habits of thought that are supposedly rooted in a dispassionate universal rationality has led us to achieve dubious goals. Too often the employment of our science has led us to the mindset of "If we can do it, we should." Unfortunately, to a person with a hammer, everything looks like a nail.[17]

While on one level it is a plain fact that we are creators, the question is whether we are co-creating anything worth the effort. We have to ask if the societies constructed in the name of modernity and its myths have left us better off. The deep gravity of human self-incurvature bears consideration for what it has brought to us. Self-deceptions have blinded the most powerful of the earth for quite some time. It would be hard to envision ancient Greek literature without this insight.

The irony of our situation is that the more powerful we become in our ability to create the world, the more in need we are of confessing our dependence upon the Creator. The need to develop a spiritual consciousness and conscience is more important now than ever. This cultivation of the spiritual dimension of all existence, human and otherwise, though found in isolated pockets among scientists and groups such as Science and the Spiritual Quest, is simply not a consideration to most scientific practice in the world today.

To suggest that we actually suffer conversion to new habits of thought, new orientations to life, new commitments to our explorations, strikes many of the most sophisticated of this world as foolish. And yet until the spiritual dimension of our lives is universally recognized as the most vital aspect of our co-creating, we will continue to stumble along, blindly grop-

ing forward into an uncertain future. If we are to avoid being captured by
the compulsions of control engendered by sin, we need communities of
grace that will proclaim different visions than the ones that presently guide
and shape us.

Case Study: Genetic Engineering

As just one example of the tension between the scientific and religious perspective, we might look at one of the frontiers of our scientific and creative
endeavors today, genetic engineering. Much in the news recently owing to
the suspect claims of human cloning, genetic engineering is the cutting edge
of present discussions concerning religion and science, and persons are lin-
ing up on all sides of the debate. In fact, the phrase "playing God" has been
invoked regarding all efforts to use our knowledge in the arena of genetic
engineering.[18]

On one side of the issue are those concerned about the Promethean role
that scientists would play in the emerging manipulation of cellular life,
especially DNA. There is some concern that our biological tinkering is a
transgression of the limits placed on humankind. In worst-case scenarios we
have the Frankenstein metaphors to point out the hubris that leads to the
creation of life. There is a sense that inviolate boundaries are being transgressed and a vague discomfort coalesces into a stance that sees the DNA as
sacred and thus untouchable. This is especially the case with something as
central to human definition as cloning.

The other side is represented by those who argue that engaging in this
type of thinking would have meant that we would not have enjoyed the benefits of modern science because of prohibitions to research that would have
been put in place. The medical advances we have enjoyed in the last century
have been due to the efforts of science. A stance of just letting nature be
would put us totally at the mercy of viruses, disease, and untold causes of
suffering.[19] DNA, while of crucial importance, should not be isolated in an
untouchable, isolated realm: "To think of genetic material as the exclusive
realm of divine grace and creativity is to reduce God to the level of restric-
tion enzymes, viruses, and sexual reproduction. Treating DNA as matter—
complicated, awe-inspiring, and elaborately coded, but matter
nonetheless—is not itself sacrilegious."[20]

How will we negotiate between these approaches, for each has a truth to
it? If faith is future oriented as I have argued, then the future should be seen
as holding the potential of the coming to be of God's intention for the earth.

Novelty and emergence have been and will be a part of this future. God has bestowed upon the human creature the ability to continue the creative activity of God. Even our technology is part of this ongoing process. If we neglect to use our intellect for the alleviation of suffering in the world, are we not in danger of sloth as we are of pride?

Nothing has been accomplished for the benefit of humanity while waiting for God to undertake full responsibility. The moral impetus rests with us to use our powers to co-create. Doesn't the great commandment to love God and neighbor mean we exercise our abilities for the common good of humankind? Wouldn't this mean that if we can take care of viruses, birth defects, and diseases in cellular manipulation, we should do so as a gift of God?

This concern does become particularly acute when we consider the issues of such technologies as germline intervention or nanotechnology. Germline intervention is "the insertion of new gene segments of DNA into sperm or eggs before fertilization or into undifferentiated cells of an early embryo that will be passed on to future generations and may become part of the permanent gene pool."[21] Nanotechnology involves manipulating atoms at the nano-level (nano is the measure 10 to minus nine, or in terms of size, as a football is to the planet earth so is a nano-particle to a football), where molecules are extracted, taken apart, and reassembled at the nano-level. The potential uses of this technology are both touted, such as molecular submarines trained to kill medical viruses, and denounced, such as we find in Michael Crichton's new book, *Prey*, in which the particles become competitors with humans for energy.

Such efforts as cloning and nanotechnology presently constitute the frontiers of genetic inquiry, especially with the recent work of the human genome project. Do we concentrate our attention on suffering persons already born, or do we also pay attention to the health of persons yet to come?[22] This type of intervention also has huge consequences for the future shape of life on our planet because it brings the issue of permanent alteration into focus. It also raises the specter in some people's minds of eugenics and the racial regime of Nazism. The fear is that our "growing power to control the human genetic make-up could foster the emergence of the image of 'perfect child' or a 'super strain' of humanity."[23]

The grasp of a genetic perfection could mean that tolerance of genetic diversity would erode, paving the way for a world where perfection becomes the desired goal. Much like the movie *Gattica*, we could construct a social ordering of society that assigns greater value to those who are best genetically suited to a technologically driven society. Those who do not measure up might find themselves faced with discrimination and marginalization.

Of course, discrimination has existed on the basis of genetic make-up since recorded history. Racism stands as just one reminder that whatever our intention, the primal wound that scars and drives us to exclusion is deep indeed. The very existence of prejudices within humankind should make us uncomfortable with a status quo that would relegate others to the position of inferior status based on genetic and biological determinations.

Does this mean we should stop all attempts at alleviating or eradicating suffering? If we are able to stop in the embryo such diseases as Alzheimer's or Huntington's, should we not take this step? For those whose first response is no, medicine and science have used their powers in the past to make this a safer and healthier world. Do we turn our backs on those responsibilities now?

The fact that we are technically capable may well be a sign of our promise for a better future. With a strong sense of moral accountability, we may have resources through stem cell research or germline intervention that would allow us to stop the untold suffering of countless numbers who would otherwise be doomed. On this reading, the advances in the medical and biological sciences are a part of the divine call to creation. Does this mean that we are playing God? No, "but we should play human in the *imago Dei* sense—that is, we should understand ourselves as created co-creators and press our scientific and technological creativity into the service of neighbor love, of beneficence."[24]

In the Christian community there are a number of thoughtful voices that suggest we receive the gifts of technical knowledge and the ability to use them as means of service to our neighbor. Is this part of moving into the future that God is calling us toward? The new creation presumably will not contain pain and suffering, thus attempts on our part to eradicate them must not necessarily be seen totally through the lenses of fear of hubris.[25]

This is where the issue of biocultural evolution is seen in all its potential as holding promise for so many. Genetic science and genome research hold keys to a transformation that stretches the imagination. If there were ever a place where the realization of the created co-creator would reach full force, here it is. This too continues the stirring vision offered by Hefner.

Before we go rushing into the sanctuary, however, Christian faith must not lose its prophetic sense. It is a commitment to transcendent reality that rests at the heart of the Christian faith, specifically to the reign of God proclaimed by Jesus. This commitment does not allow for blindness to the negative potential within humankind's endeavors. Certain questions must be asked. What are the cultural structures we have built to sustain these practices? Who benefits from the advances we make in medicine or science?

Who defines what healthy or unhealthy actually looks like? Who gets to define what humanity is? Without a deep spiritual sense of our dependence upon the Creator, can we even define humanity accurately? The vision of created co-creator is one I believe that Christians should embrace, but not without asking what are the practices of life that are sustaining us now. Do these seem to be vehicles for bringing forth the full promise of co-creation, which is ultimately redemption?

Take the one industry that would be a major institutional arena for genetic work. Is it profit and power that presently drive our health care system? Certainly among many health care professionals we find a deep compassion and commitment to their work, but the industry itself does not serve the poor or disenfranchised of society unless forced to do so by law. Who gets left out of the present systems of health care and who gets taken care of the best? Not to put too simplistic a line on this, but self and corporate interests drive the health care system currently in America. The society we have constructed contains large numbers of persons who have no access to health care. Is this the system we should invest our hopes in for a world-constructing, human-defining genetics? The powerless and poor are in danger of being left out of this system just as they have always been (Amos 8:4–6).

This does not mean we should shove our heads in the sand and refuse the knowledge we have been given, but it does mean we should be intentional about building more informed faith communities of those whose lives have been shaped by values that extend beyond profit. These communities should in turn offer rigorous ethical and spiritual critiques of the present social structures under which genetic work is being done.

This is so unacceptable for many in the research community that the idea sounds ludicrous on the face of it. The religious dimension is so neglected within our public spaces that many would see the demand for a specifically Christian moral ethic as unwarranted intrusion into areas where it does not belong. But when we are casting about for how health and well-being are defined, it will always be those who possess the power of culture formation that decide. If Christians take the vision of co-creating seriously, they should bring their concerns to the discussion.

When we consider the cultures that are being shaped and shaping us today, we must ask whether or not it is a coincidence that societies that exhibit the greatest amount of ecological damage and consumption as well as economic inequality are the most scientifically literate and technologically sophisticated. Within these societies and in relation to other global communities we find cause for suspicion about who benefits from the technological advances we have made. Just think of how prescription drugs are regulated around the world to get a view of what the new world would look like if we continue creating within the present structures.

The visions that presently sustain our practices and form our communities are in need of revision. Christianity must move beyond its current cultural captivities to such transitory aspects of human existence as nationalism, capitalism, and politics. More often than not, Christian faith finds itself on the periphery of public discourse. Its ideological hijacking by politicians who espouse a superficial and idolatrous understanding has left Christianity a faint voice in cultural evolution. The authentic priestly and prophetic voice that Christianity possesses has been marginalized in the face of forces that are inimical to faith.

Science, too, has its myths that cause a blindness. Believing that there is a universal human rationality that would transcend such factors as social location, cultural limitation, and self-interests, science lives in its own form of illusion to which it clings. The myth of transcendence that grounds the modern worldview in its scientific guise is increasingly coming under suspicion. We are more able to recognize that the quest for knowledge is a form of power and the desire for power too easily leads to control. Our intellectual quest has supposedly been engaged in order to serve humankind, not dominate it or nature. However benign the narrative, the reality has turned out far different. What are our energies being directed toward? "Science in the service of concupiscent human nature is likely to prove tragic, as much in the twenty-first century as in the twentieth."[26]

These are considerations that call for more wisdom than we presently seem to possess. Our knowledge and technological employment far outpace our moral and spiritual ability to form communities that will fashion and sustain the type of persons that will see their lives as being created co-creators. The self-knowledge of this as our true orientation to the creation might bring more caution and thoughtfulness as we use our abilities to serve God and not mammon. The church is the community that should sustain practices and participation in God that would inculcate habits of heart and mind not ensnared by the powers at work today. We should at least insist on a voice in what is happening in the world that is coming to be.

The church is also the location where we can hear the truth about ourselves and learn the disciplines necessary to create the future. There is an ontological dimension of life that reveals a distortion between God's intention and earthly reality. Our neglect of that reality causes us to lose the wisdom necessary for the healthy and true ordering of life. How we view the universe will have crucial consequences for how we use it. Christianity, in faithfulness to the triune God, may have to reconstitute itself in directions that lead it to understanding the universal and cosmic dimensions of our own narrative. We turn now to how this reconstruction might proceed.

NOTES

1. Dorothee Soelle, *The Silent Cry: Mysticism and Resistance* (trans. Barbara and Martin Rumscheidt; Minneapolis: Fortress Press, 2001), 110. This desire of the present age to vacate the earth of sacred space and time is in no small part at the root of the struggles of the contemporary world. There are those who see the emptying of the world of sacredness as being a profaning of the living God and thus they commit their lives to seeking to restore their understanding of what constitutes God back into the public square. The political forces behind these movements though often betray the type of commitments for which I am arguing here.

2. The interested reader can start with Philip Hefner's *The Human Factor: Evolution, Culture, and Religion* (Minneapolis: Fortress Press, 1993). Hefner's writings also appear in a number of other works, such as "The Evolution of the Created Co-Creator," in *Cosmos as Creation: Science and Theology in Consonance* (ed. Ted Peters; Nashville: Abingdon, 1989), 211–33; and "Theological Perspectives on Morality and Human Evolution," in *Religion and Science: History, Method, and Dialogue* (ed. W. Mark Richardson and Wesley J. Wildman; London: Routledge, 1996), 401–23.

3. Philip Hefner, "The Evolution of the Created Co-Creator," in *An Evolving Dialogue: Theological and Scientific Perspectives on Evolution* (ed. James B. Miller; Harrisburg, Pa.: Trinity Press International, 2001), 399–416.

4. Philip Hefner, "Biological Evolution and the Created Co-Creator," in *Science and Theology: The New Consonance* (ed. Ted Peters; Boulder, Colo.: Westview Press, 1998), 172–86.

5. An interesting article on this subject can be found in *The Chronicle of Higher Education* (October 18, 2002): 19–21. "Trapped by Evolution" tells the story of how our cultural constructions are having a huge impact on life.

6. Ibid., 20.

7. Hefner, "Biological Evolution and the Created Co-Creator," 176.

8. Neil Postman, *Technopoly: The Surrender of Culture to Technology* (New York: Vantage, 1991), 74. For a decidedly Christian take on this issue, see Peter Gay, *The Way of the (Modern) World: Or, Why It's Tempting to Live as if God Doesn't Exist* (Grand Rapids, Mich.: Eerdmans, 1999), 79–120.

9. Hefner, "Biological Evolution and the Created Co-Creator," 181. The emphasis is Hefner's.

10. Hefner, "The Evolution of the Created Co-Creator," 406–7.

11. Hefner, "Biological Evolution and the Created Co-Creator," 183.

12. Ibid., 184.

13. Hefner, "The Evolution of the Created Co-Creator," 413.

14. In all fairness, Hefner is aware of this dimension of human existence and sees evil and sin as intruding on the working out of the contours of our co-creating. *The Human Factor,* 241ff.

15. John Milbank, *Theology and Social Theory: Beyond Secular Reason* (Oxford: Blackwell Publishers, 1990), 269.

16. Ibid., 270.

17. Postman makes this observation, but another one is corollary to it. Science has become as much a technically driven enterprise as a conceptually driven one. Given this, we might want to revisit Thomas Kuhn's notions of scientific revolutions and ask whether the emergence of technique is a paradigm shift that should occupy the centrality of our responses to the world of science. Jacques Ellul saw this coming decades ago.

18. Ted Peters has written a book about this with the title *Playing God: Genetic Determinism and Human Freedom* (New York: Routledge, 1997).

19. For example, see Ronald Cole-Turner, *The New Genesis: Theology and the Genetic Revolution* (Louisville, Ky.: Westminster/John Knox, 1993); *Beyond Cloning: Religion and the Remaking of Humanity* (Harrisburg, Pa.: Trinity Press International, 2001); and his text with Brent Waters, *Pastoral Genetics: Theology and Care at the Beginning of Life* (Cleveland: Pilgrim Press, 1996); or J. Robert Nelson, *On the New Frontiers of Genetics and Religion* (Grand Rapids, Mich.: Eerdmans, 1994).

20. Cole-Turner, *The New Genesis,* 45. To be fair, Cole-Turner sees a significant problem with human misuse of our knowledge: "One never reads of co-creation and sin in the same sentence. But our technology, for all its good, is constantly on the edge of sin, exploitation, and greed. It is, after all, human technology, beset by our weaknesses. To ignore this danger, as the language of co-creation so easily does, is to fail to guard against it" (102).

21. Peters, *Playing God,* 144.

22. Ibid., 145.

23. Ibid., 147.

24. Ibid., 161. This is a common line of argument among the proponents of genetic work. Cole-Turner makes the parallel between the diseases that Jesus heals and our attempts to heal (*The New Genesis,* 91ff.), but this notion of Jesus' healing needs to stand within the context of the social structures of his time as well. Some of his healings had significant social implications that were revolutionary to the established social order. See Wendy Farley, *Tragic Vision and Divine Compassion: A Contemporary Theodicy* (Louisville, Ky.: Westminster/John Knox, 1990).

25. See, for instance, Nancy R. Howell, "Co-Creation, Co-Redemption, and Genetics," *American Journal of Theology and Philosophy* 20, no. 2 (May 1999), 147–63. In this article Howell proposes that "a theology of redemption, informing both theological anthropology and theodicy, is key to discerning how genetics should address human suffering" (147).

26. Holmes Ralston III, "Science, Religion, and the Future" in *Religion and Science: History, Method, Dialogue,* 76.

9

DRAWING DOWN
THE FIRE

If you wish to understand the Creator, understand the Creation.
—Columbanus

Someday after we have mastered the winds, the waves,
the tides and gravity, we will harness for God the energy of love;
then for the second time in the history of the world,
[humankind] will have discovered fire.
—Teilhard de Chardin

This morning my wife Jan and I watched the Leonid meteor shower from our back deck. Not quite as spectacular as the one last year, this one still had plenty of amazing streaks of light flashing through the sky, leaving images of lines being drawn and then disappearing. I wondered as I looked at these lines blazing their way across the sky what the ancients must have thought when they saw sights like this, or even more spectacular, the comets that hang in the night sky, trailing a glow of light behind them. Did they marvel at those streaking lights in the night sky? Did they believe that the earth was calling down fire?

Think for a moment what the world would look like without light. Consider the effects on the earth of no light. No photosynthesis at work to bring forth the amazing diversity of life and color we experience around us. No evolutionary nudge toward the development of an incredibly complex and sophisticated organ like the eye. No rainbows, aurora borealis, or flowers. We would not be able to behold a sunset over the ocean spreading amazing color like an artist smearing a canvas with paint from her palette. The beauty of a clear blue sky on a fall day would not be a part of our enjoyment of life. All reality as we know and experience it is mediated to us through the phenomenon of light. Without it, life would not be possible.

Now consider the emergence of the world as described by the statement "Let there be light." According to our best understanding of contemporary physics, light would have been the first perceptible reality to our eyesight if we had been present to observe it. From 10^{-43} to 10^{-33} seconds after the big bang, the universe is thought to have been a vast primal stew, a primary ingredient of which were photons. Light would have bathed the entire universe. Photons are formed by the fusion reactions of immense gravitational pressure. The pressure of a star's mass releases quanta or packets of energy that carry heat and light into the universe. These packets of energy, photons, are experienced by us as light and heat, but the photons themselves are never seen by us. They are elusive because every time we try to "capture" them, the attempt changes them into something else.

If this were all there were, we should have a mystery to keep us entertained for quite some time. However, this elusive wave/particle of energy also mediates to us the electromagnetic force that holds the universe together. This force, mentioned previously, is invisible and massless, observed only in its effects. It carries light and also radio transmissions to us. The photons it carries are in turn the primary carriers not only of light and heat, but of information throughout the entirety of the observable universe, information necessary for the appearance and sustaining of life. In this sense, we could even see photons as holy mystery.

One of the more interesting pieces of information they bring to us is the experience of color. The energy of a photon is usually described as part of its wavelike character. The closer the waves are to each other, the more energy the photon contains. We experience this vibratory pattern as color because red light consists of 4×10^{14} vibrations per second and blue light consists of 7.5×10^{14}. This knowledge provides us with clues when we are observing clusters of galaxies with our telescopes, because clusters moving away from one another generate a red color, and clusters moving toward one another have a blue glow.[1]

Not only color, but the very nature of reality itself is manifested by the photon. The world of atoms consists of wavelike particles separated from each other by a void and held in place by the never seen massless photon traveling at the speed of light among particles that are not only particles, but also waves. This means, for example, that the solidity of iron is 99.999999999999 percent vacuous space made to feel solid by fields that have no material reality.

At bottom, all reality we experience and know is composed of energy. Some of the most famous names in science tell us of a world difficult to describe and even imagine. Max Planck discovered that this expression of energy at the atomic level is intricately connected and counterintuitive to our best attempts at logical explanation. The French physicist Louis de Broglie claimed that "as a result of a great law of nature every bit of energy of proper mass is intrinsically related to periodic phenomenon of frequency."[2] Under this understanding, all matter was related to a particular wavelength and frequency, or wave cycles per second. The universe hums with the zoom of being.

Welcome to the wave/particle zoo. There is underlying the universe a commonality of energy, mediated by fields, composed of photons, which bring us a world of amazing complexity. Quantum weirdness indeed! We are so embedded within this array of forces, frequencies, and motions that they overwhelm our imagination to describe them; when we try, we usually have to resort to metaphor. We call quarks by names like "charm" or "up." Life is so bizarre in its various manifestations as to sometimes escape our capacity for contemplation of it.

The human body contains somewhere around 75 trillion cells. These cells in turn contain somewhere around 10^{27} atoms, all in a continual state of motion. As they zoom throughout their world, an amazing thing happens when they "become focused on a single act when a sperm cell adds its message of genetic material into a receptive egg cell."[3] In the wave energy that goes into this moment, the potential exists for a new life to emerge into the world.

When I start to contemplate the energies present in my body, I become even more amazed. I find interactions of such complexity as to defy common sense. How did carbon, nitrogen, oxygen, hydrogen, sulfur, and phosphorous decide to join together to create life? One response to this question is that these elements did not "decide" to do anything at all, that life is the product of random occurrences, happening over vast periods of time. But what form of random processes and information exchanges led to us?

Over an incredible amount of time, life developed a cellular society composed of gatekeepers that regulated chemical and biological reactions that would allow for the emergence of creatures that could view the sunset and be filled with awe and appreciation. Molecules possessing extraordinary complexity emerge to create cells that would recognize them and accept the enzymes the molecules bring to them, keeping out the unnecessary or unwanted elements.

Take just one small part of this cellular life, mitotic division. In this process, duplicated DNA chromosomes align along a central plane of the cell. Each parent cell produces spindle fibers that reach out from opposing walls of the cell, attach themselves to each of the pairs of duplicated chromosomes, and pull the pairs apart, separating the chromosome sister pairs into two sets of twenty-three pairs. Is it just blind purposeless nature that taught the cells to invent and train these amazingly clever fibers?[4]

From the explosion of galaxies to the most intricate biological interactions, we find a reality that is at heart composed of energy in motion. Why does this energy possess the properties to bring forth a type of consciousness that functions intelligently? Is it all random chance, atoms and quarks blindly colliding into each other to produce a being who wonders at the night sky filled with meteors? Or does the universe's energy hint at something else, a consciousness pervading all life that allows life to explore and come to be?

> Could the consciousness we perceive as the mind be as fundamental as, let's say, the phenomena of gravity generated by mass, or the electrical charge generated by a photon? . . . Might consciousness also be an intricate, all-present part of nature, of the universe? In that case every particle would have some aspect of consciousness within. The more complex the entity, the greater would be its awareness of the consciousness housed within.[5]

This consciousness is brought to us by the effects that photons produce. The effects are not separable from their source, which resides in the mystery of energy. Such an understanding focuses attention on a reality that runs through our explorations. The source of photons is always distinct from yet present in its effects. Energy is the underlying source of all existence.

Light Inaccessible?

When members of the early church were struggling to articulate their understanding of God, they used a variety of languages, metaphors, and images to try and grasp some of the deeper connections of faith. They were exercised by their cultures to account for how Christian faith offered a vision of God that would witness to God's revelation in Jesus Christ. When the Orthodox tradition was struggling with how to articulate the incomprehensibleness of God made known in Christ, they appealed to the category of energy: "As a way of holding in tension strict monarchy and the idea of a common *ousia,* the Cappadocians, Gregory of Nyssa in particular, took refuge in the distinction between the absolutely unknowable and incomprehensible divine ousia and the manifestation of God through the divine energies *(energeiai).*"[6]

While the definition of these energies can be complex, and certainly they were meant to address the uncreated energies of God such as we find in redemption, "the primary image the tradition uses to describe these energies is light."[7] These energies were to be seen as communicable aspects of God's nature, but if we are right in asserting that the connection between God and the world is so close, then the presence of light in the world is a redemptive aspect of God's nature, since it brings forth life itself.

Light is the fundamental and primary carrier of reality for us. In the physical sense we can say that light might even be an abstraction; certainly it has an impersonal dimension to it. Consider the analogy that says God's goodness is like the light of the sun, shining on everyone. All creation shares in the undifferentiated reality of photons.

Yet in the context of the triune God, light becomes revelatory. It illumines the darkness. Consider the biblical accounts of light. People sit in great darkness, but then see the light (Matt 4:16), or Jesus proclaims he is the light of the world (John 8:12). The transfiguration of Jesus takes place in the midst of white light (Matt 17:2). The light shines in darkness and the darkness has not overcome it (1 John 2:8). Light illumines the God who is present within the created order. The apophatic tradition leads to cataphasis, hiddenness reveals disclosure, because we are truly able to "see" and therefore we can interpret the world with a new level of sight.

A closer look at nature, at quarks, leptons, fields, trees, galaxies, and all life, shows that it is becoming increasingly difficult to think of life in terms of particular things existing in total distinction from one another. The larger picture would appear to be that nature is a mass of energy exchanges, patterns of life built among the constant communication taking place, resulting in the continuing of life.

Viewed from the light that faith offers, we find in these processes the world moving in a certain direction, even though this cannot be defined by the means of science as such. Though the world of science interprets the movement of the world on the basis of mathematical rules, physical properties and laws, and, counterintuitive to "laws," random processes, faith sees something different, though it is difficult at times. We look beyond the great myths of progress and efficient causality to see a world, even in its estrangement from God, being shaped by grace.[8]

In our reflection upon the energies of the world, the Trinity is where both the personal and impersonal dimensions of God as light are joined together. On the one hand the doctrine of the Trinity allows us to understand that the power manifested in the world is not the pantheistic expression of nebulous energy. On the other hand it makes us alert to the reality that God's common graces are present to the entire creation and there is much that will simply remain beyond our grasp.

Trinitarian faith speaks to the ways in which God's intention for creation and humanity is set in the context of desire for relationship and communion. This relationship is not just between humankind and God, but is set within the matrix of all life. We are summoned to exist within the web of life, embracing it all as gift. We exist within a universe constituted by its relations. The universe is no longer seen from a fixed perspective, and we require a new language and an imagination in reflection upon creation.

Christian faith should have the resources to embrace new languages, while keeping faith with the previous ones, to express the cosmic dimensions of God's life. That God's intention for the creation is seen in deep measure in Jesus of Nazareth suggests that commitment to God's way in the world will be a commitment of suffering love. This places us into territory that many are fearful of occupying, because for us it may mean a form of life we had not previously contemplated.

As discussed earlier, this solidarity with creation means life can no longer be lived under the convenient delusions that creation is a mere matter of blind choices and total randomness. If the creation is truly "groaning in travail," we will have to be attentive to its cries. The pain of the earth in some respects is created by humans. We are the ones who pour vast amounts of our time and energy into finding new levels of violence and destruction to visit upon the innocent. We are ones who abuse our responsibility as co-creators of life, sometimes in favor of creating death.

But creation itself contains its own form of violence. Viruses, natural selection, planetary life itself with galaxies colliding and stars dying, exhibit a certain form of violence that can make us look like mere amateurs at the processes of destruction. The shadow side of creation is a very present reality and we will sometimes have to stand mute and helpless before the forces that pull galaxies together. Even as we recognize our powerlessness, we will also discover the God who experiences these moments with even more sensitivity than we possess. We will also realize that we are called to an adventure that is a part of the coming to be of the world. We are called to manifest the presence of God.

This reading of the natural order should call forth from us the desire for communion among life and God. Just as the Trinity has been understood as Being-in-Communion, so, too, we shall realize that to be in communion with God and the earth means attention to the dimensions of a common grace, shared by all life. Existing within the context of this grace, we will grasp that much of the world of exploding stars and biological death may not be about us, but about God. We will have to live in this tension; the question is, how will we respond?

On the basis of faith we should embrace the created order to help us shape our spiritual awareness. This is the world that forms the interpretive context within which we live and move and have our being. Though this interpretation cannot be done apart from revelation and the beliefs and practices that have shaped the community of faith, done from this context the world serves as potential to illumine God's life for us. We are shaped by a distinct faith to discern the world we exist within even though a plurality of interpretations may result.[9]

This becomes difficult because we are so embedded within both the world and a certain interpretation of faith that it is hard to gain perspective to see other interpretations. In scientific observation it is understood that the way we look for things is sometimes determined by what we believe is actually there in the first place. It becomes hard, even in science, to gain new perspective if we are committed to an interpretation as the reality itself. As science advances, it does so on the moments of revision that extend our conceptual capacity to understand.

Following the Light

This is where the necessity of leave-taking mentioned earlier becomes of acute importance for us. We can become so wrapped up in images of God that we hold and cling to that we become prisoners of our own theologies. In the Scriptures we find that God is continually calling for persons to go on pilgrimage in order that God might do a new thing. All through the biblical narrative we have stories of those who have to take leave of all secure and comfortable supports in order to draw deeper into the life of God.

Sometimes it is the most deeply held and believed notions of God that are called into question. The heart of the Christian faith rests on the gospel accounts of Jesus, who is continually calling persons out of old habits of faith in order to be receptive to the reality of the God who goes beyond our projections or wish-fulfilling desires. Think of the story of the Good Samaritan, for instance, where Jesus addresses the prejudices of his hearers about who serves God better, those included in the covenant or those outside it who do the right thing (Luke 10:25–37). Think of other places in the Gospels where Jesus calls persons to let go of their images in order to experience the life of God (Luke 11:37–44), or the parables of reversal that reveal a deeper grace than many of us believe in (Matt 20:1–16). This letting go is painful and not often accomplished.

The greater part of the pain comes because we have confused our images of God with God and so cannot see the difference. Even with a foundational belief in the Trinity, for example, we can still entertain feminine images of God. This seems like a direct contradiction to a Trinity that is expressed in terms of Father, Son, and Spirit, yet contemplate the image of a world waiting to be born. A mother giving birth is one of the most compelling images for the way in which creation develops from the matrix of maternal care and emerges into the world to become independent from but always connected to the source of divine life.

At other times letting go is painful because it means that the relationship with God becomes deeper and therefore more dangerous than before. We are stripped of all our excuses for ignoring the life of God in the world. We are exposed for seeking our own concerns rather than risking the presence of God in the world. We lose our bearings because we have left the comfort of our religious institutions and theologies. Creation itself summons us to a deeper awareness of God's creative energies.

Christian theological reflection must assume the crucial position of trinitarian belief, though there may be a host of trinitarian perspectives that will be faithful to the true centrality of the Christian story, Jesus Christ. All theological construction must remain, like science, open-ended. This does not mean that it takes place without commitments, because we are constrained by the reality we do understand. However, as we are trying to articulate the presence of God, we must realize that our attempts cannot adequately contain the reality we are seeking to behold. Like the photon, God carries the mystery of the universe, but this mystery is elusive, and in some measure unknown to us.

We are formed as persons by the context of a particular tradition, but are we trapped by the thought forms of this tradition? Though we are illumined by them, are we constrained by Latin or Greek worldviews when we seek to express our understanding of Christian faith? Is the language of *hypostases, ousia, prosopon,* or *persona* the language in which to understand the life of the triune God today? More, is the metaphysics of perfection the sole grounds on which to comprehend the contours of God's being? If God's ongoing redemptive relationship with the world is truly in process, then the universe is still being created and we find ourselves part of that journey.

This sense of change and motion is difficult for us to entertain because for many of us the life of God must be secured from any connection with change. That the life of God also grows is simply not acceptable to many. In Aquinas, for instance, the creation proceeds in such a way that the goodness of creation reflects the goodness of God, but creation adds nothing to the divine goodness. God's total independence from creation means the creation really adds nothing to the life of God.[10]

Would a trinitarian approach allow for a sense of God's becoming within the life of God? God, differentiated from creation, is nonetheless joined to it through the Son (from whom creation originates) and the Holy Spirit (who is the sustaining presence of all existence). God becomes God fully in relationship, not only within the community of internal relations, but in relationship with what God has created. The source of light is always distinct from, yet present in, its effects. God is the underlying source of all existence, but is also joined to it.

If we take seriously the implications for faith, the Trinity suggests that we cannot easily separate the physical from the spiritual. Would it be too much to suggest that we cannot separate mass from energy either? The deep connections between the creation and the life of God offer us the challenge to develop a "worldly" Trinity. Rooted in the biblical witness, it will address the contemporary world by engagement with the sciences and all understandings of the world.

In trinitarian belief, God's life consists of Being-in-Communion, desiring for the creation the willingness to live life as reflected by the Father, Son, and Spirit. We have been exploring the contours of what this willingness looks like for the last several chapters. All Christian interpretations of the world must be viewed in this light. Trinitarian belief does not necessarily lead to patriarchal theology. It speaks not to hierarchy of rule, but of a community of life. This doctrine, once abstracted from God's redemptive intent revealed in Jesus of Nazareth, becomes unhinged from the full implications of God's relation to the creature.

The triune God stands at the seam of reality and interpretation because Christianity understands that God seeks embodiment and relationship.

This may seem like an innocent statement, but it is extraordinarily destabilizing. If true, then all theologies of creation or God that perpetuate prevailing social structures of oppression or exclusion or fail to critique with a prophetic witness those cultural expressions of disobedience to God's intention for the creation revealed in the teachings of Jesus are to be regarded with suspicion. God's embodiment is seldom found in the maintenance of the status quo, but in all avenues of life and the protection of it.

As Christian faith explores the energies that are manifest in the created order, it will have in mind an answer to the question of why matter behaves the way it does. This does not entail a reduction of all properties to physical explanations, because there are some questions that escape our best attempts at interpretation. Still, when we look at one form of physical life we are most connected to—the human brain—we find something there that offers us material for reflection.

The adult human brain contains approximately one hundred billion neurons. So does the brain of an infant, though many of the connections among the nerves have not been formed. In an adult brain the axon of each neuron connects with as many as one hundred thousand dendrites of other neurons. From these connections the branching defies common sense, a million billion connections. We have 1,000,000,000,000,000 points within our heads at which neurotransmitters are exchanging information from nerve to nerve. All this occurs within an incredibly small space, leading to a biochemical complexity that leaves those with the heart for it on the cusp of mystery: "From the isolated cell to the interaction of nerve and muscle, through to the 10^{15} neural connections within a brain, a depth of information surfaces that annoyingly has not any iota of justification being there."[11] And this just barely scratches the surface.

Every experience we have affects those neural connections and becomes embedded within our consciousness. At what point in this concentration of neurons, each extending a thousand or more axon terminals, did the brain "go critical" and give rise to the mind? How does a purely physical process give rise to an aesthetic sense of beauty, or even a notion of morality? Though this process has been interpreted as the product of meaningless forces, resulting in a universe that has no meaning, it also lends itself to the interpretation that nature has been kinder than we have a right to anticipate.

The complete complexity of the brain is due to energy; the massless wave/particle duality we label as a photon has brought us to this moment. In this process nothing is isolated; rather, all has been extending itself by building communities of life. The atom joins with atom, the molecule with cell, the protein with acids, and so on, one vast society of life. Life itself, like God, seeks a community of being. Does the very consciousness that permeates all coming to be of life reflect the providence of God?

This question is of great concern to Christianity as it seeks to discern the life of God in the world. In trinitarian belief, God's being exists for others, in communion as well as distinction. All of life is being called to the future of God and we are no different. The world is distinct from, but participates in, the divine life through God's sustaining presence. As life is drawn closer into the life of God, Christian consciousness is informed by faith to see that life is being called to move toward being in communion with all that is, seen and unseen.

How will we express the triune life of God that honors this movement? One place to start is by suggesting that perhaps we can consider another model of Christian interpretation of the world that offers us promise for understanding Christian life in the world. When we were exploring the ways in which the Christian story had acquired certain interpretive authority such as we find in the tradition expressed by Augustine, we found resources in Irenaeus of Lyon for a reframing of Christian life.

Irenaeus believed that the space between humankind and God is a space not of exile, but of promise and potential. Creation in his mind was the space of becoming, the space for the divinization of the earth creature, the mud creature. In a close reading of the biblical witness as he knew it, Irenaeus saw the world as being the arena for salvation, but this was not just a matter of individual salvation, but of a completion of the world. Paul, also, saw this as the future of the world.

Salvation is not so much being saved *from* our sins (though this is a crucially necessary element) as it is being saved *for* God. A close reading of the biblical texts will show that from the prophetic concern for justice to the admonitions from Paul on how to live our lives in order to manifest God's presence, we were not created to escape earthly life but to make the presence of God a reality in it. In living into this reality, we find ourselves participating in the divine life.

In a partial way we can respond to this salvation by worship of God and participating in communion with God and the community of life that God extends to the world through the church. There are also resources for the cultivation of spiritual disciplines in the tradition. Reflections of the spiritual life found in such pieces as Benedict's Rule or in the writings of more contemporary authors such as Thomas Merton, Henri Nouwen, and Kathleen Norris offer spaces for the cultivation of spiritual graces.

The depth and richness of this life is seen in God's own willingness to be in communion with us, but it goes even deeper. Irenaeus, in responding to the gnostic separation of spirit and matter, not only saw God accustoming the creature and creation for divinity, but God being accustomed for the creature. The life we experience all around us can be interpreted as a world growing away from God, lost in its own rebellion to God, or it can be viewed as a world growing toward God even as God grows toward the world.

That this is especially hard to see in a world poised on the knife's edge of annihilation or in love with its own destruction means a commitment to faith is evidence of "things not seen." We cannot deny the effacement of the creation by creatures who do not respond to God's call to participate in this grace. However, faith should see that ultimately God will have the final word in the matter, even if humankind refuses the summons to grace.

The time between the already and the not yet is a time of both peril and promise. In the unrelenting violence of the contemporary world, which is a manifestation of our blindness of the way of God for the world, we may be brought at some point to the stark reality that the world and human community as they are presently constituted may not survive. Awaiting God's Sabbath rest does not mean the embrace of utopian visions, for we must stay rooted in the realities within which we are embedded. However, we are called to an unremitting, unceasing proclamation of an alternative vision of human society and the expression of God's life in the world.

Perhaps we have to take leave of stories we have lived that interpret the world in terms of its deficiency rather than as the space of promise and potential. If the past is a perfection lost, then the future is a wandering away from home; but if the past is a promise we have forgotten, the future is an adventure we are moving toward. That Christian faith seems not to live in this vision is profoundly discouraging.

The more we are compelled to move into the life of God, the more we will move into the world. The communion between God and humankind will necessarily result in an intensification of life within the world, both ours and God's. The life of God being totally accustomed to Being-in-Communion is reflected in our willingness to be in communion with God, internally in cultivating God's presence and externally in living in creation in the full knowledge that it is given to us as gift.

There is no linear way of conceptualizing this; it is in a very real sense a matter of quantum relations. The relationship between God and humankind is in continual interaction and movement and cannot be conceived of in a locality of cause and effect exchanges. When Irenaeus pointed to the great exchange occurring between God and the world, he was not pointing to a space of power or knowledge or timeless perfection. It is God's own space of suffering love. In a truly significant way, the cross interprets the world.

It is this quality that creates the means whereby we find ourselves growing into God and God growing into us. In the inner intensification of our consciousness we find the space whereby we experience the pain and loss of deep suffering, but we also find an overwhelming joy of beholding beauty, love, and faithfulness. In this process we have the potential to make manifest the presence of God in a way that allows for an authentic communion with divine life.

Appearances to the contrary (and God knows it appears extremely contrary these days), nature and the human creature are all responding in their own way, in their own means, to the invitation to communion, union with God. Sometimes this response takes the way of rebellion and unnecessary pain and violence is the result. In responding positively, however, our lives become richer, fuller, and clearer, even though there may be increased suffering. We can see the universe in ways that mark it as the ground for the journey to completion.

Our receptivity to the presence of God creates the conditions for the intensification of God's own presence in the world. In the created order we find a sacramental grace in the sense that God is present there, seeking relationship with all that exists. This sacramental presence is found in the entirety of the creation, for the Word made flesh is also the same Spirit that seeks embodied expression.

What is even more amazing to contemplate is that perhaps God is also becoming richer, fuller, and more deeply textured within our awareness and the life of the world. God desires relationship because relationship defines the very essence of God's triune being. It is precisely in our willingness to exist in relationship with God and the world that transformation and renewal become possible. To claim this means that we should entertain the possibility that the world carries the potential to enhance the life of God, if we will be open to the possibility.

This world does not just exist as a cauldron out of which we must be plucked, or a proving ground to see if we are worthy of God's love. There is great beauty and majesty, and life has brought us to the door of mystery. Many souls have had the experience, call it mystical, of being profoundly moved by the natural world to a sense of being in the presence of mystery. The physicist or biologist, seeing through telescope or electron microscope, can find him- or herself in the presence of glory. We should be careful not to discount or negate these moments of communion with God by narrow critiques of how this worships the creation and not the creator. For the eyes of faith, these are one and the same.

But this common grace is prepared for us by the sacramental grace found within the worship of the church. In this context the Word, specifically the narrative of the crucified, suffering Messiah, and the table of bread and wine, focus our attention and consciousness upon the paradox that the awesomeness of the universe's energies, the manifestations of the grandeur and glory of God, is found in the willing embrace of powerlessness. How we respond to this story determines the means by which God is brought into the world in clarity.

Our willingness to allow this story to inhabit our lives and form our consciousness and spirit enlarges the space for God's own presence to make a home in the world. This is where the new creation takes root and is also the ground on which we position ourselves to accept the responsibility of co-creation. God accustoms Godself to us in the measure we choose to accustom ourselves to God.

Seen from the perspective of faith, nature's present indeterminacies can be understood as vehicles of promise. Nature is unfinished because it has a future and that future is defined by promise. God nourishes the world by offering numerous possibilities to it in order that it continue its journey to the future. In those moments when we do not honor this truth, in our neglect of the gifts of God or our abuse of creation's promise, when we are lured by the siren call of security to create that which may destroy or efface God's good creation, the Creator is engaged in the most intimate ways conceivable in bringing forth life from the desolation.

In this strange journey from matter to thinking, willing, loving life, do we not find something that, regardless of the self-incurvature of sin, *responds*? Is there something inner to all life that leads to a certain beauty, even though striving, achieving, or failing are enfolded into the very fabric of the universe? There is an inwardness to all things that is responsive to the Creator's presence because nothing is separate in totality. That we are the creatures who frequently choose to say "no" is perhaps the clearest indication that freedom is a profoundly complex responsibility.

Promise and potential mark the created order as much as chaos and disorder do. Promise does not of necessity mean perfection, and evil and suffering in the world provide ample testimony that we live in estrangement from our common destiny. Ironically, the very beliefs in God that persons hold in many traditions today lead directly to exclusion, suffering, and death. While the world is the sacramental reflection of God's being, it can appear to be a place of exile.

God is most clearly seen in Christian faith as the manifestation of suffering love, and while central to the narratives of Jesus, this orientation to the world is found within the triune life of God, struggling with a world coming to be. Irenaeus may have been possessed of keen insight when he suggested that perfection rests in the future, not the past. In our pilgrimage to the future, all things are of sacred worth. None of the processes of life are removed or distant from God, for God is both source and origin, the Alpha and Omega.

In this present fragility and struggle, evolution, as we presently understand it, contains something other than struggle, survival of the fittest, and human notions of progress; it contains the biblical promise of fulfillment. Creation, mediating the sacred in the midst of our pain and suffering, exists in the context of promise because suffering love rests at the heart of the matter. Think of the risks the triune God assumes when God shares with all creatures the indeterminate future. We are participants in creating this new future, and thus we find in the end that this promise is not a plan, but a vision.

Jesus offers us the vision of the future that God intends and the picture he paints is richly textured. This is where we are enabled to see that we are called to the horizons of hope, shared by all life. The Gospel calls us to incarnate the very presence of God in a world coming to be. It invites us to manifest in our very lives the promise of reconciliation and peace. How shall we accustom ourselves to this? Has the intensification of subjectivity and inner awareness drawn down the fire of love?

How will the story of God's coming to be in the world get told if not by those who share with St. Paul nature's own longing for the completion of creation? Will we opt for the reductionism of chemistry, genetics, and environment? The church should not vacate the interpretive space of the world offered to us by scientific inquiry. However, even in the engagement of theology and science there will be a space between. For God may not be found in the 1 or the 0, but in the space between, not in the grains of sand, but in the space between, not even in our intellectual sophistication or our piety, but in the space between. Ultimately, no matter how far we journey toward the light we will find ourselves at the heart of the Paschal mystery: the One who creates the world, becomes vulnerable to it, and in that very suffering takes the world into the life of God, redeeming all things, finally becoming all in all.

NOTES

1. Sobosan, *Romancing the Universe,* 193n. 46.

2. Gerald L. Schroeder, *The Hidden Face of God: Science Reveals the Ultimate Truth* (New York: Touchstone Books, 2001), 27. This book is interesting in the number of detailed examples it offers of the processes of cellular and biological life.

3. Ibid., 50.

4. Ibid., 71.

5. Ibid., 6–7.

6. LaCugna, *God for Us,* 72.

7. Mark Heim, *The Depth of the Riches: A Trinitarian Theology of Religious Ends* (Grand Rapids, Mich.: Eerdmans, 2001), 177.

8. If readers here wonder whether I am trying to bring St. Thomas in the back door, I would suggest they read his accounts of the way in which grace fulfills nature, since humanity and the cosmos alike are oriented toward God as the goal. This vision can also be raised in our context, though we may find our explanation of this to be different than Thomas's. See, for example, *Summa Theologica,* "Treatise on Grace" II, I, qq 109–14.

9. At this point no one should assume I am making the argument that all interpretations of the world are of equal value or worth. I believe strongly that there are interpretations of creation that are at enmity with the Gospel of Jesus Christ. These interpretations may in fact come from within the community of Christianity. But a multiplicity of perspectives is going to be present, and so this book has been an exercise in asking how Christianity might address the various interpretations offered the world through tradition and the sciences.

10. See, for instance, *Summa Theologica,* I, I q 6:1, 3, 4. Karl Rahner in *The Trinity* critiques Aquinas for concentrating his attention on the essence of God common to all three persons rather than God as the source of reality and subsequent salvation history. According to Rahner, Thomas's treatment of the Trinity "becomes quite philosophical and abstract and refers hardly at all to salvation history" (16–17).

11. Schroeder, *The Hidden Face of God,* 133.

SELECTED BIBLIOGRAPHY

Aristotle. *Complete Works.* Edited by Jonathan Barnes. 2 vols. Princeton: Princeton University Press, 1984.

Armstrong, Karen. *A History of God: The 4,000-Year Quest for Judaism, Christianity, and Islam.* New York: Knopf, 1993.

Augustine. *The Confessions.* Translated by Maria Boulding. New York: New York City Press, 1996.

_____. "The Writings of Augustine," in *Nicene and Post–Nicene Fathers.* Edited by Philip Schaff. Vols. 1–3, 5. Grand Rapids, Mich.: Eerdmans, 1971–1976.

Barbour, Ian G. *Religion and Science: Historical and Contemporary Issues.* San Francisco: Harper San Francisco, 1997.

_____. *When Science Meets Religion: Enemies, Strangers, or Partners?* San Francisco: Harper San Francisco, 2000.

Barth, Karl. *Church Dogmatics.* Translated by G. W. Bromiley and T. F. Torrance. Vol. III/1–2, *The Doctrine of Creation.* Edinburgh: T&T Clark, 1960.

Behe, Michael. *Darwin's Black Box: The Biochemical Challenge to Evolution.* New York: Touchstone Books, 1998.

Benz, Arnold. *The Future of the Universe.* New York: Continuum, 2000.

Berger. Peter. *The Sacred Canopy.* Garden City, N.Y.: Doubleday, 1969.

Boff, Leonardo. *Trinity and Society.* Translated by Paul Burns. Maryknoll, N.Y.: Orbis Books, 1988.

Brown, Peter. *Augustine of Hippo.* Berkeley: University of California Press, 1967.

Brueggemann, Walter. *Theology of the Old Testament: Testimony, Dispute, Advocacy.* Minneapolis: Fortress Press, 1997.

Buckley, James and David S. Yeago, eds. *Knowing the Triune God: The Work of the Spirit in the Practices of the Church.* Grand Rapids, Mich.: Eerdmans, 2001.

Bulgarov, Sergius. *Bride of the Lamb.* Translated by Boris Jakim. Grand Rapids, Mich.: Eerdmans, 2002.

Chadwick, Henry. *Early Christian Thought and the Classical Tradition: Studies in Justin, Clement, and Origen.* New York: Oxford University Press, 1966.

Clayton, Philip. *God and Contemporary Science.* Grand Rapids, Mich.: Eerdmans, 1997.

Coleman, Richard. *Competing Truths: Theology and Science as Sibling Rivals.* Harrisburg, Pa.: Trinity Press International, 2001.

Cole–Turner, Ronald, ed. *Beyond Cloning: Religion and the Remaking of Humanity.* Harrisburg, Pa.: Trinity Press International, 2001.

_____., ed. *Human Cloning.* Louisville, Ky.: Westminster/John Knox, 1997.

_____. *The New Genesis: Theology and the Genetic Revolution.* Louisville, Ky.: Westminster/John Knox, 1993.

Cobb, John and Clark Pinnock, eds. *Searching for an Adequate God: A Dialogue Between Process and Free Will Theists.* Grand Rapids, Mich.: Eerdmans, 2000.

Cunningham, David. *These Three Are One: The Practice of Trinitarian Theology.* Oxford: Blackwell Publishers Inc., 1998.

Cushing, James T. *Philosophical Concepts in Physics: The Historical Relation Between Philosophy and Scientific Theories.* Cambridge: Cambridge University Press, 1998.

Davies, Brian. *The Thought of Thomas Aquinas.* Oxford: Clarendon Press, 1992.

Dawkins, Richard. *The Blind Watchmaker: Why the Evidence of Evolution Reveals a World Without Design.* New York: W. W. Norton, 1987.

_____. *Climbing Mount Improbable.* New York: W. W. Norton, 1996.

Dembski, William A. *Intelligent Design: The Bridge between Science and Theology.* Downers Grove, Ill.: InterVarsity Press, 1999.

_____. *The Design Inference: Eliminating Chance Through Small Probabilities.* Cambridge: Cambridge University Press, 1998.

Dennett, Daniel. *Darwin's Dangerous Idea: Evolution and the Meaning of Life.* New York: Simon & Schuster, 1995.

Deutsch, David. *The Fabric of Reality.* New York: Penguin, 1997.

Dillard, Annie. *For the Time Being.* New York: Alfred Knopf, 1999.

_____. *Pilgrim at Tinker Creek.* New York: Bantam Books, 1974.

Donovan, Mary Ann. *One Right Reading: A Guide to Irenaeus.* Collegeville, Minn.: Liturgical Press, 1997.

Drees, Willem. *Creation: From Nothing Until Now.* London: Routledge, 2002.

Eldridge, Niles. *Time Frames: The Rethinking of Darwinian Evolution and the Theory of Punctuated Equilibria.* London: Heinemann, 1986.

_____, and Stephen Jay Gould. "Punctuated Equilibrium Prevails." *Nature* 332 (1986): 211–12.

Ellul, Jacques. *The Technological Society.* New York: Vintage, 1964.

_____. *The Technological Bluff.* Grand Rapids, Mich.: Eerdmans, 1990.

Fagg, Lawrence W. *Electromagnetism and the Sacred: At the Frontier of Spirit and Matter.* New York: Continuum, 1999.

_____. "Sacred Indwelling and the Electromagnetic Undercurrent in Nature: A Physicist's Perspective." *Zygon* 37, no. 2. (June 2002): 473–90.

Farley, Wendy. *Tragic Vision and Divine Compassion: A Contemporary Theodicy.* Louisville, Ky.: Westminster/John Knox, 1990.

Feigenbaum, Mitchell. "Quantative Universality of a Class of Nonlinear Transformations." *Journal of Statistical Physics* 19 (1978): 25–52.

Ferguson, Kitty. *Fire in the Equations: Science, Religion, and the Search for God.* Grand Rapids, Mich.: Eerdmans, 1994.

Ford, Adam. *Universe: God, Science, and The Human Person.* Mystic, Conn.: Twenty-Third Publications, 1987.

Ford, Lewis. *The Lure of God: A Biblical Background for Process Theism.* Philadelphia: Fortress Press, 1978.

Gay, Craig M. *The Way of the Modern World: Or, Why It's Tempting to Live as if God Doesn't Exist.* Grand Rapids, Mich.: Eerdmans, 1998.

Gilson, Etienne. *The Christian Philosophy of Saint Augustine.* Translated by L. E. M. Lynch. New York: Random House, 1960.

Gleick, James. *Chaos: Making a New Science.* New York, Viking Penguin, 1988.

Gould, Stephen Jay. *Rock of Ages: Science and Religion in the Fullness of Life.* New York: Ballantine, 1999.

_____. *The Panda's Thumb.* New York: W.W. Norton, 1980.

Grant, Robert. *Irenaeus of Lyons.* Cambridge: Cambridge University Press, 2001.

Gregory of Nyssa. *Gregorii Nysseni Opera.* 10 vols. Werner Jaeger, ed. Berlin and Leiden: E. J. Brill, 1921.

_____. "Against Eunomius" in *The Nicene and Post-Nicene Fathers.* Edited by William Moore and Henry Austin Wilson. Vol. 5. Grand Rapids, Mich.: Eerdmans, 1973.

Gunton, Colin. *The Promise of Trinitarian Theology.* Edinburgh: T&T. Clark, 1990.

Hauerwas, Stanley. *With the Grain of the Universe: The Church's Witness and Natural Theology.* Grand Rapids, Mich.: Brazos Press, 2001.

Haught, John F. *God After Darwin: A Theology of Evolution.* Boulder, Colo.: Westview Press, 2000.

_____. *Science and Religion: From Conflict to Conversation.* New York: Paulist Press, 1995.

Hawking, Steven. *A Brief History of Time.* New York: Bantam Books, 1988.

Hefner, Philip. *The Human Factor: Evolution, Culture, and Religion.* Minneapolis: Fortress Press, 1993.

Heim, Mark. *The Depth of Riches: A Trinitarian Theology of Religious Ends.* Grand Rapids, Mich.: Eerdmans, 2001.

Hoitenga, Dewey J. Jr. *Faith and Reason from Plato to Plantinga: An Introduction to Reformed Epistemology.* Albany, N.Y.: SUNY Press, 1991.

Howell, Nancy. "Co-Creation, Co-Redemption, and Genetics." *American Journal of Theology and Philosophy* 20, no. 2 (May 1999): 147–63.

Hull, David. "The God of the Galapagos." *Nature* 352 (1991): 485–86.

Hunter, Cornelius. *Darwin's God: Evolution and the Problem of Evil.* Grand Rapids, Mich.: Brazos Press, 2001.

Hutchingson, James E. *Pandemonium Tremendum: Chaos and Mystery in the Life of God.* Cleveland: Pilgrim Press, 2001.

Irenaeus. *Against the Heresies.* Translated by Dominic Unger, with further revision by John J. Dillon. Vol. 55 of *Ancient Christian Writers.* New York: Paulist Press, 1992.

_____. "Against Heresies." Pages 315–567 in *The Ante-Nicene Fathers.* Edited by James Donaldson and Alexander Roberts. Grand Rapids, Mich.: Eerdmans, 1973.

Jenson, Robert W. *The Triune Identity: God According to the Gospel.* Philadelphia: Fortress Press, 1990.

_____. *Systematic Theology.* 2 vols. Oxford: Oxford University Press, 1998–1999.

Johnson, Elizabeth A. *She Who Is: The Mystery of God in Feminist Theological Discourse.* New York: Crossroad, 1994.

Jones, Steve. *Darwin's Ghost.* New York: Random House, 2000.

Köster, Helmut. *History, Culture, and Religion of the Hellenistic Age.* Hermeneia, I. Philadelphia: Fortress Press, 1982.

LaCugna, Catherine M. *God for Us: The Trinity and Christian Life.* San Francisco: HarperSanFrancisco, 1993.

Lindberg, David C. *The Beginnings of Western Science.* Chicago: University of Chicago Press, 1992.

Lossky, Vladimir. *The Mystical Theology of the Eastern Church.* Cambridge: James Clarke, 1991.

MacIntyre, Alasdair. "The Logical Status of Religious Belief." Pages 159–201 in *Metaphysical Beliefs.* Edited by Stephen Toulmin. New York: Schocken Books, 1957.

Mandelbrot, Benoit B. *The Fractal Geometry of Nature.* San Francisco: W. H. Freeman & Co., 1977.

Martyr, Justin. "The First Apology." Pages 163–87 in *The Ante-Nicene Fathers.* Edited by James Donaldson and Alex Roberts. Grand Rapids, Mich.: Eerdmans, 1973.

Matczak, Sebastian, ed. *God in Contemporary Thought: A Philosophical Perspective.* New York: Learned Publications, Inc., 1977.

McFague, Sallie. *Models of God: Theology for an Ecological, Nuclear Age.* Minneapolis: Fortress Press, 1987.

McGrath, Alister. *Historical Theology: An Introduction to the History of Christian Thought.* London: Blackwell, 1998.

_____. *Nature.* Vol. 1 of *A Scientific Theology.* Grand Rapids, Mich,: Eerdmans, 2001.

Middleton, J. Richard, and Brian J. Walsh. *Truth is Stranger Than It Used to Be: Biblical Faith in a Postmodern Age.* Downers Grove, Ill.: InterVarsity Press, 1995.

Milbank. John. *Theology and Social Theory: Beyond Secular Reason.* Oxford: Blackwell Publishers, 1990.

Miles, Jack. *God: A Biography.* New York: Vintage Books, 1996.

Miller, James, ed. *An Evolving Dialogue: Theological and Scientific Perspectives on Evolution.* Harrisburg, Pa.: Trinity Press International, 2001.

Minns, Denis. *Irenaeus.* Washington, D. C.: Georgetown University Press, 2001.

Moltmann, Jürgen. *God in Creation: A New Theology of Creation and the Spirit of God.* San Francisco: Harper & Row, 1985.

_____. *History and the Triune God: Contributions to Trinitarian Theology.* Translated by John Bowden. New York: Crossroad, 1992.

_____. *The Trinity and the Kingdom: The Doctrine of God.* Translated by Margaret Kohl. San Francisco: Harper & Row, 1981.

Nelson, J. Robert. *On the New Frontiers of Genetics and Religion.* Grand Rapids, Mich.: Eerdmans, 1994.

Newlands, George. *God in Christian Perspective.* Edinburgh: T&T Clark, 1994.

O'Meara, Thomas Franklin. *Thomas Aquinas, Theologian.* Notre Dame: University of Notre Dame Press, 1997.

O'Murchu, Diarmuid. *Quantum Theology: Spiritual Implications of the New Physics.* New York: Crossroad, 2000.

Osborn, Eric. *Irenaeus of Lyons.* Cambridge: Cambridge University Press, 2001.

Pannenberg, Wolfhart. *Towards a Theology of Nature: Essays on Science and Faith.* Louisville, Ky.: Westminster/John Knox, 1993.

_____. *Theology and the Philosophy of Science.* Translated by Francis McDonagh. Philadelphia, Pa.: The Westminster Press, 1976.

_____. "The Doctrine of Creation and Modern Science." *Zygon* 23, no. 1 (March 1988): 3–21.

Peacocke, Arthur. *Paths from Science to God: The End of All Our Exploring.* Oxford: Oneworld, 2001.

_____. *Theology for a Scientific Age.* Minneapolis: Fortress Press, 1993.

Pelikan, Jaroslav. *Christianity and Classical Culture: The Metamorphosis of Natural Theology in the Christian Encounter with Hellenism.* New Haven, Conn.: Yale University Press, 1993.

_____. *The Christian Tradition: A History of the Development of Doctrine.* 5 vols. Chicago: University of Chicago Press, 1971.

Peters, Ted. *God—The World's Future.* Minneapolis: Fortress Press, 1992.

_____. *Science and Theology: The New Consonance.* Boulder, Colo.: Westview Press, 1998.

_____, ed. *Cosmos as Creation: Science and Theology in Consonance.* Nashville: Abingdon, 1989.

_____. *Playing God: Genetic Determinism and Human Freedom.* New York: Routledge, 1997.

Pinnock, Clark, ed. *The Openness of God: A Biblical Challenge to the Traditional Understanding of God.* Downers Grove, Ill.: InterVarsity Press, 1994.

Pittenger, Norman. *The Lure of Divine Love: Human Experiences and Christian Faith.* Cleveland: Pilgrim Press, 1979.

Plato. *Dialogues of Plato.* Translated by B. Jowett. 2 vols. New York: Random House, 1937.

Polkinghorne, John. *Belief in God in an Age of Science.* New Haven, Conn.: Yale University Press, 1998.

_____. "Creation and the Structure of the Physical World." *Theology Today* 44 (April 1987): 53–68.

_____. *Faith, Science, and Understanding.* New Haven, Conn.: Yale University Press, 2000.

_____. *Science and Theology: An Introduction.* Minneapolis: Fortress Press, 1998.

_____. *The Quantum World.* London: Penguin Books, 1986.

Polkinghorne, John, and Michael Welker, eds. *The End of the World and the Ends of God.* Harrisburg, Pa.: Trinity Press International, 2000.

Rahner, Karl. *The Trinity.* Translated by Joseph Donceel. New York: Herder & Herder, 1997.

Ralston, Holmes, III. *Environmental Ethics: Duties to and in the Natural World.* Philadelphia: Temple University Press, 1988.

_____. "Does Nature Need to Be Redeemed?" *Zygon* 29 (June 1994): 205–29.

_____. *Science and Religion: A Critical Survey.* Philadelphia: Temple University Press, 1987.

Raymo, Chet. *Skeptics and True Believers: The Exhilarating Connection Between Science and Religion.* Toronto: Doubleday Canada Limited, 1998.

Richardson, W. Mark, and Wesley J. Wildmans, eds. *Religion and Science: History, Method, Dialogue.* London: Routledge, 1996.

Sandmel, Samuel. *Philo of Alexandria.* New York: Oxford University Press, 1979.

Santmire, H. Paul. *Nature Reborn: The Ecological and Cosmic Promise of Christian Theology.* Minneapolis: Fortress Press, 2000.

_____. *The Travail of Nature: The Ambiguous Ecological Promise of Christian Theology.* Minneapolis: Fortress Press, 1987.

Schroeder, Gerald L. *The Hidden Face of God: Science Reveals the Ultimate Truth.* New York: Touchstone Books, 2001.

Sharpe, Kevin. *Sleuthing the Divine: The Nexus of Science and Spirit.* Minneapolis: Fortress Press, 2001.

Sheldrake, Philip. *Spirituality and Theology: Christian Living and the Doctrine of God.* Maryknoll, N.Y.: Orbis Press, 1998.

Sobosan, Jeffrey. *Romancing the Universe: Theology, Science, and Cosmology.* Grand Rapids, Mich.: Eerdmans, 1999.

Soelle, Dorothee. *Theology for Skeptics: Reflections on God.* Minneapolis: Fortress Press, 1994.

_____. *The Silent Cry: Mysticism and Resistance.* Translated by Barbara and Martin Rumscheidt. Minneapolis: Fortress Press, 2001.

Tavel, Morton. *Contemporary Physics and the Limits of Knowledge.* Piscataway, N.J.: Rutgers University Press, 2002.

Torrell, Jean-Pierre. *Saint Thomas Aquinas: The Person and His Work.* Translated by Robert Royal. Vol. 1. Washington, D. C.: Catholic University of America Press, 1996.

Torrence, Thomas F. *Space, Time, and Incarnation.* London: Oxford University Press, 1969.

Tracy, Thomas. *God's Action and Embodiment.* Grand Rapids, Mich.: Eerdmans, 1984.

Turner, H. E. W. *The Patristic Doctrine of Redemption: A Study of the Development of Doctrine during the First Five Centuries.* London: Mowbray, 1952.

Von Rad, Gerhard. *Genesis.* Translated by John H. Marks. Philadelphia: Westminster Press, 1972.

Ward, Keith. *God: A Guide for the Perplexed.* Oxford: Oneworld, 2002.

Weinberg, Steven. *The First Three Minutes.* New York: Basic Books, 1977.

Williamson, Clark. *A Guest in the House of Israel: Post-Holocaust Church Theology.* Louisville, Ky.: Westminster/John Knox, 1993.

Wills, Garry. *St. Augustine.* New York: Lipper/Viking, 1999.

Wolfson, Henry. *Philo: Foundations of Religious Philosophy in Judaism, Christianity, and Islam.* 2 vols. Cambridge, Mass.: Harvard University Press, 1947.

Worthing, Mark William. *God, Creation, and Contemporary Physics.* Minneapolis: Fortress Press, 1995.

INDEX